EARTH

ELECTIVE 5

PATTERNS AND PROCESSES IN THE HUMAN ENVIRONMENT

MICHAEL ORGAN

educate.ie

educate.ie

PUBLISHED BY:
Educate.ie
Walsh Educational Books Ltd
Castleisland, Co. Kerry, Ireland
www.educate.ie

EDITOR:
Dog's-ear

DESIGN:
Kieran O'Donoghue

COVER DESIGN:
Kieran O'Donoghue

LAYOUT:
Design Image

PRINTED AND BOUND BY:
Walsh Colour Print, Castleisland,
Co. Kerry, Ireland

Copyright © Michael Organ 2016

ISBN: 978-1-910468-75-3

ACKNOWLEDGEMENTS

To my family, your support means more than you will ever know. I hope I can always make you proud of me. To Ciara, for your unconditional love, support and perfectly timed cups of coffee. To the students and staff of Scoil Pól, Kilfinane, for your infectious enthusiasm and support. Thanks to the team at Educate.ie and all those who worked so hard in the producing of this book, especially Emma and Claire.

PHOTOGRAPHS AND ILLUSTRATIONS

For permission to reproduce photographs, the author and publisher acknowledge the following copyright holders:

© **Alamy**: 8T, 43, 44B, 85T, 89, 95, 98T, 98C, 99T, 100, 135T, 135B, 136T, 138, 156, 165, 167T, 169B, 170, 176 • © Barrow Coakley Photography: 97T, 106, 123, 127, 150, 151, 152 • © Bill Flynn/ Waterford County Museum: 112 • **cartoonstock.com**: 41T, 78B • © Declan Corrigan, Working Pictures Photography: 168• © Derek Speirs: 77C • © Getty Images: 18, 45T, 85C • © Google Earth: 157B • © Irish Defence Forces: 81 • © ***The Irish Times***: 86, 158B, 164B • © **John Ditchburn/inkcinct.com**: 149 • © **iStockphoto.com**: 45B, 46, 48B, 69, 90B, 113, 133, 137T, 157T, 161B, 162B, 173, 174T, 174B • **Courtesy of the National Library of Ireland**: 76 • © **Ordnance Survey of Ireland**: 105, 108, 119, 120, 122, 125, 128, 129 • © Photocall Ireland: 75, 78, 88T • © **Shutterstock.com**: 2, 6B, 11, 17B, 56T, 70, 74T, 82, 109T, 134, 137B, 146BR, 161T • **Wikicommons**: 96B

Ordnance Survey Ireland Permit No. 9072
© Ordnance Survey Ireland/Government of Ireland

osi Ordnance Survey Ireland
National Mapping Agency - www.osi.ie

Contents

Preface iv

Chapter 1 Population Change Over Time and Space 2

Chapter 2 Overpopulation and Development 39

Chapter 3 Migration 67

Chapter 4 Settlement 95

Chapter 5 Urban Land Use and Planning 133

Chapter 6 Urban Problems 156

Index 184

Preface

Earth is an up-to-date and comprehensive package for Higher and Ordinary Level Geography students. The *Earth* package includes a textbook, elective books, a Teacher's Resource Book, posters and digital resources.

This elective book covers:

- Elective 5: Patterns and Processes in the Human Environment.

Key Features of *Earth: Elective 5*

- Content is developed in line with the requirements of the marking scheme.

- The text is written with both Higher and Ordinary Level students in mind.

- Fully developed, Significant Relevant Points (SRPs) give students exactly what they need to know. Text in bold clearly shows the information required to gain marks for SRPs. This allows for independent learning and study.

- Each topic begins with **Key Words** and **Learning Outcomes** to inform the student and to facilitate teacher planning.

- The **Geo Dictionary** feature provides a focus on literacy throughout and gives simple definitions of key terms and new words. The **Geo Numeracy** feature gives information on how to carry out important calculations.

- **Active learning** questions and tasks are included throughout each chapter to engage students. The questions range from comprehension questions to more detailed ones involving class discussion.

- Relevant, accurate diagrams are carefully drawn in a style that is easy for students to reproduce. Up-to-date maps, photographs, satellite images and statistical data further aid learning.

- **FACT** boxes provide additional information to enhance student interest and promote further independent research.

- **Why** textboxes explain difficult concepts.

- There is a strong study and exam focus:

  - End-of-chapter Higher and Ordinary Level past-exam questions give students an insight into the wording of exam questions and test their knowledge.

  - End-of-chapter Exam Focus model answers show clear links to the marking scheme.

  - End-of-chapter Topic Maps aid understanding and revision.

  - The **Educate Yourself** feature highlights key points in each topic. These promote focused and logical ordering of information and enable the student to write informative answers that are topic specific. Educate Yourself tables for *Earth: Elective 5* are available online at **www.educateplus.ie**.

I hope you enjoy your journey through this wonderful subject and that this book becomes the perfect companion.

Michael Organ

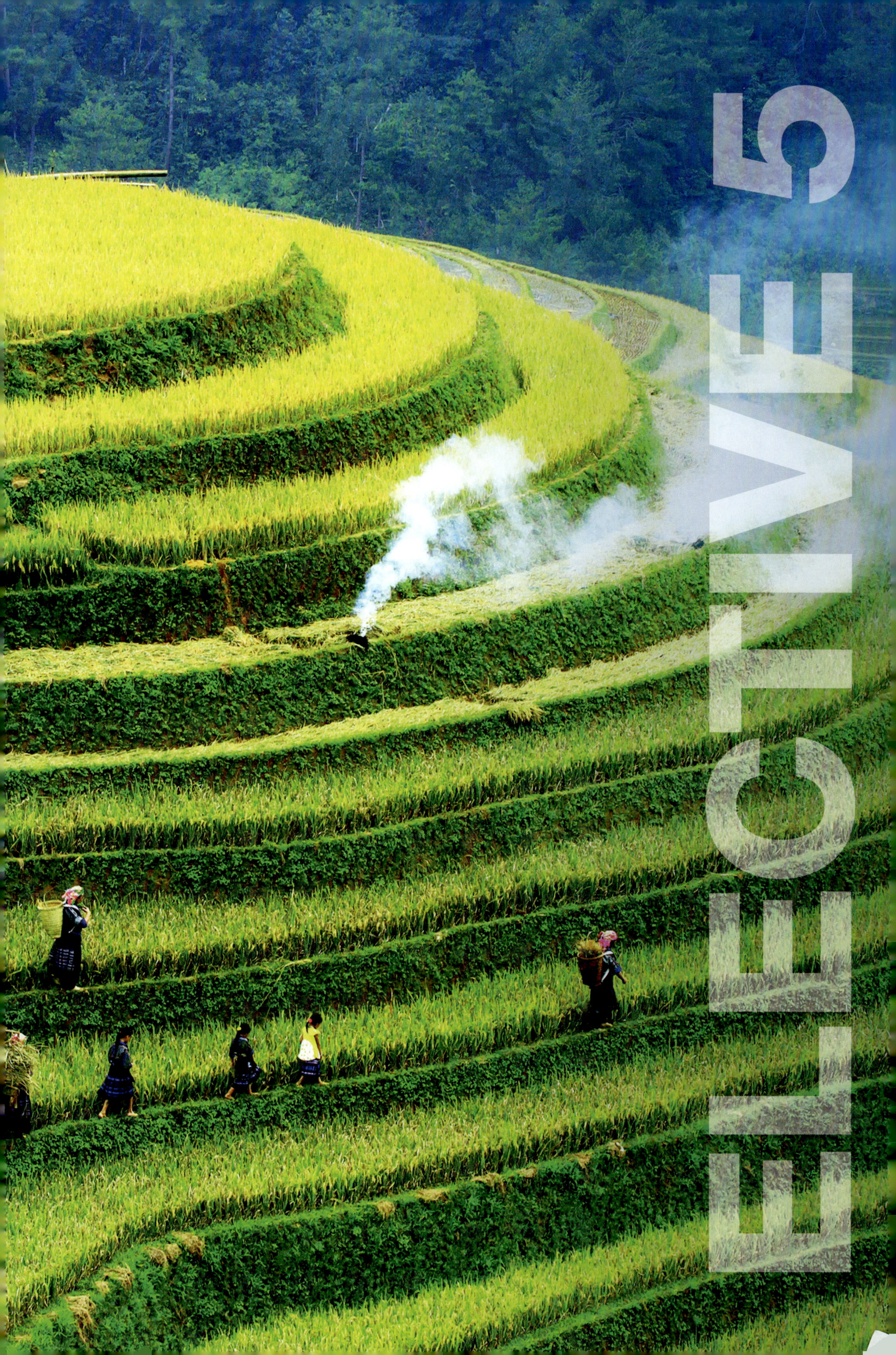
ELECTIVE 5

CHAPTER 1

Population Change Over Time and Space

In this chapter, you will be introduced to demographics – the study of human population. Many of the ideas discussed in this chapter will already be familiar to you from your studies of human processes in the regional section of the core Geography course. You will learn about the factors that influence the density and distribution of people throughout the world. You will learn how various factors impact on population patterns, birth rates and death rates. It is important that you gain a good understanding of how population characteristics vary over time, and from country to country, as well as the ways in which population can be measured and shown. The key terms and ideas presented in this chapter are the driving force behind all other aspects of human geography discussed in this elective.

KEY WORDS 🔑

- Population distribution
- Population density
- Dynamic
- Physical factors
- Human factors
- Physiological density
- Agricultural Revolution
- Industrial Revolution
- Birth rates
- Death rates
- Total fertility rates
- Life expectancy
- Migration
- Natural increase
- Natural decrease
- Demographic Transitional Model
- Population pyramid
- Dependency ratio

LEARNING OUTCOMES 🧠

What you MUST know
- The ways in which population distribution and population density can vary over time
- The factors that impact on population growth
- Demographic Transitional Model and the characteristics of countries in each stage
- Population pyramids and the differences between the pyramids for developed and developing countries
- Changing population characteristics of Ireland over time

What you SHOULD know
- Population distribution and population density of France
- The challenges facing Ireland's population in the future
- Examples of population characteristics of countries in the developed world and in the developing world

What is USEFUL to know
- The history of population growth

Introduction

On 21 October 2011, the world's population **reached 7 billion** people for the first time in its history. As well as causing a stir among the media, who searched for the '7 billionth baby', geographers took notice for reasons other than finding a new celebrity. Since 1750, the world's population has been increasing rapidly, with an even sharper increase occurring since 1960. As of March 2016 the world population is estimated to be 7.4 billion people – meaning an increase of some 400 million in just four and a half years. In this chapter, we will look at **the factors that influence the growth and distribution of population** across the globe. In particular, we will examine:

- Where the world's population lives
- The factors that influence population change
- The impacts of population growth and the patterns of population growth.

World population growth

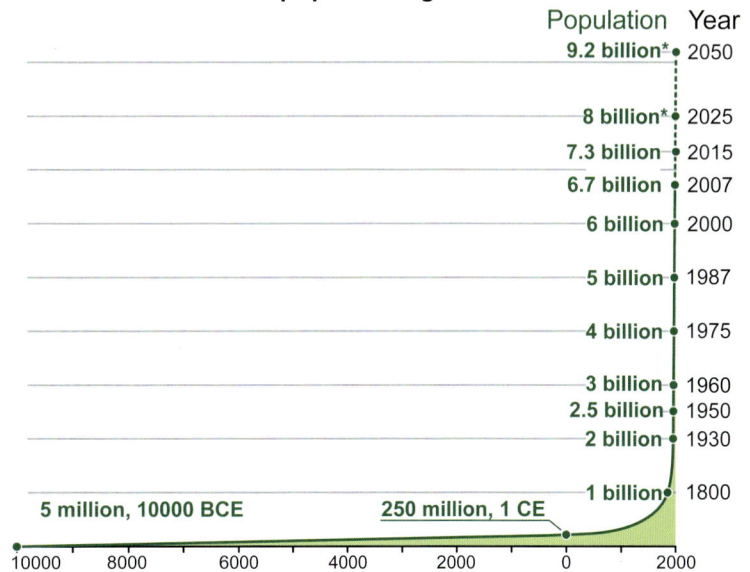

Population	Year
9.2 billion*	2050
8 billion*	2025
7.3 billion	2015
6.7 billion	2007
6 billion	2000
5 billion	1987
4 billion	1975
3 billion	1960
2.5 billion	1950
2 billion	1930
1 billion	1800

5 million, 10000 BCE   250 million, 1 CE

🔴 **Fig.1.1** Population growth has increased rapidly since 1750.

FACT

In 1960 there were 3 billion people in the world. After 15 years there were 4 billion people. After another 13 years there were 5 billion. After another 11 years there were 6 billion. After another 12 years there were 7 billion. At this rate, it is estimated that there will be over 11 billion people in the world by 2100.

1.1 Population Distribution and Population Density

Population distribution and *population density* are the terms used to describe where in the world people live. In this section, both terms are explained.

Distribution

Population distribution refers to the **spread of people across the world** or across a region. In simpler terms, it means **where people choose to live** and where they choose not to live. The distribution of **people across the world is very uneven** due to a number of factors that make areas either suitable or unsuitable to live in.

Some regions of the world are very difficult to live in because of their physical processes. For example:

- The Sahara Desert is extremely hot and dry.
- The Antarctic is extremely cold.
- The Himalaya Mountains are cold and oxygen is low at higher altitudes.

As you can see in Fig. 1.2, some areas of the world are far more desirable for people to settle in. These areas are:

- South East Asia
- Indian Subcontinent
- Central Europe
- Lowland coastal regions.

GEO DICTIONARY

Population distribution: the spread of people across an area

Population density: the number of people per square kilometre (km²)

FACT

The discovery and subsequent popularity of tea-drinking in England during the eighteenth century led to a significant increase in life expectancy. This was not because of the tea itself, but rather because the water used for tea was boiled, and therefore purified.

There are three main reasons why humans find these regions more desirable to live in. These regions have:

- A comfortable climate
- A plentiful supply of fresh water
- Rich, fertile soils for cultivation and agriculture.

Fig. 1.2 Population distribution and population density across the globe

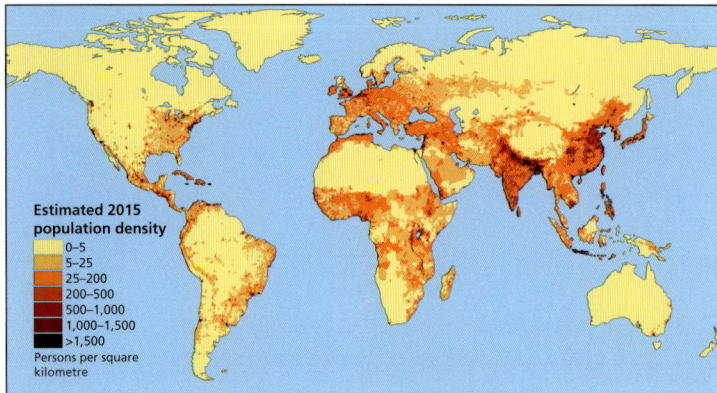

It is important to realise that the distribution of humans around the world changes over time (i.e. it is dynamic). We know this from looking at the movement of human settlements throughout history. Currently 90 per cent of the world's population is living in the northern hemisphere in tropical, subtropical and temperate latitudes (20°–60° north of the equator).

Density

It is clear that **population distribution** greatly **affects the population density** of an area. **Population density** is the **average number of people living per square kilometre of land** in a country/region. **A densely populated** region is generally accepted as one with more than **500 people per km²**.

From looking at the calculation on page 5, we can see that Ireland's population density currently stands at **68 people for every km²**. However, this does not give us an accurate reading of Ireland's population distribution. When we look at Fig. 1.3, it is clear that most of the population live along the east and south-east coast. **Dublin** City has a **population density** of over **4,500 per km²**, while the average population density of urban areas in Ireland is **1,736 per km²**. Parts of the **Gaeltacht in Connemara** have population densities as low as **6 per km²**.

Population density of Ireland
persons per km²

Fig. 1.3 Population distribution and population density in Ireland

1.2 Factors that Influence Population Distribution and Population Density

In order to explain why these differences in the distribution and density of populations occur across the globe, we need to look at both:

- Physical factors
- Human factors.

Physical Factors

Physical factors refers to:

- Relief
- Climate
- Soils
- Drainage.
- Resources

Relief

Relief of land has a **major impact** on the population **distribution** and population **density**. Areas of **flat, low-lying land** tending to have **the highest population densities**. Examples of this can be seen throughout the world. In your study of regional Geography you learned how the **upland relief in the West of Ireland discourages settlement**, while the **lowlands of the east encourage settlement**. This pattern is **repeated in Europe**, with the **highest** concentration of **population** occurring along the **lowlands of the North European Plain** and **sparse populations** existing along the **Alpine Mountains**. Outside of Europe, areas such as the **Andes Mountains** or the **Himalayas** have very **low population densities** as they have **severe climate conditions** and are **too steep** to build on.

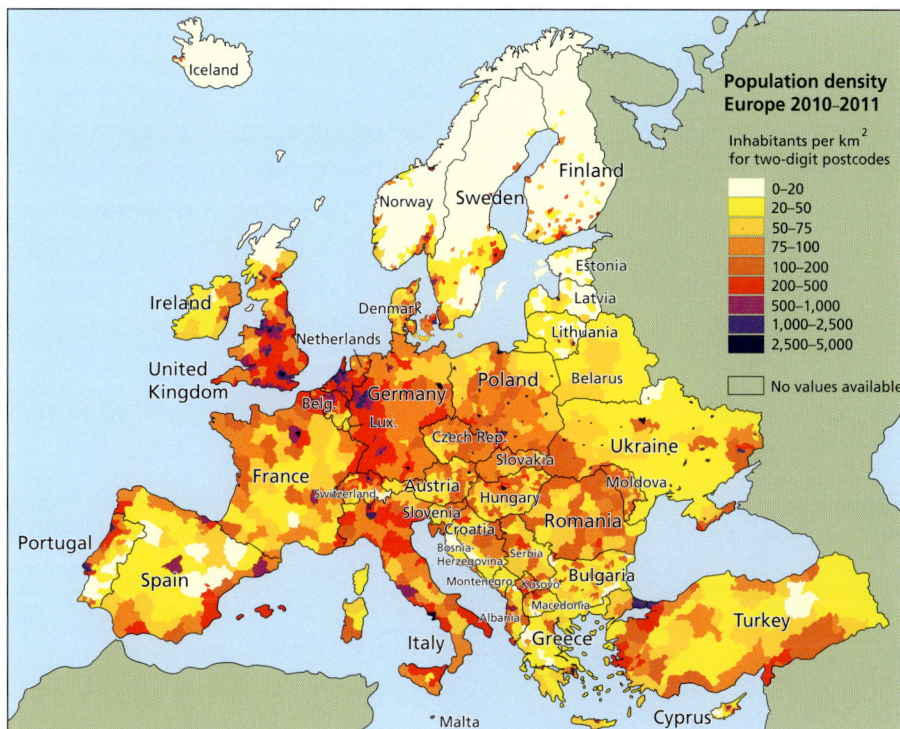

Fig. 1.4 The highest population densities of Europe are found along the North European Plain.

Today, over **80 per cent of the world's population** live at an altitude of **less than 500 m**, as the **building of settlements** and **transport networks** is much **easier on flat land**. The only **exception** to this is in **hot, tropical, equatorial regions** such as **Brazil**, where people prefer to **live in mountainous regions** as these areas are relatively cooler, e.g. **Rio de Janeiro**.

GEO NUMERACY

Population density is calculated by dividing the total population of the country/area by the total area of land (km^2) in the country/area:

$$\frac{Population}{Area\ (km^2)}$$

Using Ireland as an example:

Ireland's population: 4.7 million

Area of Ireland (km^2): 70,282 km^2

$$\frac{4,757,976}{70,282} = 67.70$$

Rounded to the nearest person, this gives Ireland a population density of 68 per km^2.

ACTIVE LEARNING

1. Define *population density* and give an example of a region with a high population density and a region with a low population density.

2. Why would Central Europe have a higher population density than areas such as the Sahara Desert?

3. Why does Ireland's population density of 68 not give an accurate picture of population distribution in the country?

Climate

Climate affects where **people can live comfortably** and it also has an impact on the **crops that can be grown** in an area. People prefer to **live in temperate climates** – 90 per cent of the world's population live in the **northern hemisphere's temperate zones**. In these temperate zones, **food crops are easily grown** and there is a **plentiful supply of fresh water**. The climate is comfortable and does not suffer from extremes such as **drought, severe flooding, freezing conditions**, etc. In contrast to this, regions with extreme climates are **too harsh for dense human settlement**. Hot desert climates are **too hot and dry to support large settlements** and require **irrigation schemes** to allow for **productive agriculture** capable of feeding a large population. Similarly, regions with **extremely cold climates** are **sparsely populated** (e.g. Northern Scandinavia, Northern Canada) as food production is impossible.

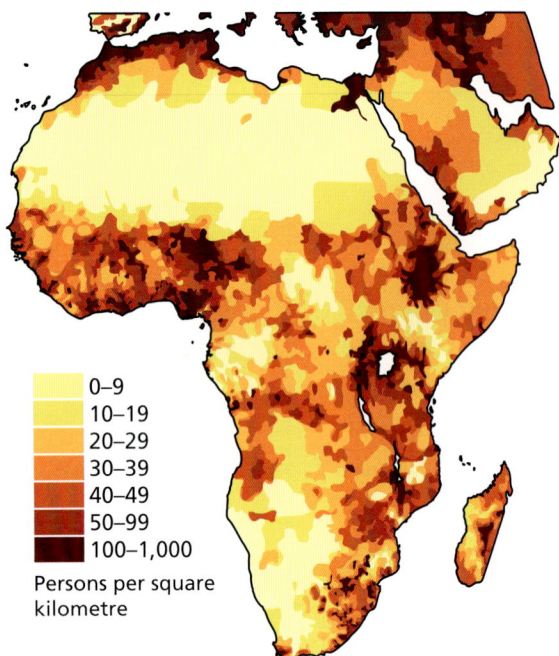

⌃ **Fig. 1.5** The Sahel region has low population densities because of its harsh climate.

Legend (Persons per square kilometre):
- 0–9
- 10–19
- 20–29
- 30–39
- 40–49
- 50–99
- 100–1,000

Soils

Areas of **flat land** usually have **more fertile soils** than mountainous areas. For example, the flat **North European Plain** has **fertile brown earths** and boulder clays which allow for **easy cultivation**. These **flat, fertile regions** attract settlement, as they are able to **support** the intensive growing of **crops** for food. This can also be seen in **Ireland**, where the **flatter**, more **fertile soil** of the **east** is more **densely populated** than **the poor mountainous soils** of the **west**. Mountainous **soils** are generally **thin and infertile**, which **discourages settlement**.

Drainage

Areas near a river are more **densely populated** than areas without **fresh water**. Rivers provide rich, **fertile alluvium** as well as transport, **food**,

⌃ **Fig. 1.6** Areas along the River Ganges are densely populated.

drinking water and (in earlier times) **defence**. Some of the **most densely populated parts of the world** are located in **river valleys**. For example:

- River Rhine (Central Europe)
- River Ganges (India)
- River Nile (Egypt).

FACT

Egypt's population is over 82 million; 90 per cent of the population live within 6 km of the River Nile.

GEO DICTIONARY

Extreme climate: a severe climate that experiences extremely high or low temperatures or extremely high or low levels of precipitation

Resources

Areas with a **plentiful supply of natural resources** are more **densely populated** than areas that lack basic resources. For example:

- **Europe** has a **plentiful supply** of resources and a **high population density**.
- The **Sahel in Central Africa** has **a low level of resources** and therefore a **low population density**.

Regions with a large supply of **resources attract business** and **industry**. However, **not all areas with resources are suitable for settlement**. For example, the **outback of Australia** contains small settlements that exist only because of the presence **of gold mines**. **Northern Sweden** also has a **low population density**, with mostly miners living there because of the presence of **iron ore deposits**.

Human Factors

Human factors relate to the way in which **humans interact with one another** or how their society is organised. We will look at three of the main human factors that impact on population density and distribution:

- Historic factors
- Government
- Socio-economic development.

Historic Factors

Events of the **past** can have an **effect** on **population density and distribution**. **Examples** of this can mainly be seen by the **colonial past** of European countries: English and French colonisation of North America; Spanish and Portuguese colonisation of South America; the Ulster Plantation, etc. The **Great Famine (1845–9)** had the **largest impact on Ireland's population** as **1 million people died of starvation** and another **1 million emigrated to countries such as Britain and the United States**. In the years following the Famine, Irish people continued to emigrate to these countries, and today there are **39.6 million Americans who claim Irish ancestry**.

Where Irish-Americans Live

Dark green shows areas with a higher density of Irish-Americans, while light yellow shows areas with a lower density of Irish-Americans

| 0–2.5% |
| 2.5–5% |
| 5–10% |
| 10%+ |

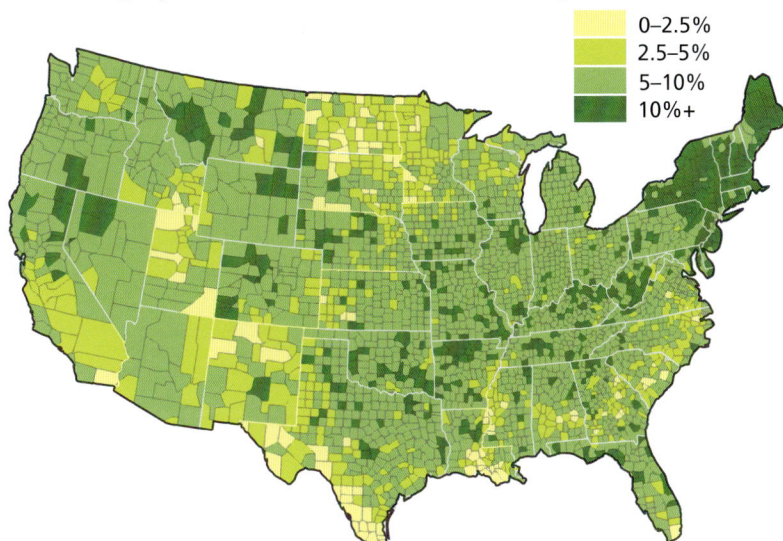

ACTIVE LEARNING

1. Explain how climate and soils influence the distribution and density of population.

2. Where are the most desirable places in the world to live? Why?

3. Go to **www.youtube.com** and search for 'population distribution and density'. There are several videos which explain the factors that influence population distribution and population density.

GEO DICTIONARY

Colonisation: the formation of a settlement in order to take control of territories or countries, typically to exploit their people or resources

◀ **Fig. 1.7** Population density of Irish-Americans living in the United States, shown by postcode

Elective 5: Human

CHAPTER 1

Government

Areas that have **stable government** tend to have **higher population densities** compared to regions where there is political unrest. For example:

- **Western Europe** has had **political stability** since the end of World War II in 1945.

Fig. 1.8 A UN-run refugee camp for Syrians in Jordan

- **Syria is suffering from a civil war** which began in 2011 due to political unrest. By July 2016, the United Nations estimated that **400,000 Syrians have been killed, 4.5 million people have fled Syria** and another **6.5 million people are displaced within Syria**.

Areas of **political unrest** tend to have **high levels of forced emigration** as refugees leave to escape danger. Since the conflict began in Syria, refugees have taken to desperate measures to escape the fighting and make their way into Europe.

Government policy can also **affect population distribution**: grants are offered to **live in certain areas** (e.g. the Gaeltacht in Ireland) or **resettlement schemes** can be implemented. An example of such a resettlement scheme occurred in **Brazil** where the **government encouraged people to move from Brazil's crowded cities** on the eastern coast to the specially **built capital Brasilia** further inland.

Socio-Economic

Places with **high levels of employment** are **more desirable** to live in than regions with **few job opportunities**.

Socio-economic conditions change over time and can cause **changes** in **distribution and density**. From **1995 to 2008** Ireland was a **desirable destination** for members of the EU who were **seeking employment**. However, since the **economic downturn of 2008**, many Irish have been **forced to emigrate** to the United States, Canada and Australia in search of work. Between **April 2013 and April 2014** over **81,900 people emigrated** from Ireland (225 per day).

ACTIVE LEARNING

1. Explain how historical factors have impacted on the population density and distribution of Ireland.
2. Why do areas with a stable government tend to have higher population densities?
3. Visit **www.iamsyria.org/conflict-background.html** for more information on the Syrian Civil War.

> **GEO DICTIONARY**
>
> **Forced migration:** when a person or group of people are unwillingly moved from their homes

Urban growth, 2005–2010

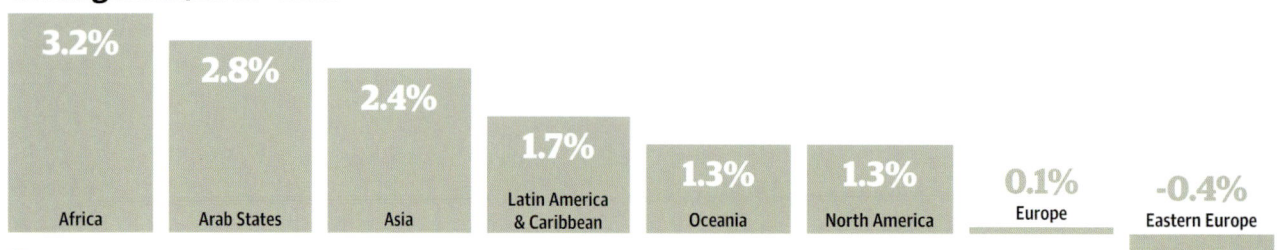

3.2%	2.8%	2.4%	1.7%	1.3%	1.3%	0.1%	-0.4%
Africa	Arab States	Asia	Latin America & Caribbean	Oceania	North America	Europe	Eastern Europe

Fig. 1.9 The world's urban population

1.3 Physiological Density

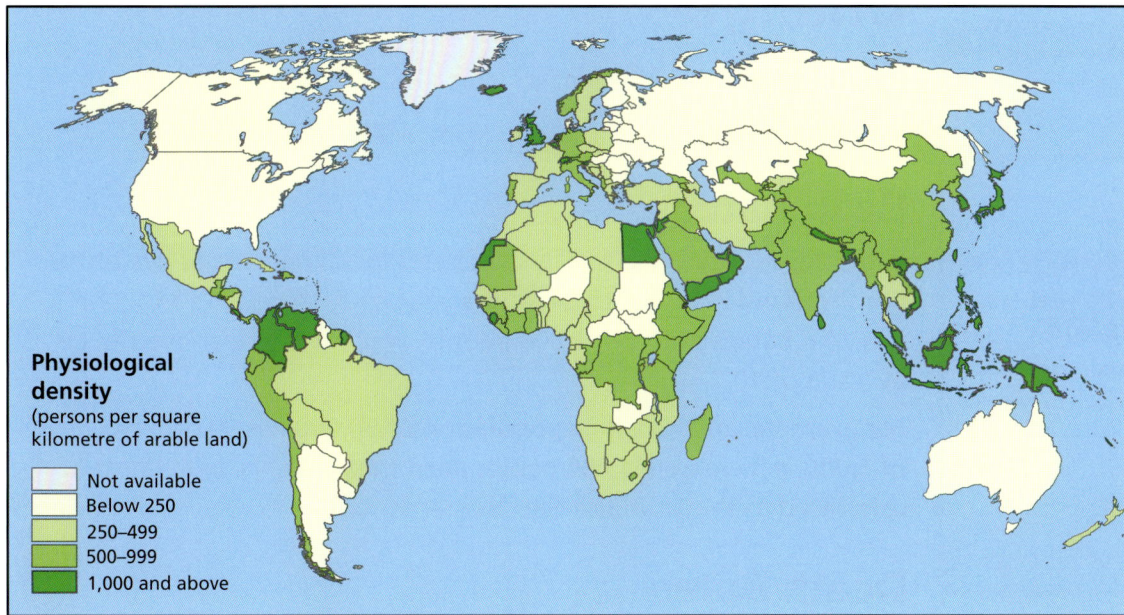

Fig. 1.10 Physiological density across the globe

As you can see, a wide variety of factors affect where people live. Therefore, the **basic calculation of population density** (total population divided by total area of land) **does not give** us an **accurate reflection** of how **population densities** are **distributed throughout a country**. For example, **Ireland** has a **population density of 68 per km²** but this does not reflect the fact that there are certain parts of the country where very few people live. Places with **low population densities** in Ireland include the **Burren**; mountain ranges, such as **MacGillycuddy's Reeks** and the **Wicklow Mountains**; and parts of **Connemara**.

Demographers use a **better measurement** known as **physiological density** to get a more accurate figure. Physiological density is the **number of people in a country per area of agriculturally productive land**, i.e. all agriculturally **unproductive areas of land** (such as mountains or boglands) are **taken away** from the area of the country. The population is then divided by the remaining area.

> **19** GEO **NUMERACY**
>
> **Physiological density**
>
> $$\frac{\text{Population}}{\text{Productive area of land}}$$
>
> Population: 4.7 million
>
> Productive area: 11,821 km²
>
> $$\frac{4{,}757{,}976}{11{,}821} = 402.5$$
>
> Ireland has a physiological density of: 402.5 per km²

> **A2** GEO **DICTIONARY**
>
> **Physiological density:** the number of people in a country per area of agriculturally productive land, i.e. agriculturally unproductive areas of land are not included

1.4 Measuring Population Change

Population growth is affected by:

- Birth rates
- Death rates.

GEO NUMERACY

Example of birth rate: a population of 50,000 has 1,000 babies born in a year

50,000 = 50 groups of 1,000

Divide the number of births (1,000) by the number of groups of 1,000 (50)

i.e. $\dfrac{1,000}{50}$

This gives us 20 births per 1,000

i.e. for every 1,000 people there were 20 babies born.

GEO NUMERACY

Example of death rate: a population of 50,000 has 800 deaths in a year

50,000 = 50 groups of 1,000

Divide the number of deaths (800) by the number of groups of 1000 (50)

i.e. $\dfrac{800}{50}$

This gives us 16 births per 1,000

i.e. for every 1,000 people there were 16 deaths.

Birth Rates

Birth rate, also known as fertility rate, refers to the **number of live births per thousand in a country/area in a year**. In **2014** Ireland's birth rate was **14.4 babies born per 1,000 people**, which was well **above the EU average of 10.1**.

For example, an area with a **population of 50,000 has 50 groups of 1,000**. If there were **1,000 babies born that year**, the birth rate is calculated as shown in the Geo Numeracy box.

Death Rates

Death rate, also known as mortality rate, refers to **the number of deaths per thousand in a country/area in a year**. For example, an area with a **population of 50,000 has 800 deaths per year**. The death rate is calculated as shown in the Geo Numeracy box.

Natural Increase

A **natural increase** occurs when the **birth rate of a country is higher than its death rate**, e.g. **Ireland** has a **birth rate of 15.9** and a **death rate of 6.37**. Therefore, Ireland has a **natural increase of 9.53 per thousand**.

Natural Decrease

A **natural decrease** occurs when the **death rate of a country is higher than its birth rate**, e.g. **Italy** has a **birth rate of 9.23** and a **death rate of 10.9**. Therefore, Italy has a **natural decrease of 1.67 per thousand**.

GEO DICTIONARY

Birth rate: the number of live births per thousand in a country/area in a year

Death rate: the number of deaths per thousand in a country/area in a year

Natural increase: when a country has a higher number of births than deaths

Natural decrease: when a country has a higher number of deaths than births

ACTIVE LEARNING

1. Calculate the birth rates for the following:
   Births 4,500; Population 73,000
   Births 15,000; Population 108,000
   Births 11,500; Population 52,500.

2. Calculate the death rates for the following:
   Deaths 1,000; Population 72,000
   Deaths 970; Population 45,000
   Deaths 1,257; Population 39,725.

1.5 Influences on Birth/Death Rates

There are four main factors that influence birth rates and death rates in a country:

- Education and social status of women
- Standard of living
- Government policy
- Culture and religion.

Education and Social Status of Women

There is a clear and obvious **connection between** the **educational opportunities of women** in a country **and their role within the country's society**. In **developed countries**, women receive a **full education** and can therefore make **informed decisions** regarding their family size, i.e. **family planning. Women who stay** within the **education system longer** tend to have **fewer children**, as they pursue **full-time careers** and **delay having children** until they are older.

- When women have fewer children, birth rates are lowered.

- When women are better educated, their **medical and healthcare knowledge lowers infant death** rates and raises life expectancy.

- In **developing countries**, many **women do not receive an education**. They **marry at a younger age** and have more children. Since these women are less educated, **family planning** sometimes does not occur.

- When women in one generation have **more children**, the **number of births can remain high in the next generation**.

- **Lack of education** and **poor medical/healthcare** knowledge leads to **high death rates** and **low life expectancy**. In strict **Islamic countries, women** are expected to **obey their husband's wishes** regarding **how many children** they will have, e.g. **Afghanistan** has a **fertility rate of 5.6 per woman**. In **sub-Saharan countries** such as Zambia, women often begin having children in their **teenage years**, leading to **high birth rates** and a **large natural increase**. In Zambia, **one-third of girls under the age of 18 have given birth**. This has given the country a **natural increase of 38 per thousand**.

GEO **DICTIONARY**

Family planning:
planning or controlling the number of children and the time period in between having children, usually through means of contraception

Standard of living:
the quality of life and the opportunities available to a person in a country

Fig. 1.11 The education of women is a key factor for the global reduction of birth rates.

Standard of Living

Countries with a **higher standard of living** (developed countries) have much **lower birth rates and death rates** compared to less developed countries. In total, the **average cost of raising a child to the age of 21 in Ireland** is €105,000, including **clothing, healthcare, food** and **education**. Therefore, **having a child** brings an **economic pressure** which results in many **couples having smaller families**. **Death rates** are **lower in developed countries**, where people have access to **better health services**. This, combined with **clean water supplies** and **proper sanitation systems**, lowers mortality rates.

In **underdeveloped** or **developing** countries, people do not have access to quality **healthcare services, financial support** for **families** or **pensions**. Therefore, couples have **as many children as possible** to **ensure that enough children survive** into adulthood to look after the parents when they are elderly. **Child mortality rates** are **high** due to a **lack of healthcare**. In some countries, having **more male children** is considered to **raise the social status of a family**, e.g. India. A **lack of clean water, food** and **sanitation** also **raise death rates**.

Estimate cost of raising a child in Ireland €105,321

NAPPIES €505.68	**HOLIDAYS** €1,653.72	**GADGETS** €577.92	**CHILDCARE** €4,094.52
FOOD €3,197.52	**HEALTH** €647.76	**COLLEGE FEES** €4,056.24	**TRAVEL** €942.84
DAYS OUT €613.32	**PRESENTS** €499.08	**RENT** €3,320.76	

Average monthly household spend on child-related expenses €919.47

Average annual household spend on child-related expenses €11,033.64

⌃ Fig. 1.12 The cost of raising a child in Ireland

Government Policy

In some countries, **governments intervene to control birth rates** in a country. This can be carried out in order to **reduce or increase the country's population**. Government policy can have a **strong influence on the demographic trends** in a country. For example, in Ireland, **children's allowance payments, child healthcare** (medical card) and access to **primary and secondary education** are provided by the state. These factors make Ireland an **attractive country in which to have children**. However, factors such as the **high cost of living in Ireland** and the **length of time children stay in the education system** can reduce the number of children a couple may have.

Examples of government intervention in birth rates include:

- **China's one-child policy**, which lasted from **1979 to 2016** and aimed to **reduce** birth rates
- **Romania's** introduction of a **series of policies** that aimed to **increase** birth rates.

How Government Policy Reduces Population Growth

China's One-Child Policy

🔺 **Fig. 1.13** China and surrounding regions

In order to **reduce the rate of population growth** in the country, the Chinese government introduced a **one-child policy** in **1979**. The policy was **strictly enforced** by the **government**, especially in the **urban areas in eastern China**, e.g. Shanghai. Families who **obeyed the policy** were awarded through **incentives**, such as **higher wages** and better **educational opportunities**, and received additional **financial assistance** from the government. **For families who did not obey the policy**, there were a **number of sanctions**, e.g. **fines, termination of employment**, and a withdrawal of government assistance, such as children's healthcare.

There were a number of **exceptions** to the policy:

- The policy **applied strictly to urban dwellers** in the east; it was **not as strictly enforced** in the more **sparsely populated west** of the country.

- Any couple who were **both from one-child families** themselves were **allowed to have a second child**.

- Couples could **apply to have a second child**, which was more likely to be **granted** if couples agreed to wait for four years.

How Government Policy Increases Population Growth

Romania's Policies for Population Growth

🔺 **Fig. 1.14** Romania and surrounding regions

Romania has a population of **19.8 million** people, which is **declining by 0.29 per cent** annually. During the **1960s** Romania's population growth was slow, with **a natural increase of 6 per 1,000 per year**. This was a problem for the government as they relied on the **availability of a large, young workforce** for their industrial economy. In order to increase birth rates, the government **introduced policies in 1965** which:

- Made **abortion illegal**

- Made **divorce difficult**

- Introduced **tax penalties for childless citizens** over the age of 25

- Introduced **tax incentives** and rewards for larger families

- **Banned** the importation of **contraceptives**.

Effects

As **boys** are **preferred** in **China**, couples began having **scans to determine the gender** of the child. In many cases, an **abortion was carried out** if the woman was **pregnant with a girl**. This **gender bias** led to a **greater number of boys being born**. This has created a **gender imbalance** in the country, with **117 boys for every 100 girls**. In response to this, the government banned scans to determine gender in many parts of the country, although this had **little effect in resolving the problem**.

Birth rate in China (per 1,000)

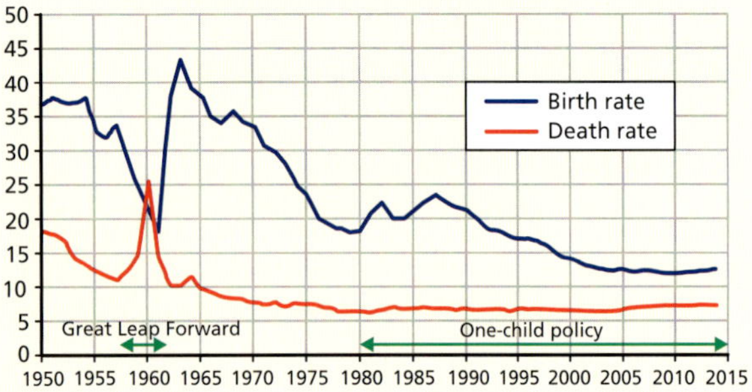

Fig. 1.15 Impact of the one-child policy on birth rates in China

The one-child policy moved China **from stage 2 to stage 4 of the Demographic Transitional Model** (see Section 1.6) very rapidly, meaning the rate of **population growth slowed greatly**. Birth rates fell below the replacement level at **1.55 children per fertile woman**, with some urban areas having **a fertility rate of less than 1.0**.

As of 2016 **China's government has removed the one-child policy** in order to **prevent the population from ageing rapidly** and to **prevent further population decline**. Couples are now allowed to have **two children**. While couples are allowed to **have larger families**, their **family planning is still controlled by the government**.

Demographers fear that the move will not be **enough** to **prevent future issues**. This is mainly due to the fact that **the old policy has led to a societal culture** of having one child or remaining childless. The first signs of this **occurred in 2012** when the **government relaxed the policy**, allowing for **12 million couples** to apply to have a second child. However, only **1.4 million**

Effects

The potential of a **financial reward** combined with the **lack of available birth control** led to a **93 per cent increase** in births between **1965 and 1967**. However, this **initial success** was counteracted by a **significant increase in infant and maternal fatalities**. As a result, by **1975**, the total fertility rate (TFR) had fallen to just **3.7 per 1,000**.

Birth rate in Romania (per 1,000)

Fig. 1.16 Birth rates in Romania

The state **failed** to **take into account** the **relationship** between **socio-economic development** and **population growth**. As most of the **government's money** was **invested in agriculture** and **heavy industry**, whose produce was **sold off to pay foreign debt**, the **standard of living declined**.

By the **mid-1980s** Romania's **standard of living** was equal to that of a **Lesser Developed Country** (LDC), with a **shortage** of even the **most basic childcare needs** such as nappies, milk formula and infant clothing.

The **high level of poverty** led to many couples placing their children in **state-run orphanages**, where conditions were terrible.

By the **mid-1990s, birth rates began to decline** to more **natural figures**. Birth rates now average **9.27 per 1,000**, while **death rates** average **11.9 per 1,000**.

families applied, indicating that **removing the policy will not solve China's ageing population problem.**

It is estimated that by **2030 China will have 219 million people** over the age of **65**, which will be almost **17 per cent of the country's population.**

FACT

Some sources estimate that the one-child policy prevented over 200 million births in China since its introduction in 1979.

It is not just China who face the dilemma of an ageing population. Countries such as the US, Canada, Russia, Australia, Japan and France are all facing the prospect of 25 per cent of their population being aged 65 and over in the near future.

It is estimated that 25 per cent of the Earth's population will be over the age of 65 by 2100. This is compared to just 5 per cent in 1950.

FACT

In 1966, the then Romanian president Nicolae Ceausescu declared that 'anyone who avoids having children is a deserter who abandons the laws of national continuity'.

FACT

The number of divorces granted in Romania fell from 26,000 in 1966 to just 28 in 1967.

Culture and Religion

Religion can hugely **affect growth rates**, e.g. in countries where **Catholicism is strong, birth rates tend to be high**. The Catholic Church is **opposed to artificial contraception and abortion**, which had led to **high birth rates** in countries with a strong Catholic ethos. **Traditionally, family planning in Ireland** was **heavily influenced by** the views of the **Catholic Church**, which promoted large families. However, as the **influence** of the church declined in Ireland, **the use of contraceptives** combined with **cultural change** led to a **reduction in family size.**

Hinduism, which is the faith of the **majority of India's population,** does not oppose birth control. However, it does **promote large families**; this, combined with India's **societal belief** that **having more sons** is **desirable,** has led to high birth rates. By having more sons, **families** will **receive dowries** from their son's future wives. Therefore, having more sons is seen as an **economic advantage.** The more **developed a country is, the less likely it is that cultural or religious issues will influence birth rates.** In a developed country, economic factors are more likely to affect family size.

GEO DICTIONARY

Lesser Developed Country: a country that shows the lowest levels of socio-economic development

ACTIVE LEARNING

1. Explain, using examples, how the educational status of women and their role in society impacts on population growth.

2. Name and explain three factors that have an effect on a country's population growth.

3. Using an example you have studied, explain how government intervention has impacted on population growth.

4. Discussion: To what extent do you think governments should have an influence on the number of children a woman may have? Do you think governments should have an input or is it an entirely personal decision?

1.6 The Demographic Transitional Model

The **rapid increase in the world's population** has led demographers to believe that **as a country develops**, both **economically and socially**, it goes through a **series of predictable changes regarding birth rates**, **death rates** and **population growth**. The changes are **outlined in a graph** known as the **Demographic Transitional Model (DTM)**, also known as the population cycle. There are **five key stages** outlined in the model:

- Stage 1: **High fluctuating stage**
- Stage 2: **Early expanding stage**
- Stage 3: **Late expanding stage**
- Stage 4: **Low fluctuating stage**
- Stage 5: **Senile stage.**

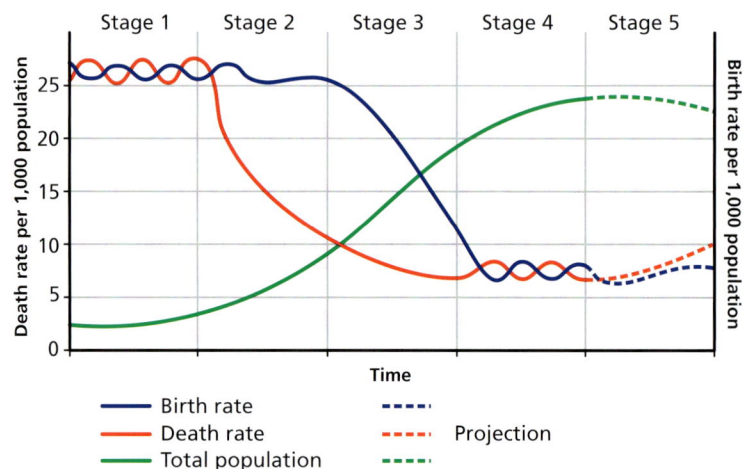

▶ **Fig. 1.17** Demographic Transitional Model

Stage 1: High Fluctuating Stage

This is also known as the **high stationary stage** and is characterised by **high birth rates and high death rates** of over **40 per 1,000**. Although there are **no countries** in the world **permanently at the high fluctuating stage**, **famine, war** and **disease** can lead to countries **returning to this stage** for a period of time. As high **birth rates** are **counterbalanced** by **death rates**, **population change** is **slow and erratic**.

Why are Birth Rates so High in Stage 1?

In countries in Stage 1, **women** are **uneducated**. This means that there is a **lack of family planning** and also that women begin having **children at** a very **young age**. Due to a **high infant mortality rate**, women have as **many children as possible** to ensure that enough children survive to look after the parents when they are older. **Agriculture** is the **main form of economy** for regions in Stage 1. Therefore, **families are large** in order to **provide enough labour** to farm the land. In this way, **children** are seen as **an economic asset**.

Why are Death Rates so High in Stage 1?

Since countries in Stage 1 are the **least developed**, they are **prone to famine and disease** outbreaks. Countries can also find themselves in Stage 1 due to **war**. One of the best-known examples of this is **Rwanda**, which experienced a **devastating civil war and genocide** from 1990 to 1994, in which nearly **2 million Rwandans died**. This **high loss of life** cancelled out the country's **high birth rate**. Poor medical knowledge can also lead to a **country experiencing high death rates**, since contagious diseases are **spread rapidly due to poor sanitation** and **hygiene practices**. This, combined with a **poor diet**, can lead to **high death rates**. An example of this is the **Ebola virus**, which has **killed nearly 11,500 people** since the outbreak began in 2014. Most of the **deaths caused by the virus** occurred in countries along the **West Coast of Africa**.

Fig. 1.18 The Rwandan Civil War returned the country to Stage 1 of the Demographic Transitional Model.

Stage 2: Early Expanding Stage

Stage 2 is characterised by a **rapid population growth**. There is a rapid **decrease in the country's death rate**, while **birth rates remain high**. The decrease in death rates is most commonly caused by **improvements in healthcare** and **medical knowledge**. Basic measures, such as **boiling water, reduce waterborne diseases**, e.g. **cholera** and **typhoid**. Greater **access to clean drinking water** from wells reduces the number of people drinking from free-flowing rivers and stagnant malarial lakes. **Vaccines against childhood illnesses**, such as measles, greatly **reduce infant mortality**. Basic **technological advances** in **food production** also contribute to the **decreasing death rate**, as simple measures such as **crop rotation** provide more stability with regard to crop yields.

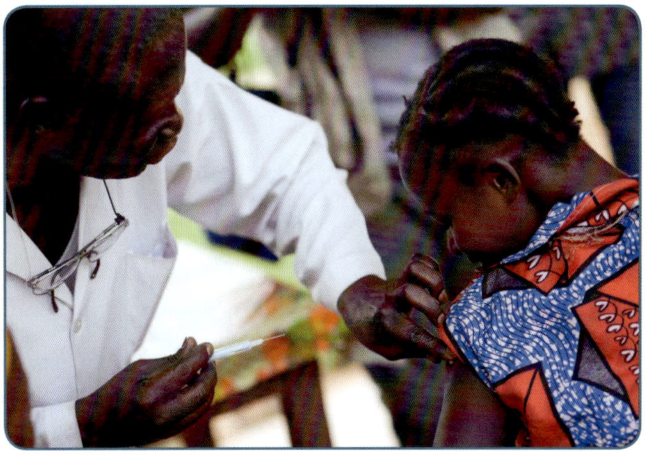

Despite the **decrease in death rates, births remain high** as women remain **uneducated and unaware** of **family planning**. As in Stage 1, women began having children at a young age, meaning they have **large families**. These children act as carers for their **ageing parents**. **Life expectancy remains low**.

Fig. 1.19 Vaccines greatly reduce child mortality.

While **Europe** passed through Stage 2 in the **nineteenth century**, many of the world's **poorest countries** still experience **rapid population growth**. Many **sub-Saharan countries** such as Nigeria, Kenya and Mali are in Stage 2, as are Asian countries such as Bangladesh, Nepal, Pakistan and Afghanistan.

Afghanistan is a **country in Stage 2** of the demographic model. Afghanistan's **population is 32.5 million**, having risen **by 12 million in just 15 years**. The country has an annual **natural increase of 2.7 per cent**, which is one of the highest in the world. Currently, Afghanistan's **birth rate is 35 per 1,000**, while its death rate is **8 per 1,000**. Only ten years ago Afghanistan's death rate was over 20 per 1,000.

Improvements in **public health** have led to **reductions in child mortality**, while increased **access to food and improved sanitation** have **increased life expectancy**. In order to progress to Stage 3, Afghanistan needs to address social and economic factors that raise birth rates, such as:

- **High levels of illiteracy for women**
- Compromised **role of women in society**
- High level of **poverty.**

⊙ **Fig. 1.20** Afghan women protest in Kabul, capital of Afghanistan.

GEO DICTIONARY

Illiteracy: when people are unable to read and write

Economic liability: when something costs money and therefore must be budgeted/planned for

Stage 3: Late Expanding Stage

Stage 3 is experienced by countries with a **rapidly improving standard of living** due to a developing economy. As the country becomes more developed, its **population can afford a better diet** and have **better access to healthcare**. As a result, **death rates continue to decline**. Birth rates begin to decline rapidly as women now have **access to family planning**. **Low infant mortality rates** mean that mothers **no longer have large families**, as it is far more likely that children will survive into adulthood. **Children** are **no longer an economic asset**, as their education, health and other needs must be paid for. Instead they are **now an economic liability** and their parents must **plan how many children they can afford** to have.

European countries passed through Stage 3 in the **first half of the twentieth century**. However, large areas of the world are **still in Stage 3**, such as **India**, **Mexico**, the United Arab Emirates, Morocco and South Africa.

Stage 4: Low Fluctuating Stage

Stage 4 is also known as the **low stationary stage** and is experienced by **highly economically developed countries**. Both **birth rates and death rates are low** due to a **high standard of living**, **high levels of education**, highly **developed healthcare systems** and **equal employment opportunities** for women. Birth rates are **low**, since **children** are seen as an **economic liability**. The **cost of raising a child is very high** and the larger a family is, the more economic pressure there is to provide for children. The populations of Stage 4 **countries are highly urbanised**, where land **prices and housing** are **more expensive**. This also **limits the number of children** a family can cater for within the home.

Ageing planet

	World average	Japan	United Kingdom	USA	Russia	China	Turkey	South Africa
	11.7% 29.2	32.3% 45.9	28% 40.2	19.7% 37.4	19% 38.3	13.9% 35.4	10.8% 29.4	8.6% 26

■ The proportion of people over 60 years (of total population)
■ Average (median) age of the population

⌃ **Fig. 1.21** An ageing world

Death rates are low, since **life expectancy is high** – roughly 80 years. Countries in the **developed world** reached **Stage 4** in the **latter half of the twentieth century**, e.g. **Ireland**, the US and France.

Stage 5: The Senile Stage

Stage 5 is characterised by **birth rates that are lower than death rates**. Birth rates are well **below replacement levels**, as **women delay having children** and can pursue careers. Therefore, women have much smaller families. As there are **very few children being born**, the population ages. This is **referred to as 'greying'**. Greying has **serious economic consequences** as there are **not enough young workers to fill the vacancies** when older generations retire. In order to fill theses vacancies, a country in Stage 5 **depends on immigration**. Stage 5 is a relatively **new population trend**, with countries such as **Germany**, **Japan**, **Croatia** and **Greece** experiencing population decline.

CASE STUDY 📁

Although **Germany** is the **16th most populous country** in the world, with **81.5 million people**, its **birth rates have been lower than its death rates** for over 50 years. In 2013, Germany's **birth rate was 8 per 1,000**, while its **death rate was 11 per 1,000**. This means that Germany should be experiencing a population decline of 0.2 per cent per year. However, Germany's **total population continues to grow** due to **immigration**.

1.7 Population Pyramids and Dependency Ratio

FACT

Women in sub-Saharan Africa today are as likely to die in pregnancy or childbirth as were women in nineteenth-century England.

FACT

Despite the fact that it is against the law, there are over 37,000 children forced into marriage each year, most of whom are young girls who are forced to marry much older men.

The **structure of a country's population** changes greatly over time, which **impacts on the needs and concerns** of the people. Because of the constant change of population, the most accurate way to show the population trend in a country is through population pyramids. Population pyramids show us:

- What percentage of the population are economically active (paying tax) and **dependent** (Aged 0–14 and 65+)
- The proportion of **males and females**
- The age of a country's population.

As a country moves through the stages of the Demographic Transitional Model, the structure of its population changes. In Stages 1–3, there is a higher percentage of children and the population is quite young. As a country moves to Stage 4 and Stage 5, there are fewer young people and more elderly. There are three general shapes that population pyramids take:

- Progressive
- Stationary
- Regressive

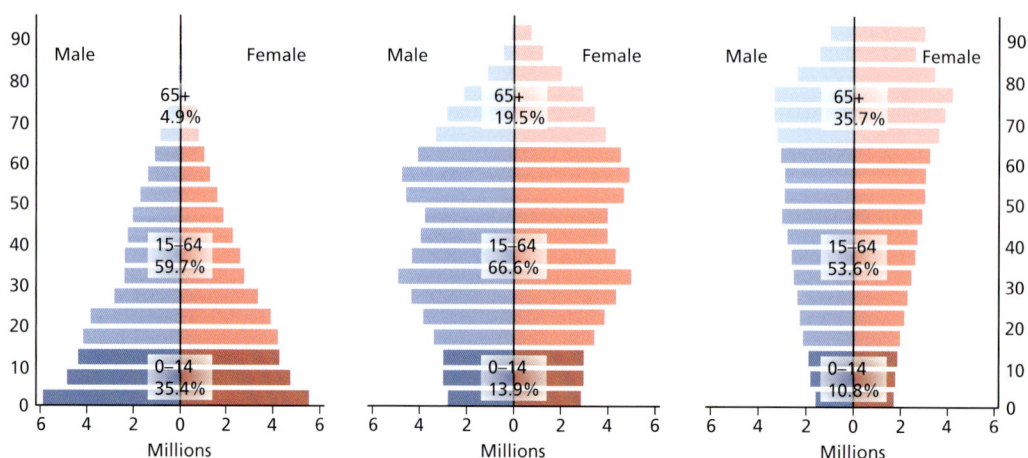

▲ **Fig. 1.22** Population pyramids can be progressive, stationary or regressive.

Progressive

A **progressive** pyramid can be identified by its **wide base** and **narrow peak**. With **each increase in age** group, the **population decreases**, causing the **pyramid** to **narrow quickly**. This shape signifies a **low life expectancy** with **high birth rates** and **high death rates**. This is typical of countries in Stages 1–3 of the DTM.

Stationary

A **stationary pyramid** indicates a **developed country** in **Stage 4** of the DTM, e.g. **Ireland**. This pyramid has a **blockier shape** as all **age** groups account for an **approximately equal percentage** of the population. A relatively **narrow base** suggests **lower birth rates** while a **wider peak** indicates a **longer life expectancy** than countries with progressive pyramids.

Regressive

Regressive pyramids represent a **developed country** in **Stage 5** of the DTM. A regressive pyramid indicates a country **suffering from low birth rates**. The **middle of the pyramid bulges**, while the **peak is wide**, indicating that the **population** is **old or greying**. As the population is old, there are **not enough births to replace the economically active sector**, which **creates issues** regarding **payment of taxes and pensions**.

CASE STUDY 📁

Population Pyramid of Japan

Japan has passed through the DTM rapidly, which can be seen in the changing population pyramids of the country.

In **1950** Japan's population pyramid was **progressive**, since the country was in **Stage 2** of the DTM. At this time, Japan's **families** were **much larger** and **35 per cent of the population was aged 0–14. Less than 5 per cent** of the population was aged **65 and over**, as **life expectancy** was much **lower** than it is today.

By **2007** Japan had **progressed to Stage 4** of the DTM, with its population pyramid changing from **progressive to stationary**.

🔺 **Fig. 1.23** Population pyramid of Japan

The **base** of the model was **narrower**, as family sizes had decreased due to **high levels of education** among **women** and a culture of **family planning**. By now, the **percentage** of the **population over** the age of **65** was far **greater than those under the age of 14**.

As of **2016** Japan remains in the **stationary pyramid shape**, although it **continues** to take on an '**inverted shape**', as the '**bulge**' **moves further upwards**, towards the peak of the pyramid.

GEO **DICTIONARY**

Replacement rate: the number of births needed in a country to maintain current population levels; this is generally considered to be 2.1 births per woman

It is predicted that by **2050**, Japan's population pyramid will be **regressive** if current trends continue. If birth rates continue to remain **below the replacement rate**, the **population will age** dramatically, with over **40 per cent above 65 years**. **Life expectancy** will also **continue to increase** as improvements to healthcare are made.

Ratio of workers to pensioners

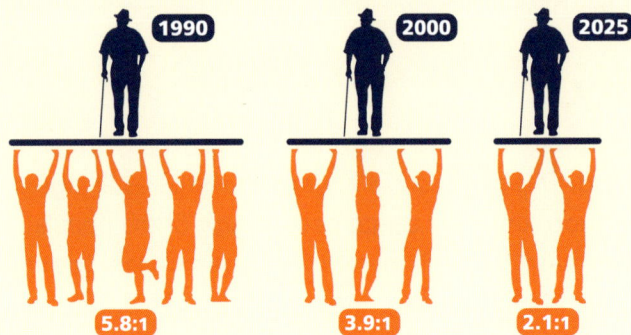

> **Fig. 1.24** Ratio of workers to pensioners in Japan

CASE STUDY 📁

Population Pyramid of Brazil

Brazil is in **Stage 3** of the DTM, which can be seen by its **progressive pyramid shape**. As the country develops, **better education and healthcare** will lead to **smaller families**, **longer life expectancy** and **slower population growth**. Although **rapidly developing**, it will take years, even decades, before the country **moves to a stationary pyramid**.

> **Fig. 1.25** Population pyramid of Brazil

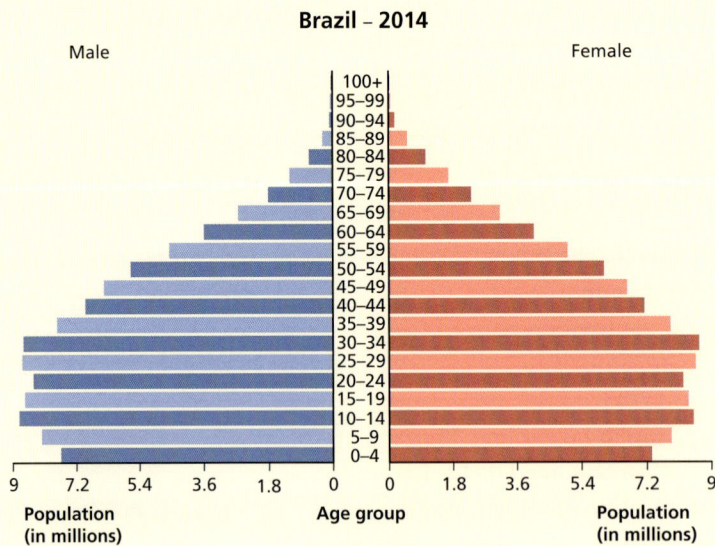

Brazil – 2014

ACTIVE LEARNING

1. Name the three general shapes of population pyramids.

2. Describe the shape of a population pyramid for countries in Stages 1–3 of the DTM.

3. In what way can a government benefit from using population pyramids?

4. Visit www.populationpyramid.net and explore how population pyramids of countries and the world have changed and will change over time.

Why Use Population Pyramids?

Population pyramids are **valuable to governments**, as they allow a government to **predict the future needs** of its population. For **example**, in **Ireland**, the **Department of Health** can **plan for the services needed** by a growing elderly population, e.g. nursing homes. Likewise, an **increase in the number of children** being born allows governments to **plan for children's health services**. Population pyramids also allow for the **planning of educational and housing needs** for a population.

1.8 The Dependency Ratio

Dependency ratio refers to the **percentage of the population** aged **0–14 and 65+** living in a country, compared to the number of people aged 15–64. Knowledge of this ratio is vital for **governments** as it allows them to **budget** and **plan** for the **future**. An **old or ageing** population leads to a **smaller ratio** between **economically active** people **and dependent** people in a country. The **economically active** population **pay taxes**, which in turn **pays for** the **country's services**. The **higher the percentage** of economically active people there are, the more money there is for the provision of services. If there is a **large dependant population**, an **increased tax burden** will be placed on the economically active.

GEO DICTIONARY

Dependency ratio: the number of people in a country who are not working (i.e. aged 0–14 and 65+) compared to the number of people who are working (i.e. aged 15–64)

Economically active: earning a wage and paying tax

GEO NUMERACY

Example of the dependency ratio: Ireland

$$\frac{\text{Children aged 0–14 + People aged 65}^+}{\text{Working population}} \times \frac{100}{1}$$

$$\frac{979{,}590 + 535{,}393}{3{,}073{,}269} \times \frac{100}{1} = 49.3$$

Therefore, there are **49.3 dependants** for **every 100 economically active person in Ireland**. This gives us a ratio of 49:100. (*based on 2011 statistics*)

CASE STUDY 📁

1.9 Ireland's Population Change Over Time

The population characteristics of Ireland have **changed greatly** over the past **150 years**. In this case study, we will examine Ireland's population characteristics with regard to:

- Population distribution and population density
- Changing birth rates
- Population structure
- An investigation of the most recent Irish census.

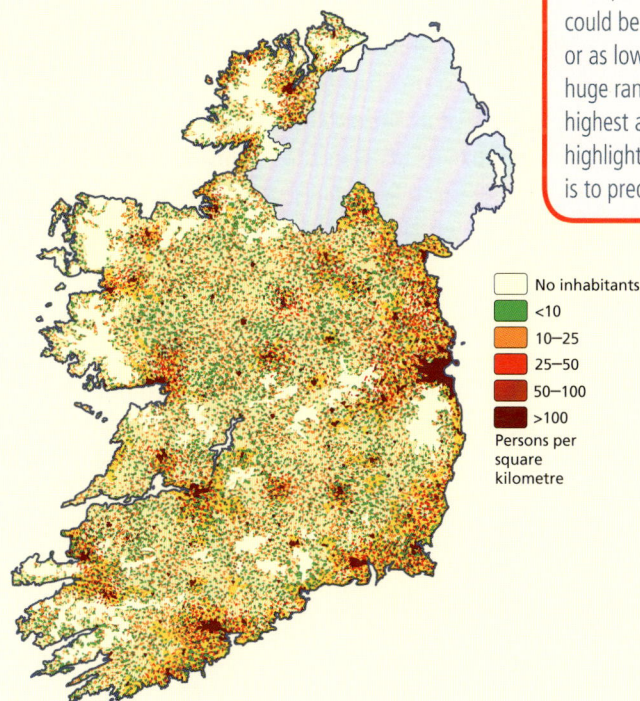

> **Fig. 1.26** Population density of Ireland

FACT

The United Nations have predicted that by the year 2100, the world's population could be as high as 17 billion or as low as 7 billion. The huge range between the highest and lowest estimates highlights just how difficult it is to predict population trends.

No inhabitants
<10
10–25
25–50
50–100
>100
Persons per square kilometre

Population Distribution and Population Density

Historic Factors

Before the **Famine (1845–9)**, Ireland's population **peaked at roughly 8 million people** (almost 6.5 million in the area of the now-Republic). At the time, Ireland's **economy** was **based entirely on agriculture**, meaning that most of the **population lived in rural areas**. At this time, Ireland's population density was **113 per km²** and **evenly spread** throughout all rural areas of Ireland. The **Famine** led to the **deaths** of roughly **1 million people**, while a further **1 million** people **emigrated**. The majority of death and emigration occurred along the **western seaboard**, as farmers there were **unable to grow crops** other than **potatoes** on their land. Furthermore, the mild, **wet climate** of the west suited the **potato blight disease** more than the drier east of the country. **Death** and **outward migration** led to a **reduced population density** along the west, while more and more families moved to Dublin.

Population fall in Ireland 1841–51

▉	0–9
▉	10–19
▉	20–29
▉	30–39
▉	40–49

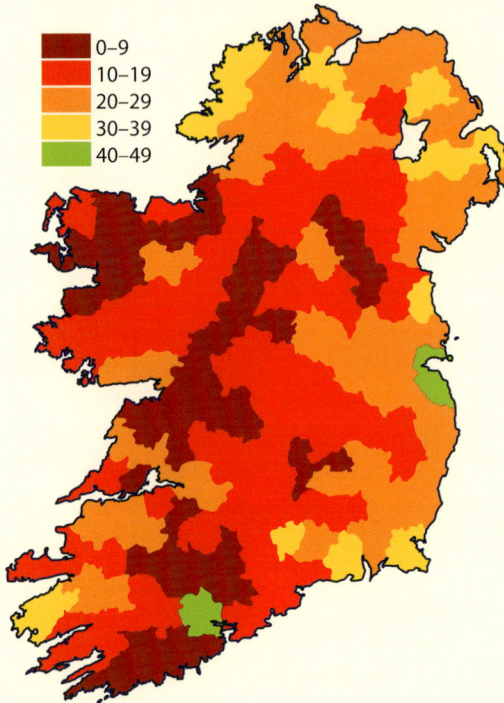

Fig. 1.27 Population fall (percentage) in Ireland as a result of the Famine

Physical Factors

A **wet climate**, **unproductive soils** and an **upland relief** make the west **unattractive for settlement**, as are the **peat soils** of the midlands and other **marshy areas** along the **River Shannon Basin**. Many of these areas have population **densities of less than 25 per km²**. It is likely that these **rural areas** will **continue to decline** as Ireland's population becomes more and more urbanised due to **rural–urban migration**.

Economic Factors

Rural–urban migration accelerated from the **1960s** onwards because of **economic policies** introduced by **Sean Lemass**. These policies attracted **multinational companies** (MNCs) to newly built **industrial estates** in Ireland's **cities and towns**. This has led to **most employment** opportunities occurring in Ireland's largest **cities**, which has **drawn people away** from **rural areas**.

As a result, **urban centres** have the **highest population densities**. Settlements surrounding these **urban centres** also have high **population densities** in **excess of 75 per km²**. Typically, these **surrounding towns** lie within the **commuter zone** of the nearest city and attract workers due to their proximity.

Fig. 1.28 Sean Lemass

Dublin is the best Irish example of this, as it is a **primate city**. Dublin has many factors that encourage settlement, such as more **employment opportunities**, **higher wages** than the national average and a **better range**

of services. As a result of this, the urban areas surrounding the city have a population density of over 75 per km². In order to **overcome high property prices** and a **housing shortage**, the **commuter zone** of the city has **spread** to **other counties** such as Wicklow, Kildare, Meath and Laois.

Changing Birth Rates

In **2014** Ireland had the **highest birth rates in the EU**, at **14.4 per 1,000**, well above the **EU average** of **10.1 per 1,000**. Generally, Ireland has always had a birth rate that was among the highest in the EU. The EU's statistical office (Eurostat) now estimates that Ireland's population has reached 4.7 million.

1950s and 1960s

By the **1950s** nearly 100 years of emigration had reduced Ireland's **population** to just **2.8 million**. Despite this being the lowest total population on record (as a result of high levels of emigration), Ireland's **birth rates remained** at over **20 per 1,000** throughout the **1950s and 1960s**. The influence of the **Catholic Church** was strong in Ireland and it **forbade the use of contraceptives**, which contributed to a **high total fertility rate** (TFR) of **four births per woman**. In rural areas of Ireland, **low levels of mechanisation** encouraged families to have more children in order to have **extra labour for the farm**.

1970s

The population of Ireland **rose rapidly** in the **1970s**, with an increase of **361,268** between **1971 and 1981**. After joining the **EU in 1973**, Ireland's **economy experienced growth**, leading to a **larger immigration** than **emigration** for the first time since the Famine. Many of the immigrants were Irish people returning to Ireland, having emigrated in the previous decade. A large percentage of these **migrants** were at the **age** where they **wished** to **begin having a family**. This led to a **decade of high birth rates**, which **peaked** around **1980**, with **74,000 babies** being born in that year.

1980s

Economic recession throughout the **1980s** led to a **decline in birth rates** due to **high levels of outward migration** among Ireland's **youngest workers** (aged 18–30). Over **200,000 young workers emigrated**, many of whom were close to parenting age. By **1995**, 15 years of economic recession led to a **low of 48,000 births that year**. Societal changes also contributed to a **decreasing** birth rate, as the **influence of** the **Catholic Church** declined and **contraceptives and family planning were accessible**. The changing **role of women in society** also meant that many **couples delayed having children** until their thirties, which meant that families were likely to be smaller.

1995–2008

Economic prosperity and **inward migration** led to an increase of population during the **Celtic Tiger era**. There were **high levels of immigration** during this time, especially from the **newly EU-joined countries** such as **Poland**. During this period, over **25 per cent of babies** were born to **foreign-born mothers**.

Today

Despite Ireland experiencing **economic recession once again**, there were over **66,240 births** in **2014**. However, this number is a **decrease** on the 74,650 births recorded in **2011**. Combined with this, Ireland has **one of** the **lowest death rates** in the world, at **6.4 per 1,000**, well **below** the **EU average** of **9.7 per 1,000**.

Population of the Republic of Ireland 1841–2011

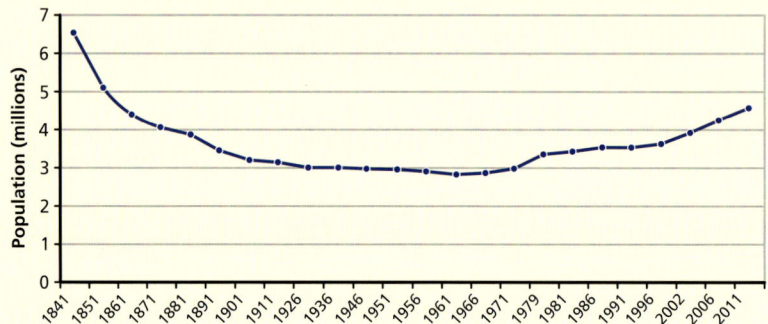

Fig. 1.29 Population dynamics of Ireland

Changing Structure of Ireland's Population

Ireland's population pyramid is **stationary**, with a **blocky shape**; however, it **narrows significantly** in the **age bracket 15–29**. This is due to **high levels of emigration** among 18–30-year-olds during the **economic recession** and it also coincides with a **low fertility rate** of just **1.9 in 2,000**, well **below** the **replacement rate**. Ireland's population pyramid is **slightly different** from **typical stationary pyramids**. The younger age groups, especially in the **0–4** and **5–9 age brackets** show a **significant increase**, coinciding with our **average birth rate being above the EU average**. There are two main explanations for this occurring in Ireland:

Ireland – 2014

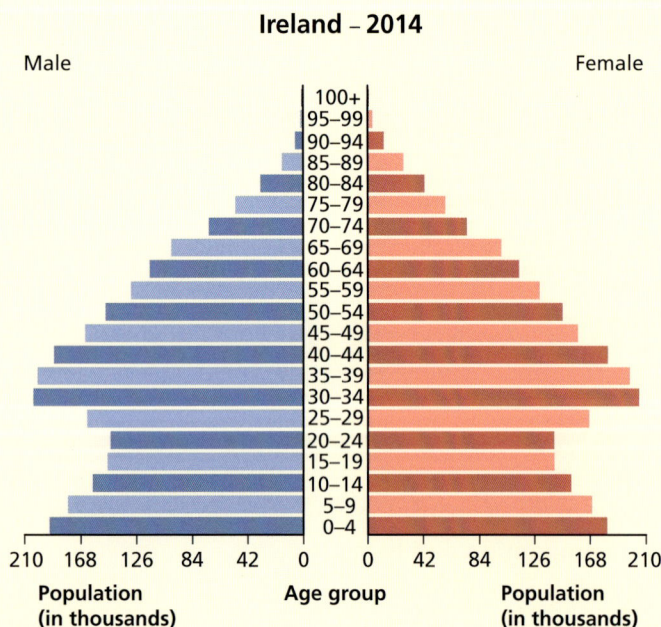

Fig. 1.30 Population pyramid of Ireland

- The economic **recession** of **2008–13** led to an increase in **unemployment**. Couples in which both people previously worked outside the home, may have decided it was the **right time** to **start** a **family**.

- The second reason is related to the **high level of young adults** who **migrated to Ireland** during the **Celtic Tiger**. This increased the number of **women of child-bearing age** in the country and hence led to an **increase in births**.

Implications of the Population Pyramid for Ireland's Governments

From looking at the shape of Ireland's population pyramid, there are two main implications for future governments:

- Experts have warned that Ireland's **current level of childcare services are not fit for purpose** given Ireland's growing young population. In order to deal with an increasing number of children, the government will need to invest more money in children's healthcare, crèche facilities and the building of additional schools.

- An **increasing life expectancy and low death** rate means an **increase in the number of people claiming pensions**. In order to pay for this, the government will have to consider broadening or increasing its taxes, reducing pensions or increasing the retirement age.

Investigation of the Irish Census

The Irish census takes place in Ireland **every five years** and provides the government with information on population growth, population density and population change. The 2016 census is the most recent to have taken place.

The 2016 census told us that Ireland's population has grown significantly since 2011. This is as a result of a **natural increase** and led to a natural increase despite a net migration of –28,558. During this period, Ireland experienced a **fertility rate of 2.1 births per fertile woman** – the highest in the EU during that period. As birth rates were higher than death rates, the **population naturally increased**. The high level of **economic growth experienced until 2008** also saw a **large number of immigrants** from **Eastern European countries** come to Ireland, many of whom stayed even during the economic downturn experienced from 2008 onwards.

Many of the **Leinster** counties have experienced **significant population increases** since the 2011 census, especially counties within the Dublin commuter zone. The population of counties such as Kildare, Meath, Louth and Wexford grew by **over 5 per cent** between **2011 and 2016**. Much of this increase occurred as **lower housing prices** attracted families to settle in these locations and commute to work in Dublin **rather than live in Dublin itself**. County **Dublin** experienced the **largest increase**, with its population growing by more than **an average of 6.1 per cent in five years**. Much of this increase has occurred as more people have moved to Dublin in search of employment during the economic

Facing the facts: The future of Ireland

128,000
Number of 80-year-olds in 2011

484,000
Number of 80-year-olds in 2046

300,000
Increase in labour force by 2046

6.7m
Projected population by 2046

860,700
Number of over 65-year-olds by 2026

1.4m
Number of over 65-year-olds by 2046

57.4 years
Male life expectancy in 1926

85.1 years
Male life expectancy in 2046

57.9 years
Female life expectancy in 1926

88.5 years
Female life expectancy in 2046

100,300
Increase in the number of children at primary school age by 2021

Fig. 1.31 The future of Ireland's population

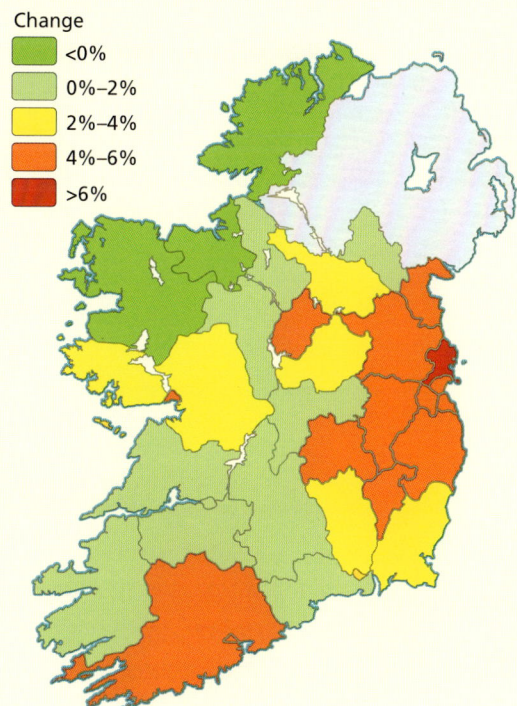

Change
- <0%
- 0%–2%
- 2%–4%
- 4%–6%
- >6%

Fig. 1.32 In the 2016 Census of Ireland, the largest increase in population was in Co. Dublin.

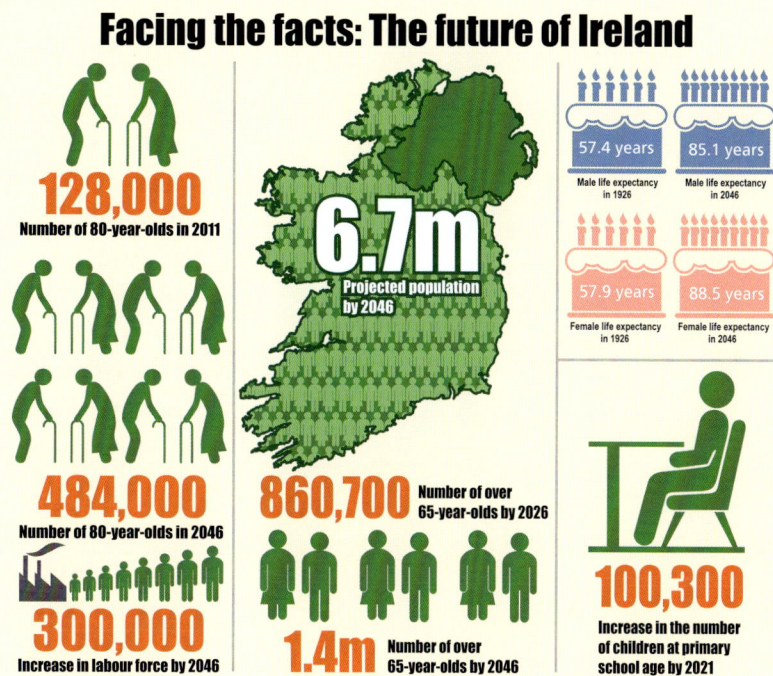

Note!

A question related to changing population patterns in Ireland frequently appears on both the Higher and Ordinary Level papers each year.

downturn. Outside of Dublin, Co. Laois has continued to grow significantly, with a 5.2 per cent increase since 2011. Motorways such as the M3, M4 and M6 have made it possible to **commute to Dublin from the midlands**. Added to this, towns such as Portlaoise and Portarlington are serviced by frequent **trains** to and from Dublin, which makes it possible to **commute to and from work without car dependency**.

Along the west coast, there were **increases of just 2.2 percent in Galway**, while county Donegal saw the largest decrease in population of –1.5 per cent. Galway City saw the **largest increase along the west**, which can be explained by its **large student population** and **improved motorway access** to the region, which has **increased employment**, especially in the medical devices sector.

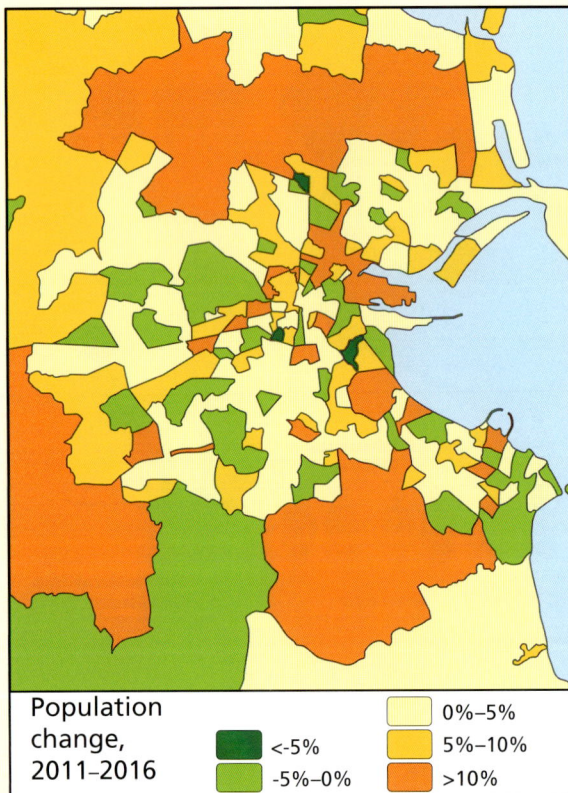

Sprawling Suburbs

If we take a closer look at the **population change in Dublin**, we notice that the **majority of inner city** areas experienced a population decline, while the **surrounding suburbs** experienced a **population increase** of between **5 and >10 per cent**. This indicates that a **people are leaving the city in favour of the suburbs** – a trend that is also seen in the **cities of Waterford, Cork, Limerick** and **Galway**. There are two main reasons for this trend:

- **High housing prices** in **inner cities** make it attractive to people to move to the suburbs, where housing is cheaper.

- When **young family members leave their parents' homes**, they will most likely move to **the suburbs**. This leads to a **population decline in the inner city**.

As the suburbs continue to be a more attractive option for young housebuyers, the **issue of urban sprawl will continue. Careful planning** will **be needed** to guarantee that space will be used in the most efficient way possible.

Population change, 2011–2016

Colour	Range
(dark green)	<-5%
(green)	-5%–0%
(cream)	0%–5%
(yellow)	5%–10%
(orange)	>10%

⌃ **Fig. 1.33** In the 2016 Census of Ireland, there was a decline in population in Dublin's inner city.

🔤 **GEO DICTIONARY**

Urban sprawl: the uncontrolled and unplanned spread of urban areas into the surrounding countryside

---

📱 **ACTIVE LEARNING**

1. Explain how physical and economic factors impact on population distribution and population density.
2. Describe how birth rates in Ireland changed from the 1950s onwards.
3. Explain why Ireland's population pyramid is different from other stationary population pyramids.
4. Explain why the populations of Dublin's suburbs are growing while its inner city is declining.
5. Go to **www.cso.ie/en/census** to find information on all previous censuses carried out in Ireland.

1.10 Population Distribution and Population Density of France

There are **64 million people** living in **France** today, making it the **22nd most populated country** in the world. The population **density** of France **averages 122 per km²**; however, this does not give us an accurate indication of population distribution throughout the country.

The Empty Diagonal

The **Empty Diagonal** (Diagonale de Vide) is a **large rural area** that passes through the Massif Central. The area has **traditionally experienced outward migration**, which has led to a very **low population density** of between **0 and 49 people per km²**. The **area's economy** is **based on agriculture**, which has become **highly mechanised**. This has **reduced** the amount of **labour needed** and has **led to outward migration**. The majority of people who leave here **migrate to Paris** or the **Rhône Valley**.

The region **lacks** major **urban centres** to **attract manufacturing**, with the companies instead choosing to locate along the Mediterranean coast.

The Mediterranean Coast

The **Mediterranean coastline** stretches from the **Spanish border to the Italian border** and is characterised by **high population densities**. **Tourism** is the **dominant economic activity** in the region, which has **developed** greatly over the **past 50 years**. As a result of this **tourist growth**, the population of the region has also **increased**. **Nice** and **Cannes** are examples of **established tourist resorts** along the French Riviera, each of which has a beach and marina.

Marseille is a city of **high employment** because of its broad range of **heavy** and **light manufacturing**, such as **oil refining**, **chemical industries** and **high-tech parks**, which have developed as a result of government-sponsored regional industrialisation.

The Nord

The Nord has been a region of **high population density** since the beginning of the **Industrial Revolution**. With large deposits of **coal and iron ore**, the region **employed tens of thousands** of people in **coal mining, steel manufacturing** and **engineering** until the **mid-twentieth century**. With exhausted coal and iron ore, the region **suffered from industrial decline** and became an area of **unemployment** and **outward migration**. To stop continued outward migration and unemployment, the **government** has **invested in redeveloping**

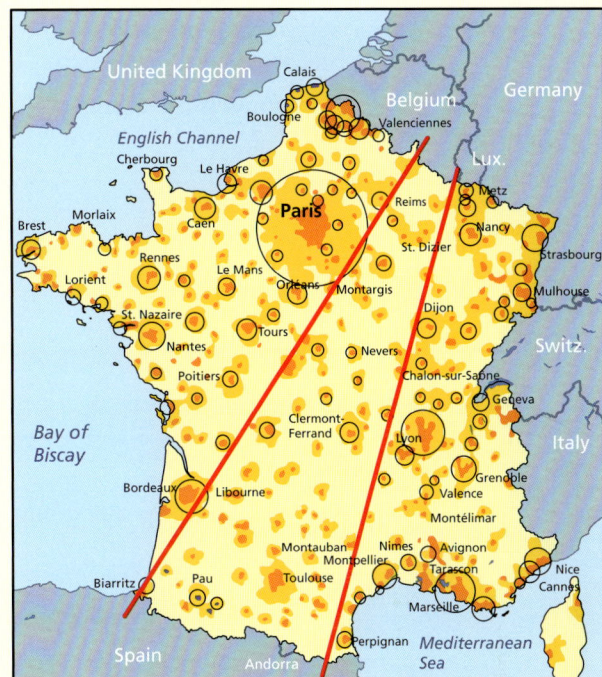

🔺 **Fig. 1.34** Empty diagonal of France

industry in the region. **Lille** is an example of a city which has **redeveloped**, with **computer manufacturing** and **modern car assembly** occurring there. **TGV lines** have also connected the region to the other **economic centres** throughout **France**, which encourages further development.

The Seine Valley

The **Seine Valley** has attracted the **highest population densities** in France, with the **Greater Paris Area** having a population of **over 11 million people**. Paris is the **core economic centre** of France with world-renowned industries such as **food**, **fashion** and **high-tech industry** having developed here. The city also has a high number of tertiary services, which **promotes the tourist industry**.

Rouen and **Le Havre** are **important ports** which are **home to heavy industry** such as **oil refining** and **chemical industries**. The high level of **employment throughout the Valley** has led to **immigration** as people seek **employment opportunities** there.

ACTIVE LEARNING

1. Explain why the Empty Diagonal has traditionally experienced outward migration.

2. Describe the reasons why the Seine Valley has the highest population densities in France.

EXAM QUESTIONS

ORDINARY LEVEL

1.

Irish population by age group in 2014	
Age group (years)	%
0–14	21
15–64	66
65–84	11
85+	2

Examine the table above showing Ireland's population by age group in 2014.

(i) Using graph paper, draw a suitable graph to illustrate this data.

(ii) State two ways that population statistics are used.

(i)
Graph paper	2m
Vertical axis labelled/Circle	3m
Horizontal axis labelled/Centred	3m
4 items @ 4m each	16m

(ii)
2 ways stated @ 3m each	6m

2015 Q10A 30M

ORDINARY LEVEL

2.

Currently, the size of the Earth's population is 7.2 billion people. It is predicted that the Earth's population could be as high as 12.3 billion people by 2100. Infectious diseases like Ebola spread faster in densely populated areas. Scientists warn that the rising population could worsen world problems such as climate change, infectious disease and poverty.

Most of the growth is expected to take place in Africa, where the population is expected to increase from around one billion today to four billion by the end of the century.

In sub-Saharan Africa, fertility levels remain high and large families – typically with more than four children – are still common.

Reductions in the death toll from HIV/Aids are said to be another contributing factor to the African trend.

Amended from Irish Examiner, 18 September 2014

Read the article above and answer each of the following questions.

(i) According to the article, what is the current size of the Earth's population and what is the predicted population by 2100?

(ii) Calculate the predicted increase in the Earth's population by 2100.

(iii) Name one problem mentioned in the article that could be made worse by this predicted increase in population.

(iv) Where is most of the population growth expected to take place?

(v) Explain briefly why this area is predicted to have the most growth in population.

(vi) Explain briefly one advantage of predicting population figures.

(i)	2 @ 3m each	6m
(ii)		6m
(iii)		3m
(iv)		3m
(v)	2 SRPs @ 3m	6m
(vi)	2 SRPs @ 3m	6m

2015 Q12A 30M

3.

Ireland – 2011

Male

Female

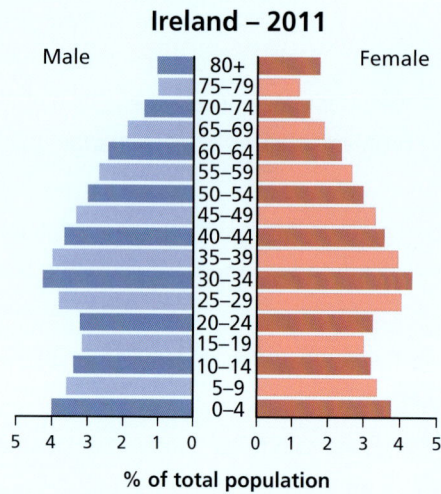

% of total population

Examine the population pyramid for Ireland in 2011 and answer the following questions.

(i) What percentage of the population was male and in the 0–4 year age group?

(ii) What percentage of the total population was in the 35–39 year age group?

(iii) Were there more males or females over 75 years of age?

(iv) Explain briefly one way the shape of this population pyramid differs from the shape of a population pyramid for a developing country.

(v) Name two ways population pyramids are used.

(i)	6m
(ii)	6m
(iii)	6m
(iv) 2 SRPs @ 3m each	6m
(v) 2 SRPs @ 3m each	6m

2013 Q11A 30M

4. 'One of the greatest challenges facing European governments in the future will be coping with ageing populations.'

Describe the difficulties that an ageing population can cause.

(i)	6m
(ii)	6m
(iii)	6m
(iv) 2 SRPs @ 3m each	6m
(v) 2 SRPs @ 3m each	6m

2012 Q12C 30M

1.

Irish birth and death rates per 1,000 of population		
Year	Birth rate	Death rate
1950	21.5	13.0
1990	15	9.0
2013	15	6.5

(i) Using graph paper, draw a suitable graph to illustrate this data.

(ii) Explain briefly one reason for the decline in Irish birth rates between 1950 and 2013.

(i)

	Bar chart, etc.	Pie chart
Title	2m	2m
Vertical axis named	1m	1m + 1m (Circle + Centred)
Horizontal axis named	1m	–
6 items illustrated	2m each	2m each

(ii)

Any valid explanation	4m

2015 Q11A 20M

2.

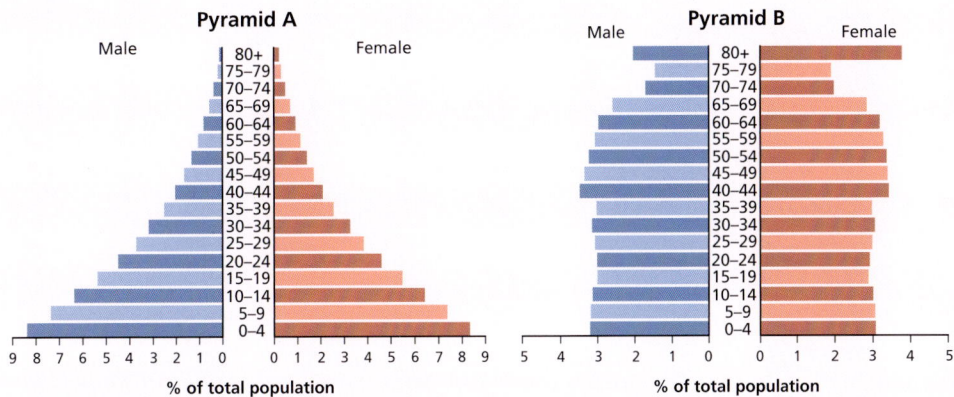

Pyramid A   **Pyramid B**

Examine the population pyramids above and answer each of the following questions.

(i) What percentage of males in Pyramid A are in the 40–44 year age group and what percentage of females in Pyramid B are in the 25–29 year age group?

(ii) Are more people living longer in the area represented by Pyramid A or Pyramid B? With reference to the structure of the pyramid, give one piece of evidence to support your answer.

(iii) Which of the pyramids, A or B, represents a developing economy? Name an example of a developing economy.

(iv) Explain briefly two challenges facing an economy with a population pyramid similar to Pyramid B.

(i)		2m + 2m
(ii)	Pyramid B & any valid piece of evidence	2m + 2m
(iii)	Pyramid A & any valid named example	2m + 2m
(iv)	Any two valid challenges explained	2m + 2m 2m + 2m

2015 Q12A 20M

EXAM QUESTIONS

3.

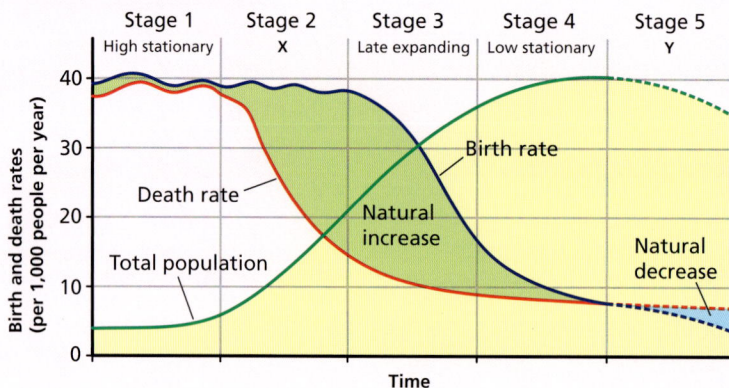

Examine the diagram above showing the Demographic Transitional Model and answer each of the following questions.

(i) In which stage of the Demographic Transitional Model is the total population at its lowest?

(ii) Name X, Stage 2 of the Demographic Transitional Model and name an example of a country in this stage.

(iii) Name Y, Stage 5 of the Demographic Transitional Model and name an example of a country in this stage.

(iv) Explain briefly one problem facing countries in Stage 5 of the Demographic Transitional Model.

(v) Explain briefly what is meant by natural increase.

(i)		4m
(ii)	2m + 2m	4m
(iii)	2m + 2m	4m
(iv)	2m + 2m	4m
(v)	2m + 2m	4m

2014 Q11A 20M

HIGHER LEVEL

4.

Components of Irish population change (average annual figures) for each inter-censal period, 1956–2011

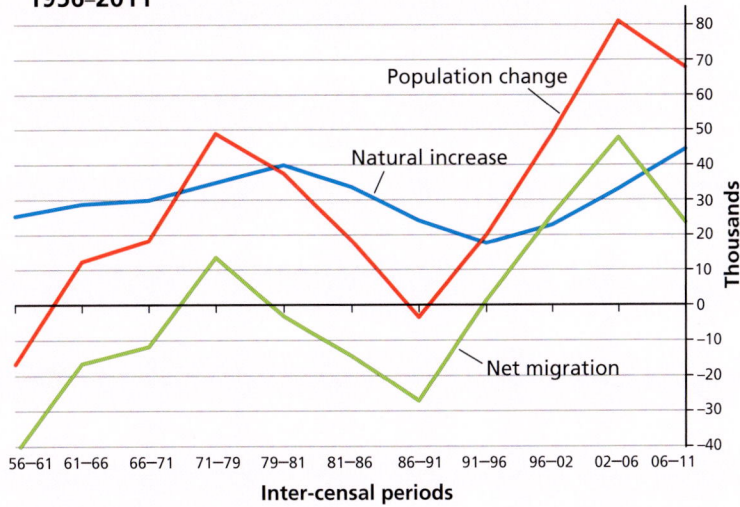

With reference to the graph above, describe and explain three changes in Ireland's population between 1956 and 2011.

3 changes @ 10 each	30m
Reference to the graph	2m
Explanation 4 SRPs @ 2m each	8m

2012 Q10C 30M

HIGHER LEVEL

EXAM QUESTION

Describe and explain, using examples which you have studied, the difference between the terms *population density* and *population distribution*.

Marking Scheme	
Define terms	2 @ 2m each
Examples	2 @ 2m each
Explanation	11 SRPs @ 2m each

2008 Q10C 30M

SAMPLE ANSWER

Population density refers to the number of people per km² in a country or region [2m]. Ireland currently has a population density of approximately 68 per km², while Brazil has a low population density of 25 per km² – both of which are considered relatively low [2m]. Population density is an average figure, and therefore does not give an accurate picture of population settlement within a country or region. For example, parts of Connemara in the West of Ireland have a population density of 6 per km², with very few people living over a wide area [2m]. On the other hand, Dublin City has a population density of >4,500 per km², with over 1 million people living in a relatively small area [*2m].

Population distribution refers to the spread of people across a country or region [2m]. The distribution of people across a country may be very uneven due to a number of factors which make areas either suitable or unsuitable to live in [2m]. Population density and distribution are closely related, as places more desirable to live have the highest population densities also [2m]. Again, this is seen in Ireland, as the eastern coast has a more comfortable climate, more agriculturally productive land and flat relief than the western coast, meaning the majority of Irish people are distributed along the east [2m].

Relief impacts greatly on the population density and distribution of land, with areas of flat, low-lying land tending to have the highest population densities [2m]. Over 80 per cent of the world's population lives at an altitude of less than 500 m, as the building of settlements and transport networks is much easier on flat land [2m]. The only exception to this is in hot, tropical, equatorial regions such as Brazil, where people prefer to live in mountainous regions because these regions are cooler, e.g. Rio de Janeiro [*2m]. Areas of flat land have more fertile soils than mountainous areas, e.g. the North European Plain has fertile brown earths and boulder clays which allow for easy cultivation [2m]. These flat, fertile regions attract settlement as they are able to support the intensive growing of crops for food while mountainous soils are generally thin and infertile, which discourages settlement [2m].

Climate affects where people can live comfortably and impacts on the crops which can be grown in an area, e.g. temperate zones [2m]. In temperate zones, food crops are easily grown and there is a

The answer is focused and follows the wording of the question (and therefore the marking scheme) carefully. The answer begins with clear definitions of both population density and distribution, as well as providing clear examples of both. This shows the examiner a clear understanding of the topic being examined. Once both have been defined, a clear understanding of the factors that influence both population and density is shown.

plentiful supply of fresh water without extremes such as drought and severe flooding [2m]. Drainage also impacts on population density and distribution as areas near a river are more densely populated than areas without freshwater [2m]. Rivers provide rich, fertile alluvium for intense agricultural activity, as well as transport and drinking water [2m]. Some of the most densely populated parts of the world are located in river valleys, e.g. River Nile in Egypt [*2m].

Marks Awarded	
Define terms	2 @ 2m each
Examples	2 @ 2m each
Explanation	Best 11 SRPs @ 2m each
Total 30/30	

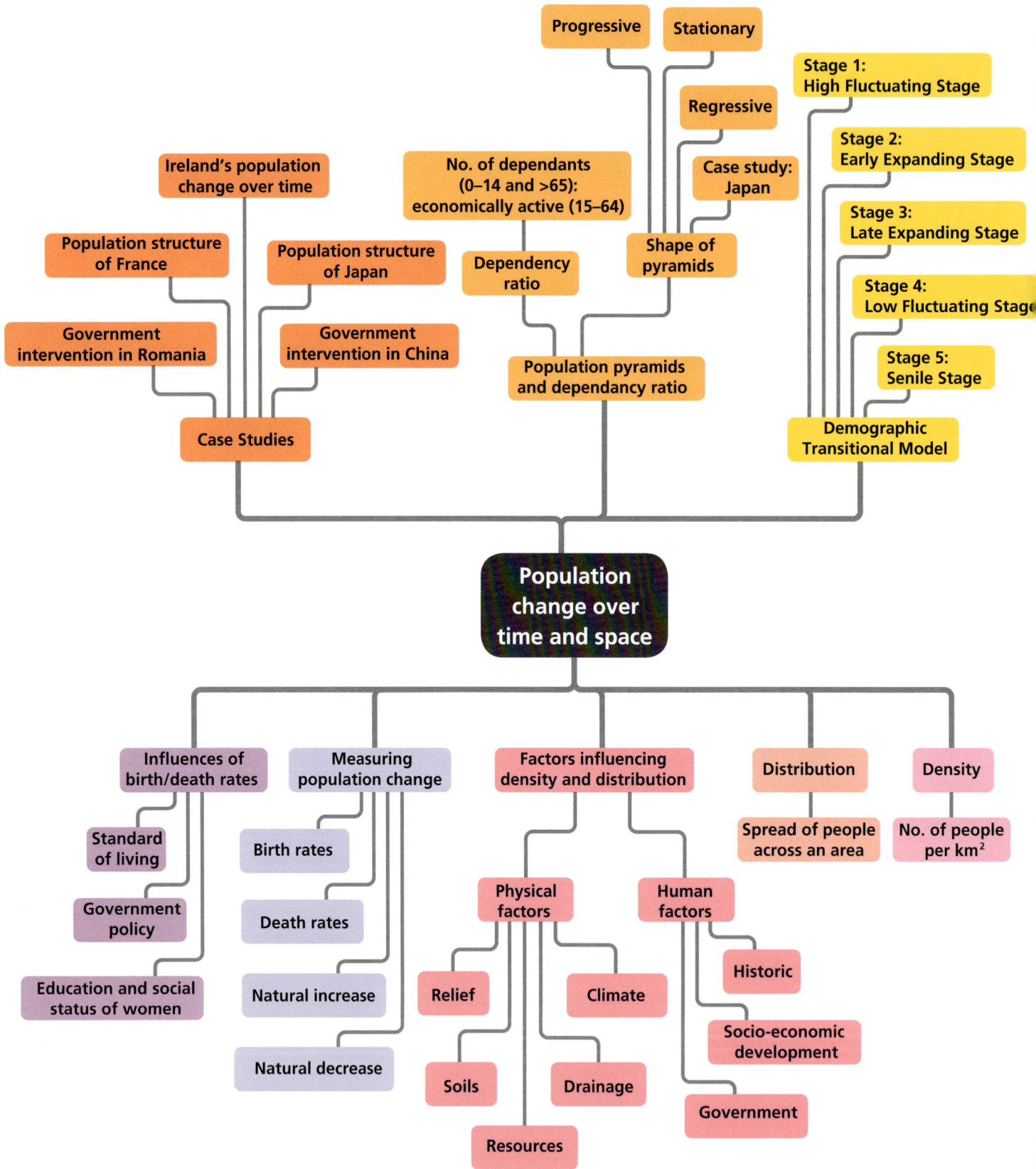

TOPIC MAP

Progressive

Stationary

Stage 1: High Fluctuating Stage

Regressive

Stage 2: Early Expanding Stage

Ireland's population change over time

No. of dependants (0–14 and >65): economically active (15–64)

Case study: Japan

Stage 3: Late Expanding Stage

Population structure of France

Population structure of Japan

Shape of pyramids

Stage 4: Low Fluctuating Stage

Government intervention in Romania

Government intervention in China

Dependency ratio

Stage 5: Senile Stage

Case Studies

Population pyramids and dependancy ratio

Demographic Transitional Model

Population change over time and space

Influences of birth/death rates

Measuring population change

Factors influencing density and distribution

Distribution

Density

Standard of living

Birth rates

Spread of people across an area

No. of people per km^2

Government policy

Death rates

Physical factors

Human factors

Education and social status of women

Natural increase

Relief

Climate

Historic

Natural decrease

Socio-economic development

Soils

Drainage

Government

Resources

CHAPTER 2

Overpopulation and Development

In Chapter 1, you learned about the factors that affect population density, population distribution and population growth. You also learned about the methods used to measure and plan for future population trends. In this chapter, we will measure the causes and effects of overpopulation – the situation whereby a country or region is unable to support its population. There are several causes and effects of overpopulation, many of which are discussed in this chapter.

KEY WORDS

- Overpopulation
- Underpopulation
- Optimum population
- Carrying capacity
- Drought
- Cash crops
- Crop rotation
- Refugees
- Mortality
- Malnutrition
- The Sahel
- Climate change
- Depletion
- Role of women
- Technology
- HIV
- Green Revolution
- Genetically modified foods
- Ecological footprint

LEARNING OUTCOMES

What you MUST know
- Definition of overpopulation
- How human interference with natural resources can lead to overpopulation
- Influence of society and culture on overpopulation
- Impact of population growth on development
- Impact of income levels on population growth
- Impact of technology on population growth
- Impacts of population growth and decline

What you SHOULD know
- Definitions of underpopulation, optimum population and carrying capacity
- Factors that increase/decrease the carrying capacity of a country/region

What is USEFUL to know
- Additional statistics on population growth/decline in the countries of your chosen studies
- Most recent developments regarding famine/drought/war in countries of your chosen case studies
- Information on the latest technological developments

Introduction

As the world's **population continues to rise rapidly**, it puts an ever-increasing **strain** on our limited **natural resources**. Water, **arable land** and **fossil fuels** are the most important natural resources in the world and are vital to human survival. As the population of the world continues to increase, these limited resources become more and more **depleted**. Examples of overpopulation are evident in many parts of the world. For example:

- **Desertification** in the **Sahel** has led to the destruction of arable land, dwindling water supplies and famine. Desertification itself is caused by increased drought due to climate change and poor management of resources.

- It is estimated that **80 per cent** of China's **arable land** has been **polluted** due to agricultural chemicals and industrial waste.

- The **slums** of **Kolkata** and **São Paulo** are examples of the impacts of overpopulation in urban areas.

⌃ **Fig. 2.1** Chemicals have polluted much of China's soil.

While the term *overpopulation* is often considered to be a developing world problem (i.e. caused by population growth in the developing world), this is simply not true. As of **2016**, **developing countries** contribute **52 per cent** of the **world's carbon output**, with the **developed world** contributing **48 per cent**. However, this alone does not give an accurate indication, as over **80 per cent of the world's population** live in the **developing world**. Also, extremely poor countries such as Mali produce very little carbon due to a lack of fossil fuels or modern agricultural or industrial systems.

It is important to understand that the people worst affected by overpopulation are often not responsible for causing it.

FACT

Mali's carbon footprint is just 0.6 tonnes per capita. This is compared to an average of 11 tonnes per capita in Ireland (17 tonnes in 2007). The US has the highest average carbon footprint at 20.4 tonnes per person.

ACTIVE LEARNING

1. Go to **www.greenhome.ie** for more information on Ireland's carbon footprint and the ways in which it can be reduced.

2. Go to **www.epa.ie** for the latest news on Ireland's environmental policies.

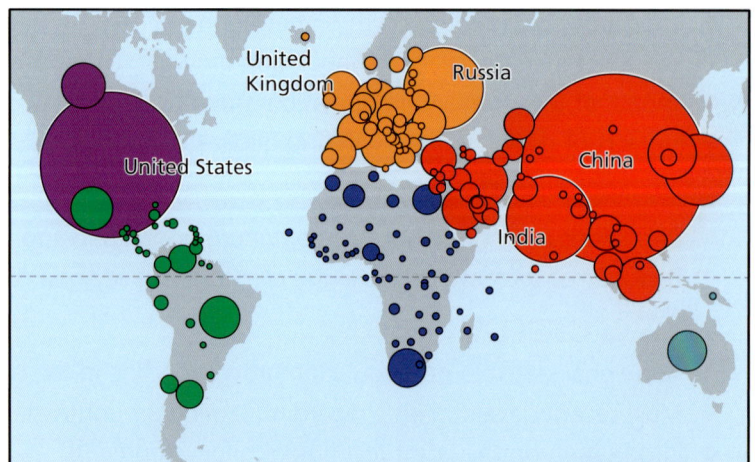

⌃ **Fig. 2.2** Earth's carbon output

2.1 Defining Overpopulation

In order to fully understand the case studies used in this chapter, you must first be able to define the key terms used.

Overpopulation

Overpopulation occurs when the **number of people** living in a region is **greater** than the capacity of the **natural resources available to them**. The **maximum number of people** a region's **natural resources can support** is referred to as the region's **carrying capacity**. Therefore, a region is said to be **overpopulated** when it has **exceeded** its **carrying capacity**.

A common mistake is to confuse overpopulation with high population density. A region with a **high population density** is **not necessarily overpopulated**. For example, the population density of the **Netherlands is 501 per km²** but is **not overpopulated** as it has a **high level of resources**. Meanwhile, **Mali** has a population density of just **14.5 per km²**, yet it is considered **overpopulated** as it **lacks** the **resources** required to provide adequate standards of living. It is also important to realise that **overpopulation** is **not** a **permanent** characteristic of a region. For example, **Ireland** was **overpopulated** during the **Great Famine** (1845–9) because of **crop failure** of the **primary food** (the potato) due to **blight**. It can be argued that Ireland remained overpopulated **until the 1950s** due to a poor economy and low standard of living.

Underpopulation

Underpopulation occurs when a region **does not have enough people** to **fully exploit** its **resources**. Underpopulation frequently occurs in developed, **highly industrialised countries** that experience **low birth rates**. Due to the low birth rates, these countries now suffer from **labour shortages**. As a result, **inward migration** is **needed** to fill the labour deficits. This occurred in **Ireland** during the **Celtic Tiger era**, when the booming economy led to a **shortage of workers** in certain professions, especially the tertiary sector.

Much like overpopulation, underpopulation is not a constant characteristic of a region. In 2008 the **economic recession** led to **large-scale unemployment** in Ireland. This led to the **emigration** of young Irish adults along with many people who had migrated to the country during the Celtic Tiger.

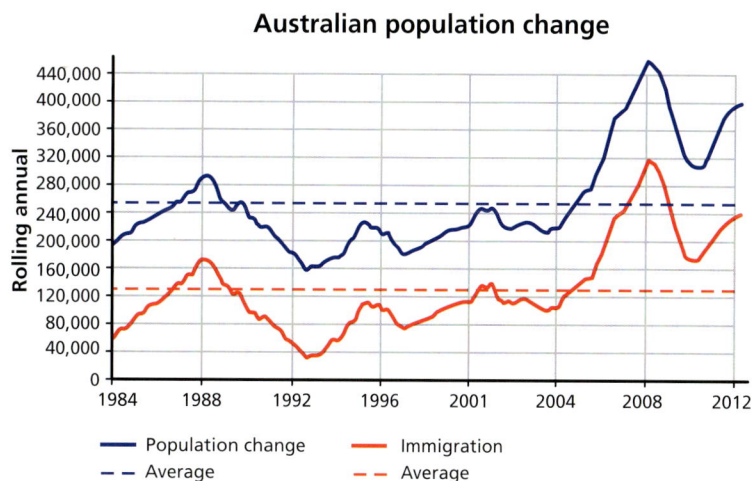

HUMAN POPULATION GROWTH CHART (including projections)

> **Fig. 2.3** What is the central message in this cartoon?

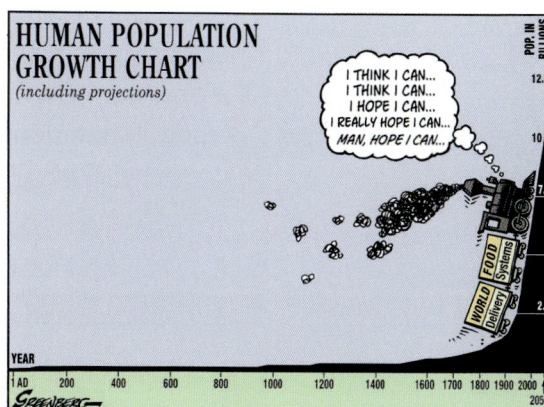

Australian population change

Legend: Population change — Immigration — Average - - Average

> **Fig. 2.4** Australia is an example of an underpopulated country that relies on immigration to fill its labour deficits.

Fig. 2.5 Optimum population

Optimum Population

Optimum population is the idea that a region has the **exact number of people** who can **exploit** its **natural resources** to a level that provides the **highest possible standard of living**. It is **highly unlikely** that any country/region remains at its optimum population for any length of time. This is because of the large number of variables, such as population growth/decline, global markets, employment opportunities and migration.

2.2 Overpopulation and the Development of Resources: The Sahel Region

The **Sahel Region** is an area of **savannah** located just **south** of the **Sahara Desert**. Traditionally, the region was made up of grassland with a sparse covering of trees, such as the **acacia**. Over **100 million people** live in the Sahel region, most of whom are **farmers** or **nomadic herders**. The Sahel region is now **overpopulated** and is unable to adequately support its population. The region is now under threat from **desertification**, as the Sahara Desert advances into the Sahel at a rate of **5–10 km per year**. Because of a limited number of resources and an extreme climate, the region has a **low carrying capacity** of just under **30 per km²** despite having a **population density** of **48 per km²**. There are three main causes for overpopulation in the Sahel:

1. Climate change
2. Rapid population growth
3. Overuse and depletion of natural resources.

ACTIVE LEARNING

1. What is the difference between overpopulation and high population density?
2. Briefly describe a point in history when Ireland was (a) overpopulated and (b) underpopulated.

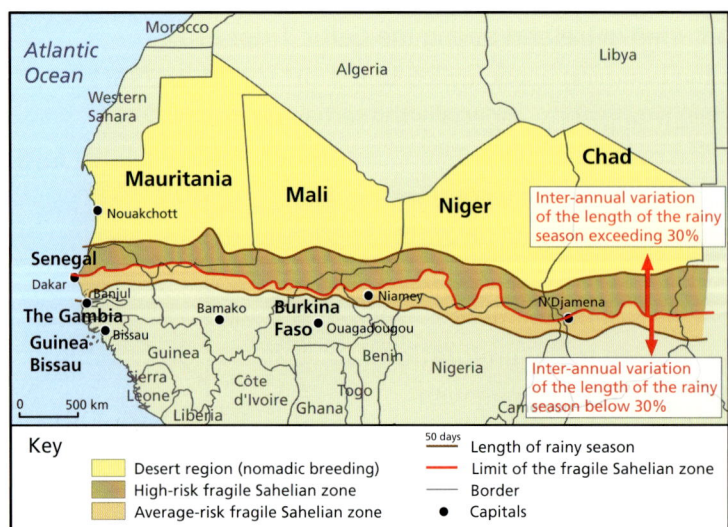

Fig. 2.6 Areas at risk of desertification in the Sahel

Cause 1: Climate Change

The Sahel region is an **arid/semi-arid region**, meaning it receives **low annual amounts** of rainfall. It has a wet season from **May to October**, with rainfall occurring in **heavy downpours**. The **high temperatures** of the region **evaporate** the **rainfall** quickly. During a **30-year spell** between **1930 and 1960**, the Sahel experienced **higher levels of rainfall**, which encouraged **inward migration** to the region. However, since this time **rainfall** has become **less reliable**, with the **wet season shortening** by **29 per cent** over the past 30 years. A **delay** in the **arrival of rain** and a shorter **wet season** has triggered several **devastating famines** as the region's population are unable to grow enough food for themselves. Examples include:

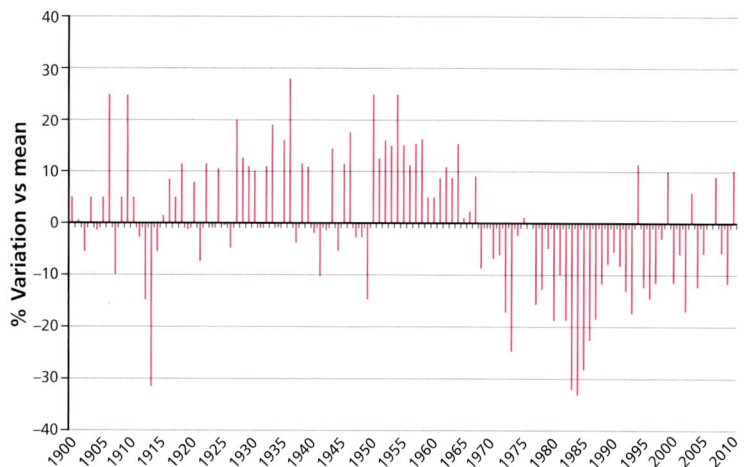

▲ **Fig. 2.7** Rainfall levels have been reducing in the Sahel.

- **1968–72:** Drought (Mauritania, Mali, Chad, Niger, Burkina Faso) – 1 million dead

- **1998:** Sudan – Famine caused by a combination of war and drought – 70,000 dead

- **2012:** Famine in West Africa brought on by Sahel drought – 18 million dead

- **2016:** An **estimated 14.28 million** people remain living with **no food security**, with an additional 2.6 million living with an immediate risk of starvation.

When the **seasonal rains** do **arrive**, they occur in **short torrential downpours** rather than longer spells of less intense rainfall. The torrential rain **damages the soil's structure**, causing **erosion** and **gullying** to occur. Gullying occurs as the rainwater carves out channels in the soil. As well as removing soil, gullying makes the **remaining topsoil** more **susceptible** to **wind erosion** as its **structure** is **damaged**. The intense heat of the region means the **rainfall** is **evaporated quickly** and is **not allowed to percolate** through the soil. This means that the **water table is** not **replenished**, and becomes increasingly dry. The high temperatures cause high levels of evaporation. This, combined with disruption to rainfall patterns through climate change, has led to wells drying up and **prolonged periods of drought**. Eventually the soil becomes hard and baked into an **impermeable laterite** soil. The topsoil is removed by the wind.

> **GEO DICTIONARY**
>
> **Gullying:** channels cut into the soil by rainwater
>
> **Percolate:** the filtering of water down through the soil
>
> **Water table:** the level below the surface in which the soil is saturated with water
>
> **Drought:** a prolonged period without rainfall
>
> **Impermeable:** water cannot pass through it
>
> **Laterite:** a hard, impermeable clay soil found in tropical or subtropical areas
>
> **Biome:** unique natural world regions, which are controlled by climate

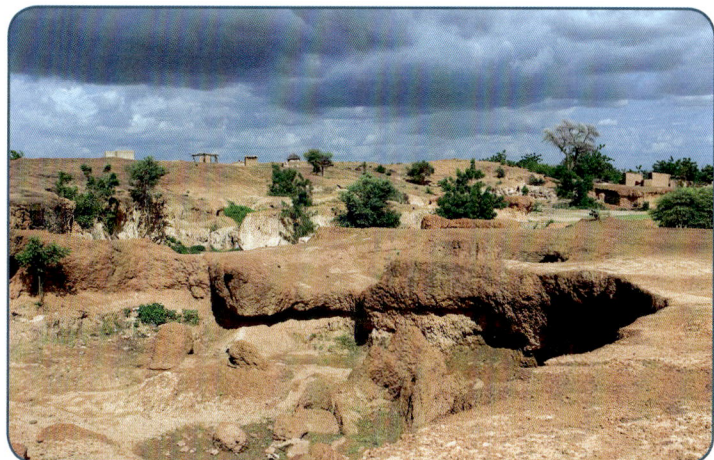

▶ **Fig. 2.8** Laterite soil of the Sahel

Manufacturing industry can **damage biomes** in a number of ways, e.g. by causing **acid rain**, **air** and **water pollution** and **altering the climate** through the release of greenhouse gases. Climate change is a serious threat to the Sahel region: high usage of fossil fuels, especially in developed countries, has been linked with the prolonged periods of drought. Climate change has caused a **rise in temperature of** the **atmosphere**, which has changed the patterns of rainfall of the Sahel. As a result of the increased temperature, the atmosphere can **hold more water vapour**, meaning **precipitation is less likely** to occur. The seasonal rains are becoming **less frequent** and last for **shorter periods of time**. In the past **25 years**, the level of **rainfall in** the Sahel has **decreased by 39 per cent**, from **720 mm to 440 mm**. Even when rains do arrive, it is becoming ever more common that they arrive **over a month late**

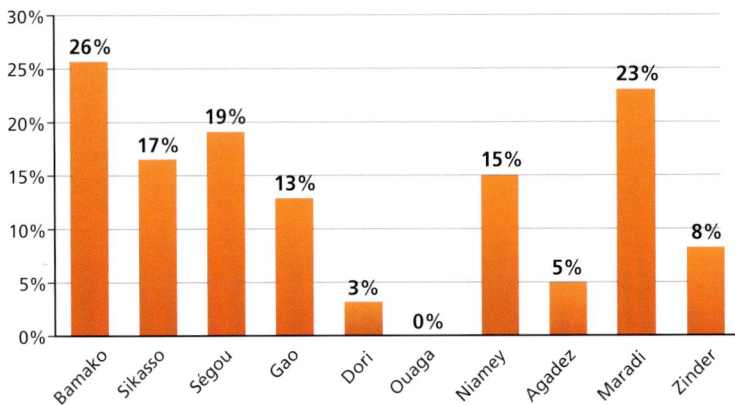

Fig. 2.9 Rising cereal prices in the Sahel during the 2012 drought

or that they last a much shorter time. The **summer of 2012** saw one of the most **severe droughts** in the history of the region. **Cereal harvests fell** by over **25 per cent**, which left over **15 million people facing starvation**. As drought continues to affect the region, the rate of desertification continues to increase.

Cause 2: Rapid Population Growth

Since the 1960s the Sahel region has experienced **rapid population growth**, with most countries in **Stage 2** of the **Demographic Transitional Model** (DTM). With **increasing birth rates** and a **falling death rate** due to **medical improvements**, the region's population is now over 100 million.

Examples of countries with falling death rates include:

- Sudan: Birth rates 39 per 1,000; Death rates 10 per 1,000
- Niger: Birth rates 52 per 1,000; Death rates 14 per 1,000
- Eritrea: Birth rates 37 per 1,000; Death rates 8 per 1,000.

Fig. 2.10 Women in the Sahel have few educational opportunities.

There are three main reasons for this trend:

- Economic poverty
- Culture/customs and the status of women
- Medical improvements.

Most of the people in the Sahel live in deep **economic poverty**. **Elder members** of families **rely on younger generations** to look after them in old age. They also rely on younger generations to provide for the family through **food provision and income**. Therefore, there is an **economic need** to have as many **children as possible** to give the best chance of security in old age. The **traditional customs** and **status of women** also increase birth rates. In many countries in the Sahel, such as Nigeria, very **few girls stay in school** for more than a few years. Many **girls are married** and **begin having children** while in their teens. The male is seen as the 'head' of the family, with the woman's role being to have as many children as possible. As a result, many countries in the Sahel have a total **fertility of over 5.0 per woman**.

Population growth has been further accelerated by the **increasing numbers of refugees** entering the Sahel region to **escape war and famine** (especially from the Horn of Africa). For example, over **1 million people** have fled from **Ethiopia to Sudan** in order to escape **prejudice, war** and **famine**. This increased influx of people puts extra **strain on** the already **limited resources** of the region.

⌃ **Fig. 2.11** Millions of people from Ethiopia and Sudan have migrated to the Sahel region to escape war and famine.

Falling death rates have also contributed to population growth. There have been improvements in **preventative medicines**, e.g. vaccines for 'childhood' diseases, such as measles and **whooping cough**. These measures, along with increased knowledge of childcare hygiene practices (e.g. boiling water to sterilise feeding utensils), have helped to lower child mortality rates.

If current population growth continues, it is predicted that the population of the Sahel will increase by an additional 15 million people by 2030.

Cause 3: Overuse and Depletion of Natural Resources

The main **natural resources** available in the Sahel are **water, soil** and **natural vegetation**. With the population continually growing, these resources are being **overused and depleted** beyond the region's carrying capacity, i.e. it is **overpopulated**.

Overgrazing

Poor **agricultural practices** cause **soil degradation**. This is particularly true in the Sahel region which is already an **environmentally sensitive** region. The increased rainfall experienced in the Sahel region between the 1930s and 1970s attracted nomadic farmers, as there was a more plentiful supply of grassland. In the

⊙ **Fig. 2.12** Overgrazing in the Sahel

GEO DICTIONARY

Horn of Africa: the easternmost part of Africa

Prejudice: harm or injury caused by bias or different beliefs of others

Preventative medicine: medicine used to prevent someone from contracting an illness or disease, e.g. vaccines

Whooping cough: a contagious bacterial disease named after the whooping noise caused by the cough

Sahel, the number of cattle a person owns is a measure of their wealth. With increased cattle herds, the land becomes **overgrazed**, meaning the soil is being used beyond its carrying capacity. Added to this, farming practices have changed, with **sedentary farming** now being carried out by many. As the animals are fenced in, the soil is not given a chance to recover its nutrients, and this damages the structure. Animal **hooves compact** the **soil**, making it difficult for water to penetrate the surface, **increasing the risk of drought** and reducing the soil's fertility. As there is less fertile soil, there is also **less vegetation**, which makes the **soil more susceptible** to **wind erosion**.

GEO **DICTIONARY**

Sedentary farming: the fencing or enclosure of animals

In order to provide **water for** their **animals**, farmers dig **wells and boreholes**. This greatly **lowers** the **water table**, which is not replenished each year.

Overcropping

With a rapidly growing population, the biggest **struggle** for the people of the Sahel is **food security**. This, combined with the growing of **cash crops** to **pay** off **international debt,** has led to the **over-cultivation of land**. In many cases this has led to **monoculture**, where one crop is continually grown by farmers. This causes **soil minerals** to become **depleted**. Farmers are **unable to pay for artificial fertilisers** and cattle dung is used as a fuel for cooking. With each passing growing season, the **soil** becomes less and **less fertile** until eventually it becomes barren.

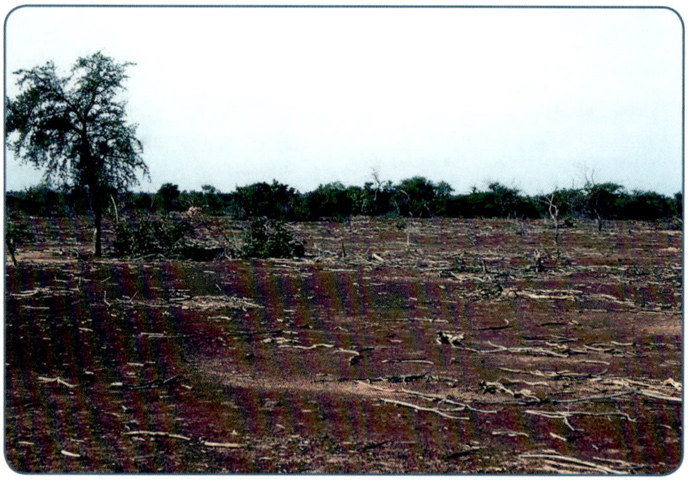

Fig. 2.13 Deforestation in the Sahel

Deforestation

Much of the Sahel region was once covered in **trees and bushes**. Many of these trees have been removed in order to make way for agricultural land or to create firewood.

Firewood is an important resource in the Sahel, as it is used for **cooking and heat**. It is the only fuel resource in the Sahel, as the region **lacks deposits of fossil fuels**. Population growth of over **3 per cent per annum** has led to an **increased demand for fuel** and has accelerated the rate of deforestation. The removal of this forest cover exposes the soil to **intense heat, flash floods** and strong winds.

Effects of Overpopulation

Environmental Degradation

Due to climate change and the overuse of natural resources in the Sahel, the region's **environment** is being **severely damaged**. Desertification (the spread of deserts) is increasing as the Sahara Desert **advances 5–10 km per year**. The exposed **dry soil** is **eroded away** by **winds** and **flash floods**. As the winds carry away the topsoil, huge dust storms are generated, often measuring several hundred metres in height. **Mauritania** is an example of a country in which this is occurring, with over **100 million tonnes of topsoil** removed each year by strong winds. The bare and barren soil left behind is now similar to the Sahara Desert and is **abandoned** for more fertile soil further south. In this way, the Sahara spreads further into the Sahel region. This increased level of desertification has a devastating effect on the lives of people in the Sahel, with **less food security** and increased likelihood of **famine** and **starvation**.

Water resources are also greatly affected as less rainfall leads to a **decreasing water table**. More **frequent drought** and increased water usage for cattle now mean that people are forced to drink from **contaminated water sources** or walk for several miles each day to secure drinking water. The best-known example of this is the **disappearance of Lake Chad**, which has shrunk to **5 per cent of its original size** in just 40 years. The lake borders Chad, Nigeria and Cameroon. It has been a vital source of fresh water for these countries and is especially **important for irrigation** schemes. The shrinking of the lake has contributed to a local lack of water, crop failures, livestock deaths, the **destruction of the local fishing industry** and increased poverty throughout the region. It is understood that **50 per cent** of the **decrease** in the **lake's volume** can been attributed to **human mismanagement**, while the other **50 per cent** has been as a result of **changing climate** patterns.

Migration and Conflict

Climate change, drought and desertification have made life in the Sahel one of hardship. As a result, **outward migration** from Sahel's rural areas has **increased** significantly. Many migrants **move to urban areas** both within and outside of the Sahel. This has led to the **rapid growth of** these **cities**. For example, Bamako (the **capital of Mali**) increased from **160,000 in 1960** to **1.3 million in 2016**.

As most of the refugees entering these cities are **ecological refugees** escaping **extreme poverty**, they have little or no personal belongings. This has led to the rapid growth of mass, **unplanned** and **overcrowded**

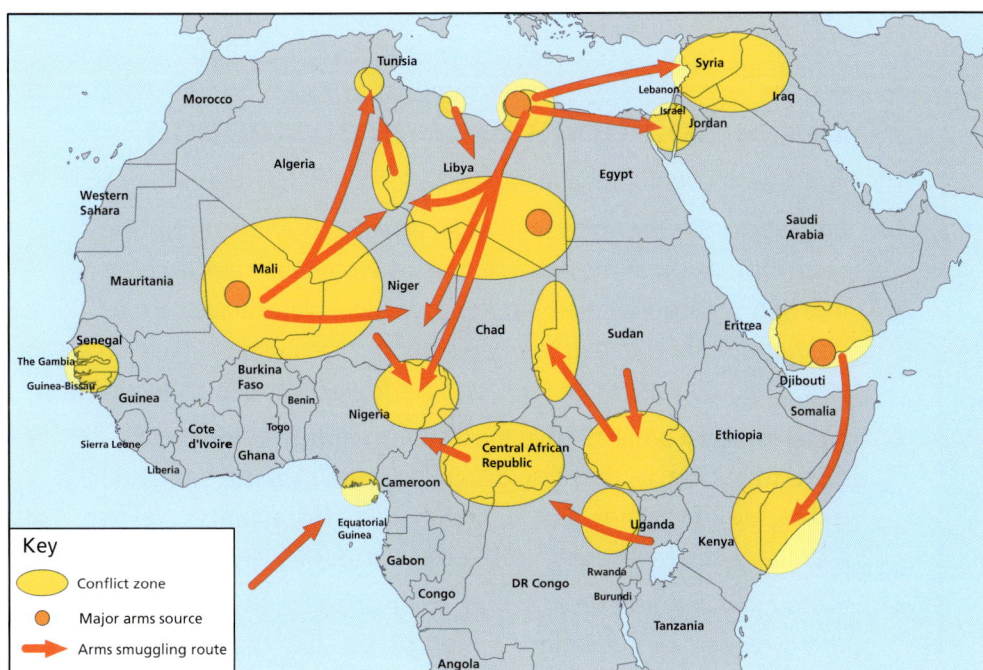

Fig. 2.14 Conflict in the Sahel

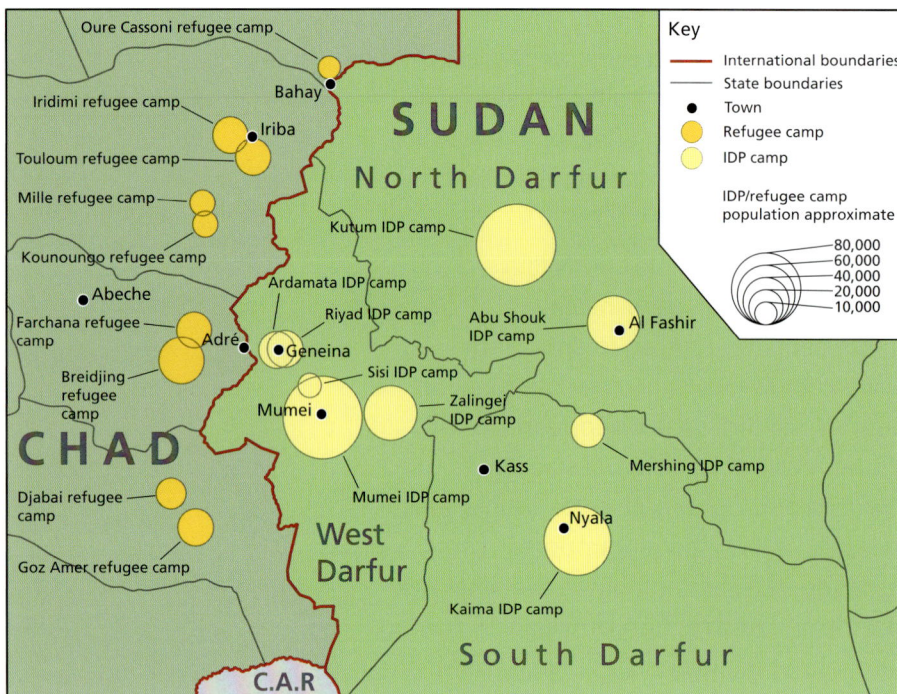

Fig. 2.15 Conflict in Darfur, Sudan

shanty towns. The outward migration of these people has had a devastating effect on the rural communities left behind. As **most migrants** tend to be **males**, the **females** are **left behind** to **look after** the **elderly members** of the **family**. This has led to **low marriage rates** in rural areas and it also **robs rural areas** of a large proportion of their **young workforce**.

In many areas, **increased migration** due to overpopulation has led to **tension and conflict between migrants** and locals. Sudan and South Sudan are examples of this, with the **root cause** of **conflict** being **cultural differences**. However, increased migration from the **Sahel region** to Sudan increased tensions before the War in Darfur began. In **2003**, **civil war** broke out in Darfur as two groups (Sudanese Liberation Army and Justice and Equality Movement) fought against the government. The rebels cited a **lack of government protection** for Darfur's **farming population** and the government's **lack of investment** in developing the region as the reasons for the conflict. The Sudanese government responded by bombing villages and arming Arab militia, who attacked civilians. As a result of the fighting, over 300,000 people were killed and over **3 million people** were **internally displaced** within Darfur. This mass internal migration has led to overpopulation in areas which are unable to support the increased populations. The majority of these deaths have occurred as a result of starvation.

Possible Solutions to Overpopulation

The problems of overpopulation can be tackled in many ways:

1. **Education of women** is seen as an effective way of **combating overpopulation** in the Sahel. Educated women are less likely to get **married younger** and are more knowledgeable in areas such as children's healthcare and family planning. When women have access to education, they are more likely to have **fewer** and **healthier children**.

2. **Afforestation** projects have the ability to **reduce** the **rate of desertification**, as they shield land from strong winds and also help to **bind soil together**. Correctly managed **afforestation** can also eventually **allow for sustainable** use of **trees** for firewood.

3. Although it is expensive to set up, **solar power** is a potential source of energy/power for the Sahel. As well as harvesting the almost constant

ACTIVE LEARNING

1. In what way has climate change caused overpopulation in the Sahel region?

2. How might the education of women help to solve the issue of overpopulation in the Sahel?

3. Of the four possible solutions to overcoming overpopulation in the Sahel (mentioned above), which, do you think, is the most likely to succeed? Which, do you think, is the least likely to succeed? Explain your reasons for both choices.

FACT

It might be difficult to believe, but just 5,000 years ago the area that now makes up the Sahara Desert was a lush, green grassland. Changes in climate around this time saw the region rapidly turn to desert.

sunshine, solar power also reduces the need for firewood. However, solar power is **expensive** and would require **large amounts** of **development aid** to be given from wealthier developed countries.

4. The introduction of **drought-resistant grasses** and crops may help to **reduce** the **impact** of **drought** and reduce the likelihood of famine.

2.3 Influence of Society and Culture on Overpopulation

In Chapter 1 we learned that the **status of women** in a **region's culture** directly **impacts on population growth**. In countries or regions where women do not have equality, birth rates are higher. This occurs due to **younger marriage ages**, **lack of education** and the view that **children** (especially males) are an **economic asset**.

Role of Women

In the **developing world**, women tend to be viewed as '**second-class citizens**' with a **lower social status** and **low levels of education**. With little or **no access to education**, women are **unaware of** the **opportunities** that exist outside of the home. Instead, women are often seen as being the property of their husbands, with the woman's primary function being to **produce heirs** to carry on the father's name. As a result, **fertility rates** in countries in the developing world are very **high**. Examples include India, Bangladesh and Niger.

Religion

In societies where there is a **strong religious influence**, we also typically see **high birth rates**. The vast majority of religions **oppose birth control** and **abortion**, while **promoting large families** and the **traditional view** of **women as mothers**. Until the late **1970s**, **Ireland** had a **strong Catholic influence** which promoted **large families** and strongly **opposed** legislation allowing for **artificial contraception**. However, as the influence of the

Catholic Church declines in developed countries, so too do **fertility rates**, e.g. **Italy** has a fertility rate of just **1.3 births per woman**. This trend is also seen in strict **Muslim countries** in which large families are promoted and **contraception** is seen as **anti-Islamic**, e.g. **Saudi Arabia**, which has a **fertility rate of 2.7 per woman**, or Pakistan, which has a fertility rate of 3.2 per woman.

Local Customs/Economic Asset

In many **developing countries, children** are seen as an **economic asset** due to the **high levels of poverty** in these areas. People in many slowly developing countries have **larger families** to ensure that enough children survive into adulthood to look after their parents in old age. Therefore, **children** are seen as a plan for economic survival. **Male children** are desirable also, since in many cultures young men who marry **receive a dowry** from their wives. Therefore, males are believed to provide an **economic advantage** for the family, while females are believed to be an economic liability.

CASE STUDY 📁

India

India has a population of roughly **1.325 billion people**, making it the **second most populous country** in the world. It accounts for **17.8 per cent of the total world population**. The **population density** of India is **446 per km²**. However, this population is **not evenly distributed**, with **32 per cent of** the **population** living in **urban regions** with **densities exceeding 25,000 per km²**, e.g. **Kolkata**. Although India's rate of **population growth is slowing** (falling from 2.8 per cent in 2008 to 2.3 per cent in 2013).

Because of the **rapid population growth** in India, its **population is young**, with a **median of 26.9 years**. Meanwhile, less than **10 per cent of the population are under 60 years of age**. It is expected that India will reach **replacement levels** (see page 20) of 2.1 by **2020**.

The status of women in India has traditionally been inferior to that of men. As a result, women have been subjected to social disadvantages compared to men in the country, which has increased the rate of population growth. Such disadvantages include:

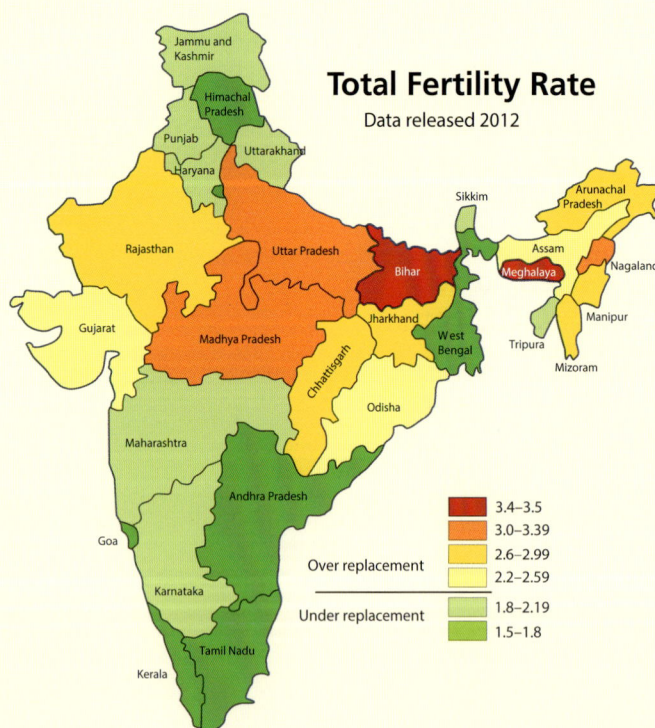
Total Fertility Rate
Data released 2012

![#a11b21]	3.4–3.5
![#f07d2e]	3.0–3.39
![#f5b731]	2.6–2.99
![#f6ea8c]	2.2–2.59

Over replacement

![#a8cf6f]	1.8–2.19
![#6bb345]	1.5–1.8

Under replacement

▲ **Fig. 2.17** Total fertility rate of India

1. Lack of education
2. Lack of family planning
3. Poor diet and healthcare
4. Arranged marriages.

Despite the Indian government's long-term commitment to **increasing female literacy rates**, more than **60 per cent** of the **female population** remain **illiterate**. This **low level of literacy** negatively affects the lives of Indian families. Illiterate women have **higher levels of fertility**, while also having **higher levels of child mortality**. This is particularly true in **rural** areas of **India**, where **illiteracy rates** are nearly double that of males: **38 per cent male** compared to **64 per cent female**. **Girls** who begin school are also **more likely to drop out** as their families ask them to **look after younger siblings**.

By the **age of 11**, over **50 per cent** of **girls** in India who started school will have **dropped out**.

If a family has to choose between educating a son or a daughter, typically the son will be chosen. **Education** of a **son** is seen as an **investment**, as a son and his wife will look after the son's parents in old age. **Educating** a **girl** is **not** seen as a **worthwhile** investment, as a daughter and her husband will look after the husband's parents, meaning the girl's family of origin will not benefit.

As **daughters** are expected to **marry young** and assume roles of **homemaker**, **wife** and **mother**, **birth rates are high**. While the **Prohibition of Child Marriage Act** states that a girl in India cannot marry before the age of 18, UNICEF estimates that **47 per cent of marriages** in India are to **girls under 18**, with an estimated **18 per cent** occurring **before** the age of **15**. As these girls have not received an education and have little say in the home, **family planning is not used**. As a result of this, the country's **birth rates are high**, leading to **overcrowding in cities**, **high urban populations** and **overpopulation**.

As males are seen as more desirable than females, couples have as many children as possible in order to produce male heirs to carry on the male family name. **More male children** are also seen as a means of **increasing social status**, as they will **receive dowries** from the bridal families. Having many children is also seen as a plan for economic survival – a kind of **insurance policy** for parents, as they will have someone to look after them in later life. As **infant mortality rates** are still **high** in India, couples have as many children as possible to ensure that enough of the children will survive to look after the parents in old age.

While the educational status of women is a major contributor to overpopulation in India, so too is the **under-utilisation of a major food resource** because of **religious limitations** placed on the consumption of **beef**. The dominant religion of India is **Hindu**, which **forbids the killing of cows**, as they are considered to be a sacred animal. Since cattle are not culled, cattle numbers have risen rapidly – despite a national shortage of food. As a result of these **poor farming practices**, **undernourished cows** have **reduced daily yields of milk**, leading to **overpopulation**.

Combined with **religious limitations** on **food supply**, the Hindu practice of **purdah** also affects women. Purdah means that **women** are **secluded** from men outside of the household. The religion also places women at a lower

India – 2014

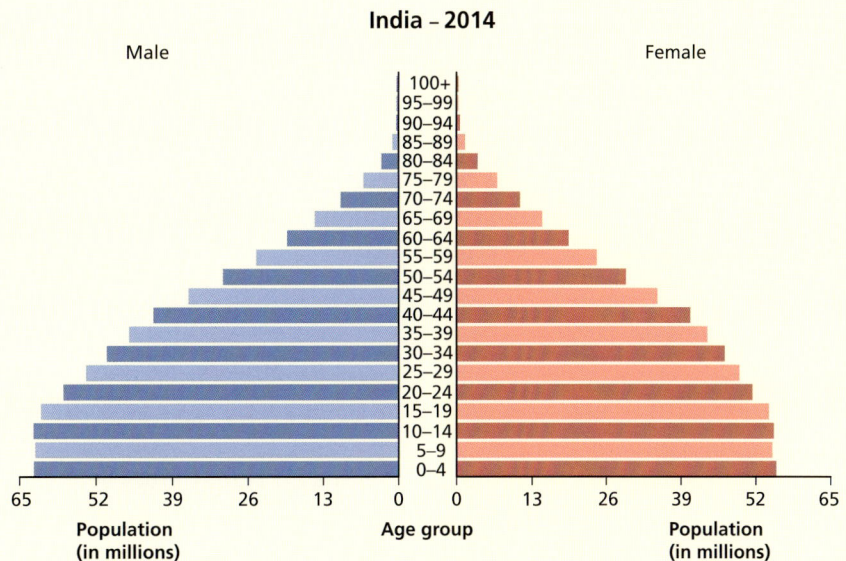

Male   Female

Population (in millions)   Age group   Population (in millions)

⌃ **Fig. 2.18** Population pyramid of India

ACTIVE LEARNING

1. Discuss how religion influences birth rates in some countries.

2. In what way has the role of women in society impacted on birth rates in India?

3. How does the practice of Purdah cause higher levels of infant mortality?

4. Go to **www.youtube.com** and search for 'role of women in Indian society' for a series of videos in which the issue is discussed.

GEO DICTIONARY

Constraints: limitations or restrictions

Utilisation: making use of something

Purdah: the practice in some Muslim and Hindu societies of screening women from men or strangers

status to men, which adds to the problem of hunger. Many Indian **women** are **malnourished** as they are required to **eat last and least** (men first, then children, then women). This also **affects** the **child mortality** rate, as **malnourished women** give birth to **malnourished children**. Therefore, the children are more prone to **fatal illness** and **disease**.

The results of these social and **cultural constraints** mean that India is a country that has **outgrown** its **natural carrying capacity**, i.e. it is **overpopulated**.

2.4 Wealth and Income Levels

There are **obvious and clear links** between the **level of income** in a country and overpopulation. Regions of the world with the **highest birth rates** are also the **regions** with the **highest levels of poverty**. Examples include the **Sahel region** and **Sub-Saharan Africa**, South East Asia, areas of India and South America. In contrast with this, **countries** with very **low birth rates** are among the **wealthiest** in the world, e.g. **Western Europe**.

Why?

In answering why population is affected by income, we must understand the conditions and societal beliefs that exist in poor and rich countries. In **wealthier countries**, **females** are free to **work outside of the home**, meaning they often choose to **pursue careers**. As they have careers, women tend to **wait until their late twenties or thirties** to begin having children. Also, women in **richer countries** are **educated and informed** about family planning and childcare. The **cost of raising children** is higher in countries with **higher incomes**, meaning that **couples will budget** as to how many children they can afford to rear. All of these **factors lower birth levels**.

In **poorer countries**, governments **do not provide financial assistance** for struggling families. Therefore, **children** are seen as an **economic advantage**. A family with more children has more workers to earn money to provide for other family members and siblings. Also **women in poorer countries** are assigned the **role of mother and minder** of the elderly.

Many **women** are **married** and begin **having children** when they are as young as **15 years old**, which means that they have **many children** during their **fertile years**. Unfortunately, **high birth rates** in poorer regions create a **vicious cycle of overpopulation**.

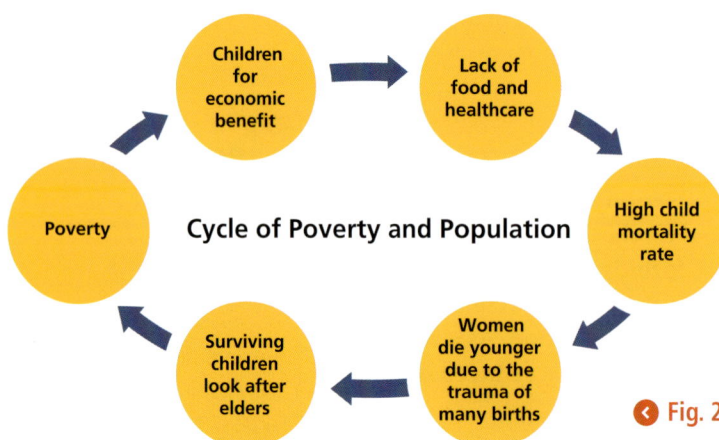

Children for economic benefit → Lack of food and healthcare → High child mortality rate → Women die younger due to the trauma of many births → Surviving children look after elders → Poverty → (back to Children for economic benefit)

Cycle of Poverty and Population

🔵 **Fig. 2.19** Cycle of poverty

Germany and Ethiopia

The effects of **wealth levels on population** can be seen through different **demographic trends** in **Germany** and **Ethiopia**. In 2008, Ethiopia and Germany had similar populations of **82 million people**. However, since that time, the population growth in these two countries has differed drastically. Germany's population has **fallen by 1 million to 80.6 million**, while **Ethiopia's population** has **risen rapidly** to **101.6 million**. Germany's **regressive population** signifies its position in **Stage 5** of the **Demographic Transitional Model**. As can be seen in the table below, women in Germany begin having children at a much later stage in life, meaning that **fewer children** will be born, i.e. **lowering** the **Total Fertility Rate** (TFR). At **1.43 per woman**, the **TFR of Germany** is much **lower than** the **2.3 replacement rate**. This occurs as couples **delay having children** in order to **finish education** and become **established** in their **chosen professions**. The widespread **availability of family planning** means that **families budget** for the number of children they can afford to rear at an **adequate standard of living**.

> **A→Z** GEO **DICTIONARY**
>
> **HIV:** human immunodeficiency virus – a virus that attacks the immune system, the body's natural defense system
>
> **AIDS:** acquired immune deficiency syndrome – a disease in which there is a severe loss of the body's immunity, lowering the resistance to infection and disease

	Ethiopia	Germany
Population growth rate	2.89 % per year	−0.18 % per year
Birth rate	37.66 births per 1,000	8.42 births per 1,000
Death rate	11.28 deaths per 1,000	11.29 deaths per 1,000
Net migration	−0.23 migrants per 1,000	1.06 migrants per 1,000
Mean mother age	19.6 years old	29.2 years old
Infant mortality rate	55.77 deaths per 1,000	3.14 deaths per 1,000
Fertility rate	5.23 births per woman	1.43 births per woman
HIV/AIDS: % / No.	1.3% prevalence / 758,600 people	0.1% prevalence / 67,000 people
Risk of infectious disease	Very high	Very low
Average years in education	7 years	16 years
Child labour: % / No.	53% / 10,693,164	0% / 0

In **Germany**, the **average cost of raising a child** to the age of 18 is **€210,000**, meaning having more children brings **additional economic pressure**. As fewer children are being born, the population of Germany is ageing. This is known as '**greying**' and it has **long-term implications** for the economy of the country, such as the provisions of **pensions and healthcare**. As Germany's percentage of **over-65s (currently 21 per cent)** continues to rise, a number of economic pressures must be dealt with. First, with fewer children being born, there will no longer be enough economically active people to pay for pensions or healthcare for the elderly. However, if taxes are raised to compensate, the income of the **economically active** is **reduced** and **couples** will be further **deterred from having children**. As a result, **Germany** now **relies on immigration** of **economically active migrants** to counteract the labour deficit and ensure a wide tax base.

Ethiopia – 2010

Male | Female

95–99
90–94
85–89
80–84
75–79
70–74
65–69
60–64
55–59
50–54
45–49
40–44
35–39
30–34
25–29
20–24
15–19
10–14
5–9
0–4

8 7 6 5 4 3 2 1 0 1 2 3 4 5 6 7 8

Percentage

Age group

Ethiopia – 2030

Male | Female

8 7 6 5 4 3 2 1 0 1 2 3 4 5 6 7 8

Percentage

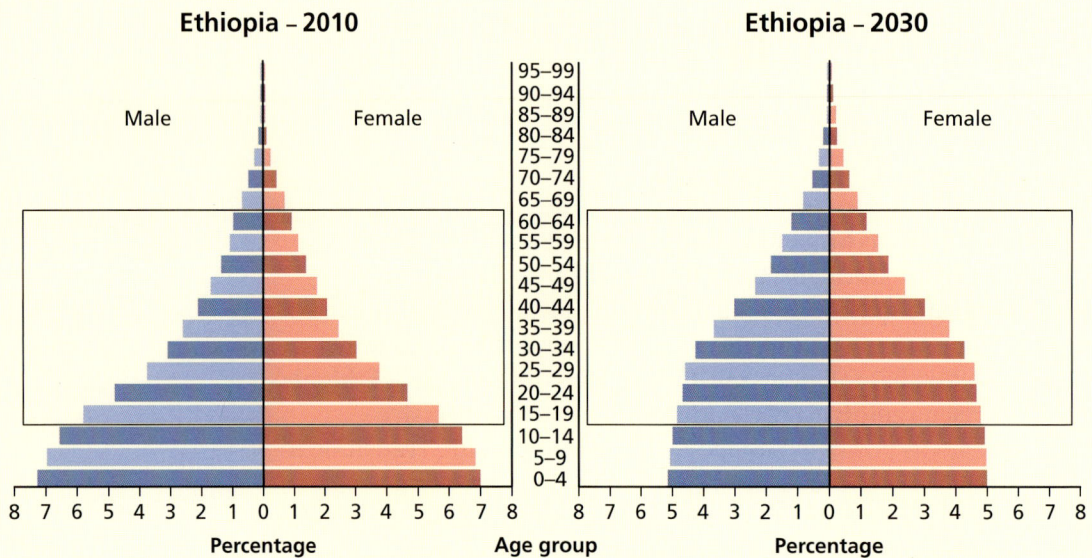

Fig. 2.20 Age of Ethiopia's population

ACTIVE LEARNING

1. Why is Germany's birth rate lower than Ethiopia's?

2. What population factors hinder Ethiopia's development?

3. Go to www.youtube.com to source videos related to population decline. Use key search terms such as 'population decline' and 'Germany falling population'.

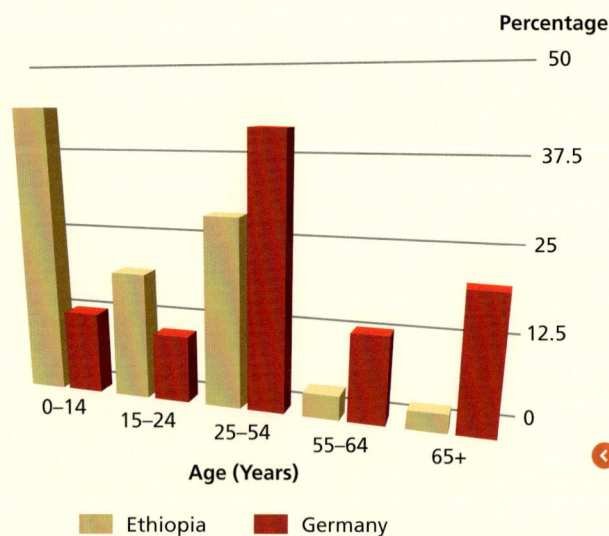

In contrast to this, **Ethiopia** suffers from **limited resources** combined with **high birth rates. Economic instability, political and religious conflict, low levels of education** and **low status of women** prevent opportunities for economic development. In **1950, Ethiopia** had a population of just **18.5 million**, with a rising **TFR of 7.17**. Due to a **lack of education** and **low status of women in society**, the population began to rise rapidly – reaching **over 100 million in 2015**.

Historically, **Ethiopia** has suffered from famine, with **six major famines** occurring **since 1900** alone. As a result, a tradition of having many children exists in order to guarantee that enough survive to look after their parents in old age. A **lack of family planning** and **education** regarding contraception has also led to an increased birth rate.

Percentage

Age (Years)

☐ Ethiopia   ☐ Germany

Fig. 2.21 Population dynamics of Ethiopia and Germany

FACT

Thirteen per cent of Ethiopian children are missing one or both of their parents; nearly a quarter of these parents died of AIDS.

With over **75 per cent of Ethiopia's population** living in **rural areas**, government aid is almost **non-existent**, with the exception of **limited food aid** in times of drought. **Low literacy rates** and **lack of education** mean that **child mortality rates** are high. **Lack of contraception** leads to a **higher than desirable TFR.** The TFR is 4.6, despite three children being the number desired by couples. This means that **birth rates** are **over 60 per cent higher** than if unwanted births were avoided. As only **35 per cent of women** receive an education, this **trend** is **likely to continue.**

The government of **Ethiopia** has **failed** to **establish** sound **economic policies** that could attract investment or develop an industrialised economy. This is highlighted by the fact that only **17 per cent** of the country's **population** live in **urban areas**. A lack of **investment in vital infrastructure** such as **hospitals and schools** has led to further difficulties such as **high risk of infectious disease outbreaks**, both as a result of **poor medical knowledge** and **poor availability of healthcare**.

Furthermore, the **lack of an educated workforce** prevents the country from being in a position to move away from an economy based on subsistent agriculture. With over **50 per cent of Ethiopia's** population **under the age of 20**, rapid population growth is likely to continue. A young population also means there is potential for economic growth. However, unless food security and government guidance is developed, **poverty** is **likely to continue**.

> **FACT**
>
> In 1990 Ethiopia had one of the lowest life expectancies in the world at 48 years for men and 50 years for women. However, this has risen significantly to 62 for men and 66 for women as of 2016.

> **FACT**
>
> Despite it being illegal, 49 per cent of girls in Ethiopia marry before the age of 18, and 1 in 5 girls are married before the age of 15.

2.5 The Impact of Technology on Population Growth/ Overpopulation

In the past 40 years, Earth's population has doubled to reach 7.4 billion people. By 2025, it is predicted that it will reach 8 billion, meaning that the issue of overpopulation will not end any time soon. As the population grows, so too does the demand for food, water, fuel and other vital natural resources. **Potable water**, the quality and quantity of arable land, rainforests and **biodiversity** are all **at risk** from overpopulation. Added to this are the **strains on medical services** across the world with ever-increasing numbers of people. It is estimated that the **world food supply** will **need to double** by **2050**, which raises a number of questions:

1. How will our environment sustain such intensive agriculture?

2. How will we increase the percentage of arable land in the world while maintaining current ecosystems?

3. How do we counteract the effects of climate change on food supply?

4. How do we address the medical needs of increased populations?

While the questions above are difficult to answer, one thing we know for certain is that technological advancements have helped, and will continue to **increase the carrying capacity** of regions across the globe. In this section, we will focus on the **role of agriculture and medical technological advancement** on population growth.

Agricultural Revolution

The Agricultural Revolution began in the **eighteenth century** in the **developed countries** with major improvements in farming practices. Ideas such as **crossbreeding of animals** and **crop rotation** significantly increased **food production** across the developed world.

GEO DICTIONARY

Infrastructure: physical structures and facilities in a country/ region, e.g. buildings, roads, power supply and telecommunications

Potable water: water which is safe enough to drink

Crossbreeding: mating two different breeds of an animal to produce a new variety/breed

Crop rotation: the growing of different crops on a piece of land each year to avoid depleting the soil's nutrients and to control weeds, pests and diseases

Fig. 2.22 Crossbreeding has created animals with more desirable traits, e.g. cattle breeds that fatten easily for beef production.

1950 vs 2008

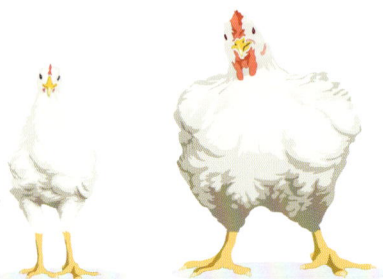

Days **68**   Days **47**

Because of these improved farming methods, **food shortages and famines declined** greatly across the **European countries** that experienced the revolution. Following improved farming methods, the development of more **specialist machinery** meant that larger areas of land could be **cultivated for food production**, while also **decreasing** the **need** for **manual labour**. As further **mechanical development** occurred, specialist machines such as **combine harvesters** greatly **increased food output**. This coincided with **improvements to transport links**, which allowed for quick and efficient movement of fresh produce to markets.

Chemicals, known as pesticides, were developed to **combat pests** that **lowered crop yields**. Pesticides led to a reduction in the **crop diseases** caused by **insects** and **fungi**, which in turn increased crop yields. The development of **artificial fertilisers** now means that food can be grown on **marginal land** that previously did not have the nutrients capable of supporting crop growth. Fertilisers also allow more intensive farming to take place, with greater yields being harvested.

Irrigation schemes, such as those used in the **Central Valley**, California or the Mezzogiorno in Italy, allow for crops to grow in times of drought. Irrigation schemes are seen as an effective means of **combating increased desertification** along the Sahel and other arid areas throughout the globe.

The Green Revolution and Genetically Modified Foods

The **Green Revolution** was the name given to the general era of **increased food production**, technology and research by scientists throughout the 1960s. From this era onwards, scientists began to develop methods to increase food production through **altering** the **genetics of crops**. In genetic modification, plants are given desirable traits, e.g. **drought- resistance** or **high salt tolerance**. As a result, genetically modified (GM) foods have the potential to greatly reduce food shortages worldwide. It is now possible to genetically alter crops to give them **higher nutritional value**, i.e. more nutrients within the food. GM foods are capable of **growing in harsh climate conditions** or within poor soils, which increases the amount of arable land available. **High-yielding crops** have had a major impact on countries such as **China** and **India**, as these countries have greatly **increased their carrying capacity** through increased yields of maize and rice. Without GM foods, India would not have been able to feed its own population, which has risen from 351 million in 1950 to 1.3 billion in 2016.

Fig. 2.23 Genetically modified chickens are much larger and grow rapidly.

What's the Catch?

With the possibility of major advantages in food production globally, there are also a number of disadvantages associated with the Agricultural Revolution and the Green Revolution.

First, technological advancement in agriculture is incredibly **expensive**, meaning it is beyond the reach of many of the world's poorest countries, i.e. the countries most in need of it. For example, **greenhouses** have proved extremely useful for farmers in developed countries, as greenhouses **control heat**, **water** and **pests**. However, greenhouses are far **too expensive** for **farmers** in the developing world to buy and install on their land.

Many **artificial fertilisers** are **oil based**, and oil is a **rapidly depleting resource**. As **oil supplies dwindle**, fertilisers will become **increasingly expensive**. Furthermore, **over-fertilisation** of **soil** can lead to it becoming **toxic**, while excess fertiliser can end up **contaminating water supplies**.

Regarding GM foods, there are a number of concerns, ranging from **declining bee populations** to our **over-reliance** on a **few varieties of seeds**. As **traditional seed varieties** are **abandoned** in favour of high-yielding GMO seeds, we become dependent on fewer seed types – what should happen if these seeds fail? Furthermore, companies who produce these seeds are allowed to patent them, which essentially means they can now patent life. These producers now have a **monopoly on** our **food production**.

A final concern is that **developed countries**, who can afford these technologies are **capable of producing surplus food**, while poorer countries have little or no food security. In the EU **'food mountains'** of surplus supplies have formed as governments prevent excess products from flooding into the EU market and reducing prices. This excess food could be used to ease food security issues in the developing world; however, it is typically **sold at a very high price**.

Medical Improvements

In general, **improvements** in **medical technology** lead to a long-term decrease in population growth. As health conditions improve, families tend to have fewer children – since more children are likely to survive to adulthood. The development of new **medications and vaccinations to prevent diseases** such as **malaria** and **measles** has greatly **increased** the **life expectancy** in countries where these medications and vaccines have been implemented. These vaccines help greatly in **reducing infant mortality** as they are **cheap** and can be administered in even the most basic of conditions.

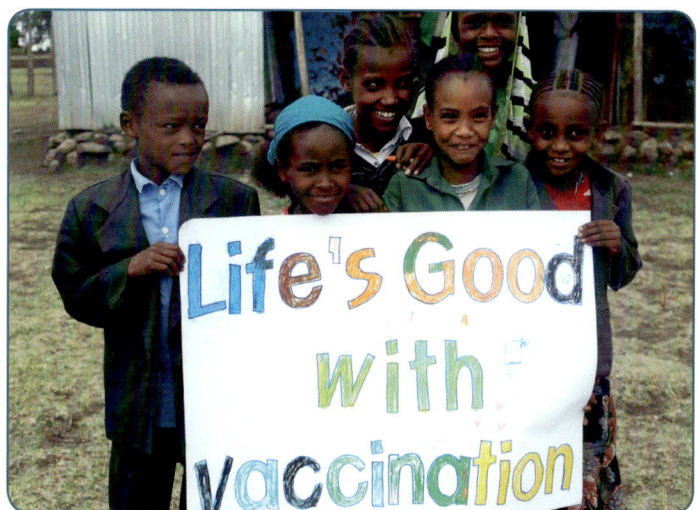

Fig. 2.24 Vaccinations reduce child mortality greatly.

HIV/AIDS in South Africa

It is predicted that populations in certain parts of the world will **decrease greatly** over the next 40 years, with over one-third of this reduction accredited to **deaths** caused **by HIV/AIDS.** The areas which will be most affected by HIV/AIDS will be **South Africa** and the **Indian Sub-Continent.**

South Africa has a population of **53 million,** of which roughly **12 per cent are infected** with HIV/AIDS. If we exclude children, the percentage of **adults infected** rises to **18 per cent.** However, this does not provide an accurate indication of infection: **13.6 per cent of black South Africans** are **infected,** compared to **0.3 per cent** of **white South Africans.** Delays in introducing **effective treatments** in South Africa have made the situation much worse than it should be, as both the **government** and **MNCs prevented** the **widespread distribution** of **antiretroviral drugs** (ARVs) to treat HIV. For many years, these treatments were **available only to South Africans** who could **afford to pay** for **private healthcare.**

> **A-Z GEO DICTIONARY**
>
> **Antiretroviral drugs:** medicines which slow down a virus's ability to reproduce or attack the immune system

Population size with and without AIDS, South Africa, 2000 and 2025

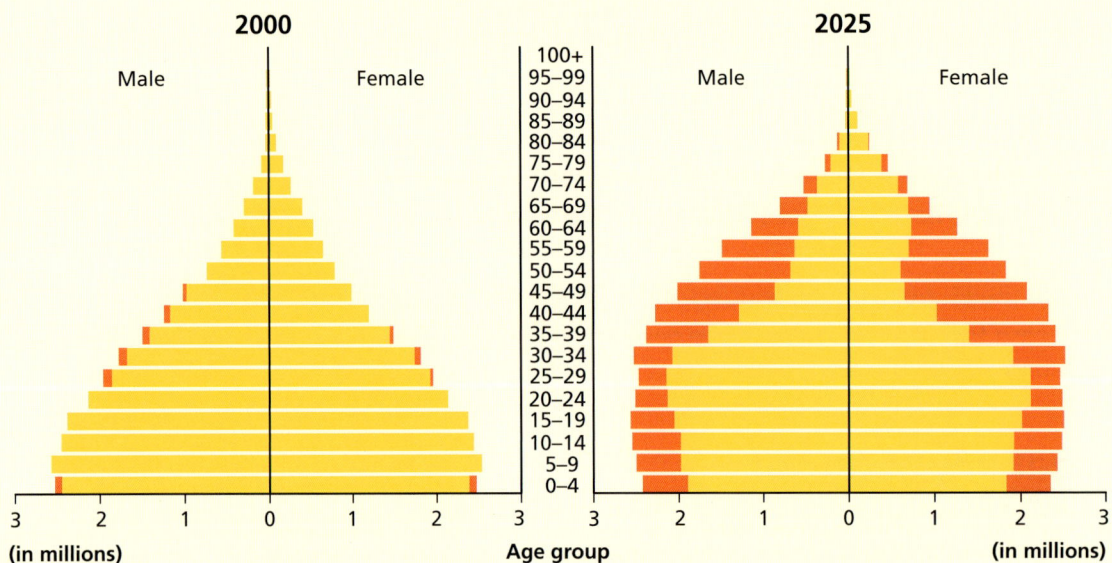

Fig. 2.25 The impact of AIDS on the population of South Africa

Legend:
- Actual estimated and projected population
- Hypothetical size of the population in the absence of AIDS

As it was mainly **white South Africans** who could afford private healthcare, the number of **black South Africans contracting** the **disease** continued to **rise rapidly.** Furthermore, treatment to **prevent infected pregnant women** from **passing** the **disease onto** their **infants** was also delayed by the government, which has largely contributed to the figure of **28 per cent** of **15–24 year olds** in South Africa being **infected** with AIDS.

Despite over two decades of media, international and national pressure, it was not until **2009,** when Jacob Zuma won the presidency of South Africa that **government barriers** were **removed** to allow for **widespread access to ARVs.** As widespread treatment with ARVs now increases rapidly, the number of **new infections** among adolescents has been **decreasing** steadily. However, the damage caused by HIV/AIDS remains substantial as older age groups continue to develop new infections, with a high percentage of deaths.

Although the education of people about the disease continues to increase, only **30 per cent of South Africans over 50 years of age** are **aware** of the true **causes** of the disease. Between the ages **25–49**, a little **over half** take **protective measures** (e.g. use of barrier contraceptives/condoms), with this figure rising to over **90 per cent** for those **under 25**. While this shows a move in the right direction for South Africa, it will take many decades before HIV/AIDS becomes a less prevalent issue.

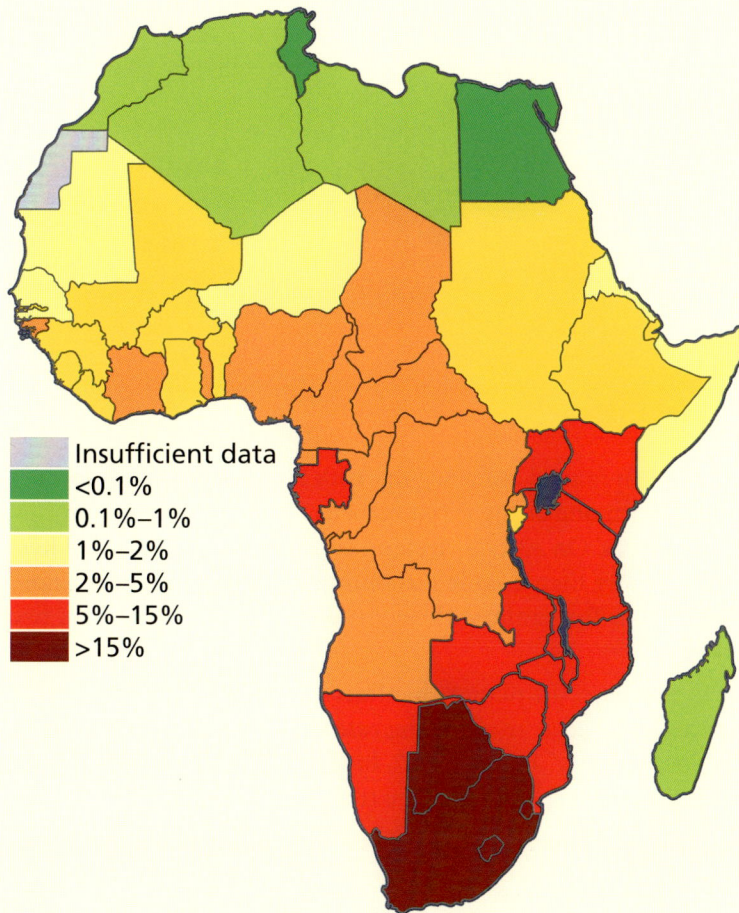

Insufficient data
- <0.1%
- 0.1%–1%
- 1%–2%
- 2%–5%
- 5%–15%
- >15%

🔺 **Fig. 2.26** Prevalence of AIDS in Africa

FACT

In 2006 the then South African Minister of Health suggested that eating foods such as olive oil, lemon and garlic would cure people of HIV and AIDS.

FACT

In 1996 South Africa's soccer team showed their support for the campaign raising AIDS awareness at the African Nations Cup by wearing red ribbons.

FACT

The first diagnosed case of AIDS in South Africa was in 1983. In 1990, 1 per cent of the South African population were infected with AIDS. This rose to 10 per cent by 1999.

ACTIVE LEARNING

1. Explain the following terms: *Agricultural Revolution*, *Green Revolution*, *genetically modified foods*.
2. Why might technological advances in agriculture be of no use to farmers in the developing world?
3. How have medical improvements increased life expectancy in developing countries?
4. For more information of global food production, watch the documentary *Food, Inc.*

The carbon footprint

Fig. 2.27 Carbon footprint

2.6 Ecological Footprint

An *ecological footprint*, also known as carbon footprint, refers to the amount of **forest land, agricultural land, recreational space** and **resources needed by a person** to live. In the **developed world** this accounts for **several hectares per person**, while in the developing world this is less than **one hectare per person**. Even within the developed world, this figure varies greatly.

CASE STUDY 📁

GEO DICTIONARY

Ecological footprint: the amount of forest, agricultural land, recreational space and resources needed by a person to live

Global hectares: one global hectare represents the average productivity of all biologically productive areas (measured in hectares) on Earth in a given year

Ireland

Ireland has been ranked as having the **10th largest ecological footprint** in the world, with **one of the worst records** for **excessive consumption of natural resources**. On average, **Ireland** consumes **over six global hectares per person** – more than **double** the **amount** used in **some European countries** such as **Romania**, with countries such as **Mali** using **0.1 hectares per person**.

If this is to continue, the **planet's habitats** risk being **completely destroyed** as **resources** are **used** at an **alarming rate** to sustain the lifestyles of wealthy societies. In the period **1970 to 2007**, **biodiversity** in the world **declined by 30 per cent** and by **60 per cent in** the **tropics**.

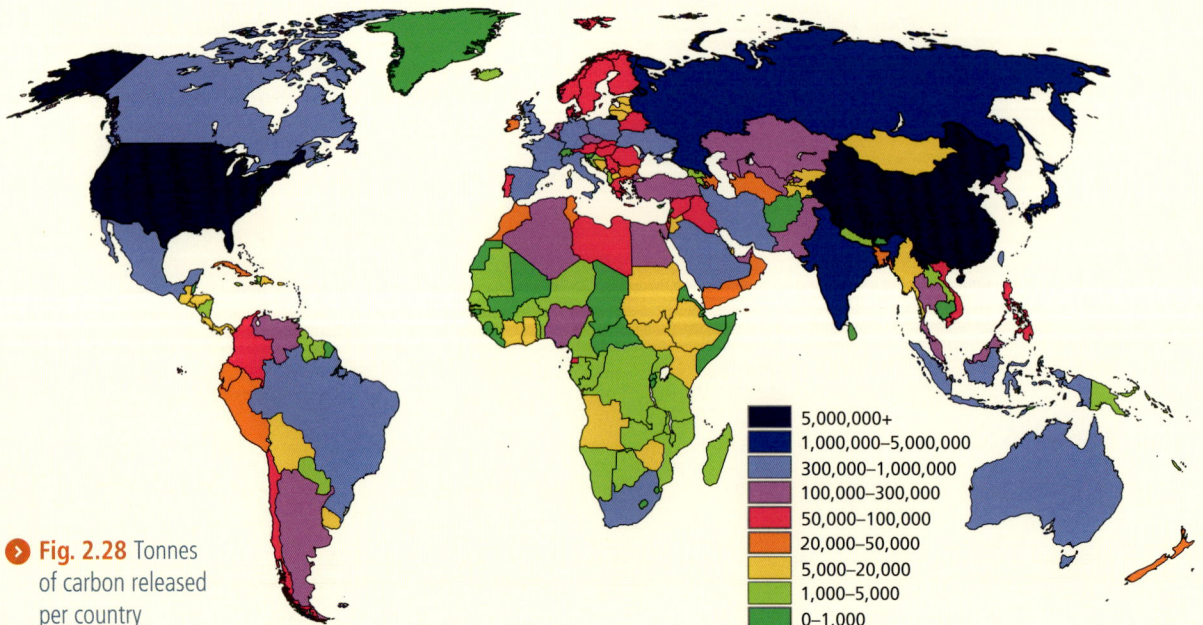

Fig. 2.28 Tonnes of carbon released per country

Colour	Tonnes
	5,000,000+
	1,000,000–5,000,000
	300,000–1,000,000
	100,000–300,000
	50,000–100,000
	20,000–50,000
	5,000–20,000
	1,000–5,000
	0–1,000

Currently, the **Earth** needs **1.5 years to regenerate** the resources we use in a year. By **2030** it is estimated that we will need the **equivalent of two planets** to meet our annual needs.

If we are to **stop** this rapid **destruction** of the planet's ecosystems, then the **lifestyles of people in** the **North (i.e. the developed world)** need to become **simpler**. More informed lifestyle choices need to be made, such as **buying food locally**, **reducing** the amount of **travel** and **reducing** our **dependence on fossil fuels**.

ACTIVE LEARNING

Visit **www.foe.ie** and click 'carbon calculator' to calculate your family's carbon footprint.

2.7 Population and Development Rates

Developed

In general, it is accepted that as a **country's economy improves**, the average **family size decreases**. The Agricultural and Industrial Revolutions of the eighteenth and nineteenth centuries caused economic development throughout Europe and provided a market for new products such as textiles. This industry, along with increasing population led to **rural–urban migration** as people moved to cities and towns in search of work. **Tax revenue** from the working populations allowed for continued **development of sanitary systems**, **health** and **education**, which **increased life expectancy** and **lowered birth rates**. As a result, the US and European countries moved through the Demographic Transitional Model faster and earlier than other countries and are today characterised by **low levels of population growth**, **ageing populations**, **industrialised economies** and **high gross domestic product** (GDP). Therefore, most of their populations are **stationary or declining**. Some countries are experiencing **underpopulation** and **labour shortages**. **Inward migration** from the **South (i.e. developing world)** is now **necessary** to sustain the standards of living in these countries.

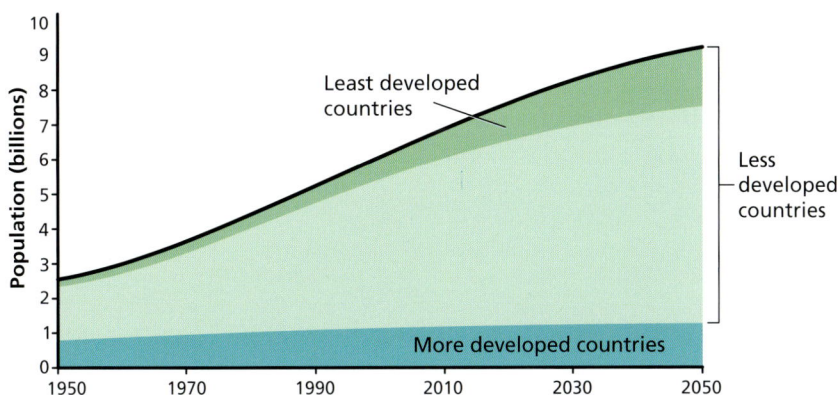

Fig. 2.29 Population growth according to development

Developing

In contrast to developed countries, developing countries face major challenges in, **controlling population growth** and increasing **economic development**. The majority of countries in the **South** are in **Stage 2 or Stage 3** of the **DTM**. In the majority of these countries, **30 per cent of the population** is **less than 14** years old. Many of these countries **experience government instability, social unrest, corruption** and **mismanagement of resources**. This makes **economic development extremely difficult** as **MNCs** are **reluctant to invest** in these countries as a result. This leaves **huge numbers unemployed**. These people move to cities in search of employment and a **higher standard of living**. Cities in the developing world can **double their population** in **less than 15 years**, which causes issues such as **overcrowding** and **violence**, e.g. **São Paolo** in **Brazil** or **Mexico City**. This overpopulation puts **pressure** on **food resources, housing** and **sanitary systems** which in turn causes **malnutrition** and **disease**.

With **fewer jobs in industry** in the developing world, the **small proportion** of **well-educated** people **emigrate to** the **developed world** where well-paid employment is available. This leads to a **brain drain** and makes the region less attractive for MNCs.

Quickly Developing

The **newly industrialised economies** (NIE) of the world are mainly located in Asia, in particular in **China**. **Labour-intensive industries** have located here to avail of **low wages** and **cheap resources**. While this high level of investment has **aided** the **development** of these economies, there are concerns regarding **poor working conditions** and the **degradation** of these **countries' environments**.

FACT

Over 80 per cent of all people live on less than $10 a day.

FACT

The poorest 40 per cent of the world's population accounts for 5 per cent of global income.

1. (i)   Name **one** region that experiences overpopulation.

   (ii)   Explain **one** cause of this overpopulation.

   (iii)   Describe the problems that result from overpopulation in this region.

   (iv)   Describe **one** solution to the problem of overpopulation.

(i)	Region named	4m
(ii)	Explanation: 4 SRPs @ 3m each	12m
(iii)	Description: 4 SRPs @ 3m each	12m
(iv)	Description: 4 SRPs @ 3m each	12m

2014 Q10C 40M

2. (i)   Explain the meaning of the term *overpopulation*.

   (ii)   Describe in detail **two** problems caused by overpopulation in any region that you have studied.

(i)	Term explained: 2 SRPs @ 3m each	6m

(ii)	Reference to country or region	3m
	Problem 1: 4 SRPs @ 3m each	12m
	Problem 2: 3 SRPs @ 3m each	9m

2012 Q10C 30M

3.   'Some parts of the world are overpopulated. Overpopulation occurs when there are too many people in a region relative to the resources available to provide an adequate standard of living.'

   (i)   Name any **one** region of the world that is overpopulated.

   (ii)   Explain in detail **one** cause of the overpopulation in the region you have named.

   (iii)   Describe in detail **one** problem caused by overpopulation.

   (iv)   Suggest **one** solution to the problem of overpopulation.

(i)	Name region	4m
(ii)	Explanation: 4 SRPs @ 3m each	12m
(iii)	Description: 4 SRPs @ 3m each	12m
(iv)	Solution discussed: 4 SRPs @ 3m each	12m

2010 Q12B 40M

HIGHER LEVEL

1. Describe and explain the causes and effects of overpopulation, with reference to examples you have studied.

Causes identified	2m
Effect identified	2m
Examples: 2 @ 2m each	4m
Explanation: 11 SRPs @ 2m each	22m

2015 Q10C 30M

2. Explain how the development of resources impacts on population change, with reference to examples that you have studied.

Impact named	2m
Examples: 2 @ 2m each	4m
Examination: 12 SRPs @ 2m each	24m

2013 Q11B 30M

3. Discuss the causes of overpopulation, referring to examples that you have studied.

Causes identified: 2 @ 2m each	4m
Named examples: 2 @ 2m each	4m
Discussion: 11 SRPs @ 2m each	22m

2011 Q12B 30M

HIGHER LEVEL

Overpopulation frequently appears on the exam paper, which means that it is a very important chapter to become familiar with. It is also important that you are fully aware of the different sections covered in this paper and are able to distinguish between the different topics. In this section, we will look at the 2011 question from the HL paper.

EXAM QUESTION

Discuss the causes of overpopulation referring to examples that you have studied.

Before we begin to answer the question, we must first be aware of exactly what we are being asked. As well as the key word *overpopulation*, what should immediately catch the eye is the fact that **plurals** are used in this question, namely the words *causes* and *examples*. Therefore, we must use more than one case study to answer this question.

Marking Scheme
Causes identified: 2 @ 2m each
Named examples: 2 @ 2m each
Discussion: 11 SRPs @ 2m each

SAMPLE ANSWER

Overpopulation occurs when the number of people living in an area is greater than its ability to support them [2m]. Two examples of regions that are overpopulated are the Sahel region of North Africa and the cities of India [2m + 2m].

One cause of overpopulation in the Sahel is climate change, as both the volume and frequency of rainfall are decreasing [2m]. Between the years of 1930 and 1960, higher levels of rainfall led to large-scale immigration to the Sahel by nomadic farmers [2m]. Since 1960 the wet season has shortened by 29 per cent, arriving later in the year, which leads to devastating famines [2m]. This drought has led to 14.28 million people living in the region without any food security should the seasonal rains not arrive [2m]. The rain that does arrive occurs in torrential downpours, which leads to erosion and gullying, making the remaining topsoil more susceptible to wind erosion [2m]. The increasing temperatures in the Sahel have led to increased evaporation rates, meaning the water table is not replenished and the soil is baked into an impermeable laterite that is useless for agriculture [2m]. The manufacturing industry of the developing world has damaged the environment of the region as it has increased acid rain, as well as air and water pollution [2m].

A second cause of overpopulation is role of women in Indian society [2m]. India is the second most populous country, accounting for 17.8 per cent of the world's population [2m]. Over 64 per cent of females in India are illiterate, as they lack the educational opportunities available to men, which leads to a lack of family planning and knowledge of childcare [2m]. Many girls are married at a very young age and begin having children while still in their teens, leading to high birth rates [2m]. As many women do not have access to basic healthcare services, there is a high infant mortality rate from preventable or curable diseases [2m]. As male children are more desirable, women have as many children as possible in order to produce as many male heirs as possible and continue on the husband's family name [2m]. Many mothers are malnourished due to the tradition of women eating 'last and least' during family meals. This affects child mortality, as malnourished women give birth to malnourished children [2m].

The answer takes its cue from the question, meaning it is well structured and examiner-friendly. All aspects of the question are dealt with separately, meaning each aspect is clearly dealt with. First, a clear definition of overpopulation is provided, showing a clear understanding of the topic being discussed. Each cause is then dealt with in its own concise paragraph, which provides clarity.

Marks Awarded	
Causes identified 2 @ 2m	
Named examples 2 @ 2m	
Best 11 SRPs @ 2m each	
Total 30/30	

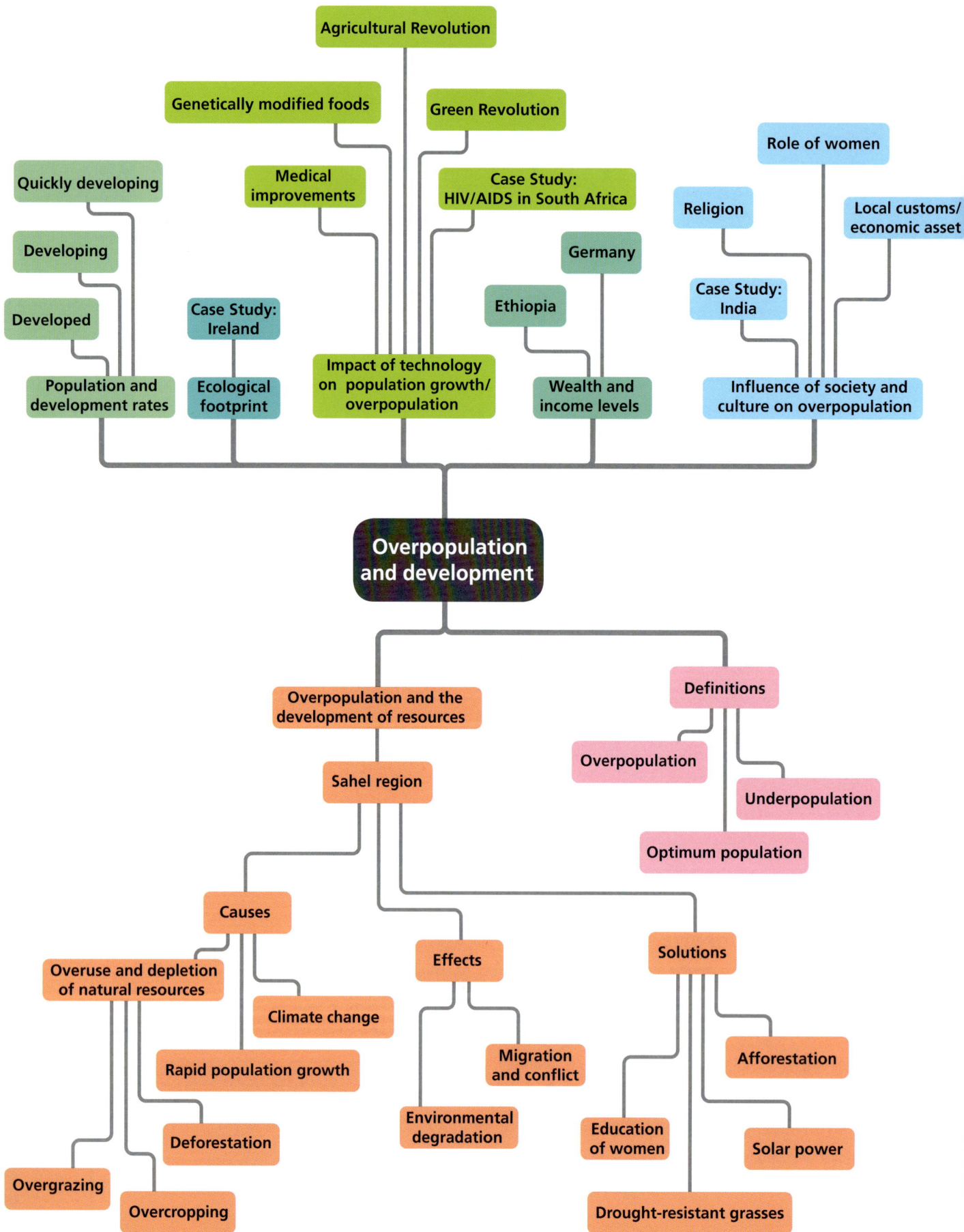

TOPIC MAP

Agricultural Revolution

Genetically modified foods

Green Revolution

Role of women

Quickly developing

Medical improvements

Case Study: HIV/AIDS in South Africa

Religion

Local customs/ economic asset

Developing

Germany

Developed

Ethiopia

Case Study: India

Population and development rates

Case Study: Ireland

Ecological footprint

Impact of technology on population growth/ overpopulation

Wealth and income levels

Influence of society and culture on overpopulation

Overpopulation and development

Overpopulation and the development of resources

Definitions

Overpopulation

Sahel region

Underpopulation

Optimum population

Causes

Effects

Solutions

Overuse and depletion of natural resources

Climate change

Migration and conflict

Afforestation

Rapid population growth

Environmental degradation

Education of women

Solar power

Deforestation

Overgrazing

Overcropping

Drought-resistant grasses

CHAPTER 3

Migration

In Chapters 1 and 2, you learned about the factors that impact population growth and decline, as well as how the limitations of the Earth's resources cause regions to become overpopulated. In this chapter, you will learn about migration and many of the reasons why it occurs.

KEY WORDS

- Migration
- Migrant
- Emigration
- Immigration
- Push factors
- Pull factors
- Donor regions
- Receiver regions
- Remittance
- Rural–urban migration
- Economic recession
- Net migration
- Multiracial
- Refugee
- General employment permit
- Asylum seekers
- Schengen Agreement
- Depopulation
- Ghettoisation
- Ethnic, racial and religious issues

LEARNING OUTCOMES

What you MUST know
- Definitions of migration, immigration, emigration and barriers to migration
- The impacts of migration on donor/receiver countries/regions
- Case Study: Changing migratory patterns in Ireland
- The migration policy of Ireland
- The migration policy of the EU
- Issues that can arise from migration
- Rural–urban migration in the developed world
- Rural–urban migration in the developing world

What you SHOULD know
- Definitions of *refugee*, *asylum seeker*, *voluntary migration*, *net migration*, *internal migration*, *international migration*, *destination region*, *source region*
- Examples of the push factors and pull factors that encourage migration
- Examples of barriers to migration, which prevent migration

What is USEFUL to know
- Additional statistics regarding migration to and from Ireland
- Current issues relating to migration issues in the EU

Introduction

Fig. 3.1 Refugees fleeing Syria

Migration refers to the **movement of people from one area to another** over a long-term period. Throughout history, humans have migrated to every part of the globe in search of basic items such as food and shelter, or in search of riches in the formation of large empires.

The first migrants were our ancestors who migrated from the East African Rift Valley to Europe and Asia, before spreading out across the entire globe. More recent trends have shown a movement from rural areas to cities and from the less developed countries of the South to the more developed countries of the North. This movement of people has major **impacts on both the receiver/host regions** and the **donor regions** – some **positive and** some **negative**. In order to progress through this chapter, it is important that you understand the key definitions in the table below.

Migration	The movement of people from one region to another over a long-term period, for a variety of reasons
Migrant	A person who moves from one place to another in order to find work or a better standard of living
Emigration	People who leave a region (E for exit)
Immigration	People who come into a region (I for in)
Barriers to migration	A factor that makes migration difficult or impossible, e.g. immigration laws, cost of travel, distance, family ties
Temporary migration	The repetitive movement of a migrant worker between home and host areas, e.g. someone who works away from home during the week and returns during the weekend
Forced migration	A person who is forced to leave their own country/region
Voluntary migration	A person who freely decides to leave their own country/region
Net migration	Also referred to as migration balance; this is the difference between the number of immigrants and the number of emigrants in a country/region
Push factor	Factors that make a person/people want to leave a country/region, e.g. war, famine, unemployment
Pull factor	Factors that attract a person/people to a region/country, e.g. employment opportunities, safety, religious freedom, better climate
Refugee	Someone who leaves their country because of fear of persecution on the grounds of religion, race or politics; refugees are granted protection under international law not to be returned to their original situation
Asylum seeker	A person who has left their country and has applied for refugee status in the country to which they have moved
Internally displaced person (IDP)	A person who is forced to leave their home due to persecution, conflict or environmental disaster but remains within their own country

3.1 Why People Migrate

A starting point in studying migration is to ask the question: *Why do people migrate?* Typically, the answer is due to a combination of push factors and pull factors.

Push Factors

As the term suggests, *push factors* refer to the **reasons that pushed the migrants from their donor countries**. Some of the main push factors are:

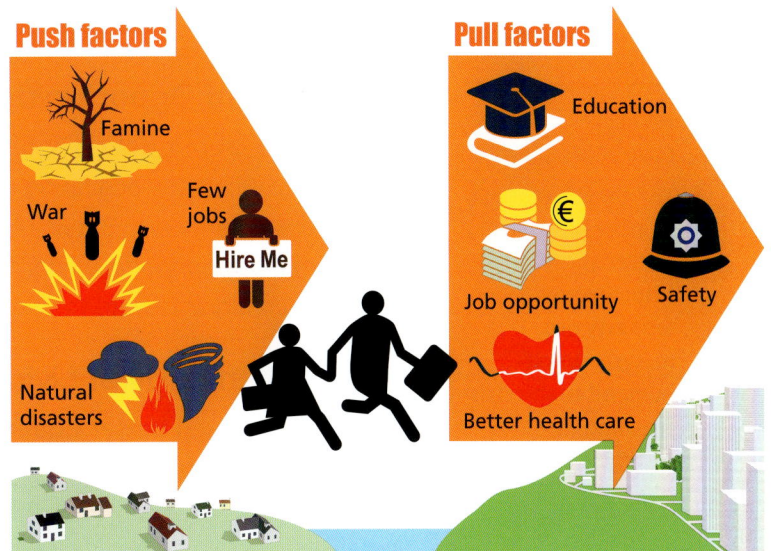

Push factors

Famine
War
Few jobs — Hire Me
Natural disasters

Pull factors

Education
Job opportunity
Safety
Better health care

Fig. 3.2 Migration occurs because of push factors and pull factors.

Unemployment

Regions with **high levels of unemployment** tend to experience **emigration**. An example of this would be the high levels of emigration experienced in Ireland in the years following the economic recession that began in 2008. Emigration levels peaked between April 2011 and April 2012, when 46,500 people left the country.

Poverty

Poverty and **lack of opportunities** force people to **migrate** to regions with **better opportunities** and a **higher standard of living**. Recent trends indicate that this usually occurs in the form of **Rural–urban migration**.

Overpopulation

As we have already seen in Chapter 2, overpopulation (e.g. in the **Sahel region**) has forced people to migrate.

War, Violence and Civil Unrest

Europe is currently experiencing one of the largest influxes of **immigrants and refugees** in its history. Much of this is as a result of **civil war and terror** occurring in countries such as **Syria**, Iraq and Afghanistan. In **2015 alone**, more than **1 million migrants** and **refugees** crossed into Europe – 80 per cent of whom arrived by boat.

Religious/Racial Persecution

Many people flee countries in which there is **political instability** or there are **extreme views** regarding religious practice or ethnicity. Well-known examples of this include the persecution of **Jewish people** in **Nazi Germany** or the persecution of black people by the former **apartheid regime** in **South Africa**.

Natural/Human-made Disasters

Natural disasters are capable of causing **widespread migration**. Examples of this include the **Ireland's Great Famine** (1845–9), the **Ethiopian famine** in 2011 or the **flooding disasters of Pakistan** in 2010.

FACT

The idea that migration is caused by dividing factors into two groups (push factors and pull factors) was devised by Everett S. Lee in 1966 in a paper entitled *A Theory of Migration.*

GEO DICTIONARY

Apartheid: a system of segregation or discrimination on the grounds of race

Ethnicity: belonging to a group of people with a collective identity

FACT

In April 2008, the then Taoiseach Bertie Ahern noted in his resignation speech that he was proud to have 'delivered a modern economy with sustainable growth in employment and brought an end to the days of forced emigration'. Less than six months later, Ireland's emigration rate had increased by 350 per cent.

Pull Factors

Pull factors are the opposite of push factors and refer to the reasons **why a region/country is attractive** for migrants. Some of the main pull factors are:

Employment Opportunities

Areas with a **labour deficit** or **high levels of employment** attract immigrants. Since the beginning of the economic recession in 2008, Irish people migrated to Britain, Australia and Canada where there were employment opportunities. Prior to this, Ireland had a labour deficit which attracted immigrants from the newly joined EU countries such as Poland.

Higher Standards of Living

Higher wages and **better quality services** such as health, education and recreation attract migrants.

Barriers to Migration

Barriers to migration are factors that **prevent people from being able to migrate**. Such barriers include the **cost of travel**, **fear** of living in a different country/culture, **language barriers** and migration laws. For example, many European countries such as Macedonia have closed their borders to migrants fleeing civil war in Syria.

3.2 Effects of Migration on Donor and Host Regions

Migration has many **positive and negative impacts** on both the **donor countries/regions** (the area they have left) **and receiver/host countries/regions** (the regions they migrate to).

Advantages of Emigration for Donor Regions

Reduction of Unemployment Rate

Emigration acts as a **pressure release** valve for **countries** experiencing **high levels of unemployment**. For example, **Ireland's unemployment** rose from **4 per cent in 2007** to **14.8 per cent in 2012** due to economic recession. The unemployment rate would have been **much higher** if it had not been for the **large-scale emigration** of Irish people to Britain, Australia, etc.

Approximately **300,000 Irish people emigrated** from Ireland **since 2008**. This **reduced** the **burden** on the **Irish government**, which would otherwise have had to **pay Jobseeker's Allowance or other social welfare payments**. This also occurred in Ireland during the recessions of the **1950s and the 1980s**. In some cases, the emigration of young adults aids the donor country as its **birth rates are reduced**. This in turn **reduces** the **need** for future generations to emigrate.

Remittance Money

Remittance money refers to **money sent home** by **migrant workers**. This occurred in Ireland as emigrants living in America sent money home to their families. Remittance money is a **major source of income** for countries in the **developing world**. Money **sent** home to **ageing parents** can provide them with a **more comfortable lifestyle** or can **lift younger family generations** above the **poverty line**. Migrants working in Ireland send money home to their families. Donor nations often have lowered costs of living and so the money sent home is worth much more. In 2015, a total of €1.8 billion of remittance money was sent home from Ireland – equalling 1 per cent of Ireland's total GDP.

Acquiring New Skills

Many migrants eventually return to their native countries. When they do so, they bring the **new skills** they have **acquired** while **working abroad**. An example of this can be seen in the **migrants** who **returned** to **Ireland** during the **Celtic Tiger**, having previously emigrated during the 1980s recession. Many who returned used the **business skills** they had acquired abroad to start up their own businesses in Ireland. This also helped to **attract foreign direct investment** (FDI) from MNCs such as Microsoft. Similarly, many Polish construction workers returned home after 2008, with many using skills they had acquired to set up their own construction companies.

Disadvantages of Emigration for Donor Regions

Brain Drain

The majority of **young migrants** are **economic migrants** who leave in search of **better employment opportunities**. Therefore, the **donor region loses** a highly **skilled** and **talented generation** of workers, who have been **educated at a cost to** the **state** and their families. When they **leave**, the State loses its investment and the **migrant's skills benefit** the economy of the **receiver region**. This has occurred several times throughout Irish history with the most recent example being the economic **recession of 2008–13**, as the **majority of emigrants** had **third-level qualifications** or were highly **skilled construction workers**.

A recurring issue for Ireland has been the **loss of young medical graduates** such as junior doctors, who are choosing to emigrate to **avail of higher wages** and **less stressful working conditions** abroad. By doing so, the HSE has had to recruit an increasing number of foreign-national doctors and nurses.

Rural Depopulation

As you have already learned from your studies of regional Geography, the **West of Ireland** suffers from **rural depopulation**. This creates **socio-economic issues** as a loss of young, skilled workers means regions are **unable to attract MNCs** or **government investment**. As young people leave, **services** such as post offices, banks and family shops **close down**. Education and **health** services are also **disrupted** as **smaller numbers of children** lead to smaller enrolments in schools and the withdrawal of GP services. Local **clubs** such as GAA, Community Games and youth clubs also **struggle to recruit members** or volunteers. **Agricultural land** is also **abandoned**, as younger generations do not take over farms. In the longer term, the **migration of people aged 18–30** leads to a **decrease** in **birth rates**, which in turn leads to **further rural depopulation** and decay.

Fig. 3.3 Rural depopulation affects the west of Ireland.

Advantages of Immigration on Receiver/Host Regions

Enrichment of Employee Skills

Host regions benefit from an **influx of highly skilled workers** who bring their expertise to the country/region. This gaining of skills makes host regions more **attractive for MNCs** and further **FDI** as there is an adequate availability of a skilled workforce. Many host regions experience **labour shortages** which are **filled by incoming migrants**. This was the case in Ireland during the **Celtic Tiger** in which **immigrants from Eastern Europe filled labour shortages** in areas such as **construction** and **food processing**, which fuelled economic growth. By **2006, migrants** were **filling over two-thirds of all new job vacancies** in the country and accounted for over **50 per cent of the food processing industry's workforce**. Migrants also filled medical labour shortages and brought their own expertise to the HSE.

Migrant workers also contribute to the economy through the **payment of taxes** and increase the **demand for goods and services**.

Fig. 3.4 Ireland has become culturally enriched as a result of migration.

Cultural Enrichment

As more migrants enter a country, they **bring** their own **cultures and traditions** with them. Since joining the EU in 1973, **Ireland** has become a **multicultural society**. This has had a **positive impact** on Irish culture. By 2014, **11.8 per cent** of the **Irish population** was made up of **foreign nationals**. Foreign nationals have introduced **new food**, **music**, **dance** and **customs**, e.g. Indian and Thai food. As well as specialist food shops opening in Ireland, supermarket chains now dedicate full aisles to foods not traditionally seen in Ireland. By becoming more culturally aware, **Ireland's own culture** is enriched.

Disadvantages of Immigration on Receiver/ Host Regions

Lack of Integration

In a survey carried out by the **Economic and Social Research Institute (ESRI)**, the two biggest **difficulties** experienced by migrants living in Ireland were **language barriers** and 'trying to fit in'. **Over half** of the **immigrants** interviewed reported being **victims of racism** through **verbal or physical** assault. Therefore, a **lack of support** in terms of **integration** of migrants can lead to issues such as **ghettoisation**, **discrimination** and **racism**. **Ghettoisation** occurs when **immigrants locate** in the **same areas** of towns and cities. As more immigrants arrive to the town/city, they too locate in that area as they are guaranteed to be surrounded by the same language and share the same cultures. This **prevents integration** of migrants into society and creates the idea of 'their part of town'. In 2007 the **Irish government** appointed a **Minister for Integration**, which was later replaced by the **Office for the Promotion of Migrant Integration**. The aims of the office are to develop and implement **policy** relating to the **integration of migrants** into all aspects of Irish society such as schools, workplaces and social activities.

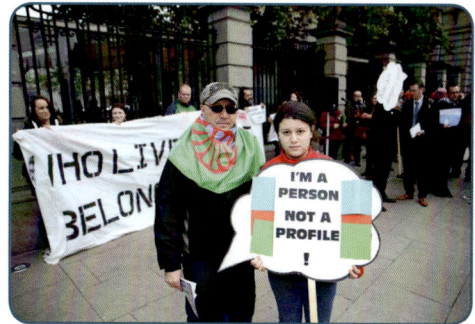

Fig. 3.5 Protests outside Dáil Éireann.

Language

Despite bringing about **improvements**, integration issues such as **language barriers remain** a concern. Nearly **40 per cent of migrants** report **language** as being their **biggest concern**. Migrants who are **unable to speak the main language** of a country find it **difficult to gain stable, fair-paying employment**, e.g. in 2015 it was revealed that **migrant fishermen** on some Irish trawlers were **paid 50 per cent less** than **Irish fishermen**. The language barrier also makes it **difficult for migrant children** to **access** the **Irish curriculum** or make friends in school.

GEO DICTIONARY

Rural depopulation: substantial reduction in the number of people living in a rural community or area

General Practitioner (GP): is a doctor based in a community who treats patients from the surrounding area

Ghettoisation: the formation of a ghetto. A ghetto is an urban area that is occupied by a minority group. Ghettos prevent migrants from integrating into their host country, as the migrants are surrounded by their own culture, language and religion.

Racism: prejudice or discrimination against a person on the grounds of race; in other words, the belief that someone is inferior as a result of their race

3.3 Changing Migratory Patterns in Ireland

Note!

This question appears very frequently on both the Higher and Ordinary Level papers. More recent questions on the topic have asked students to begin discussing migratory patterns in Ireland from 1950 onwards.

Throughout Irish history, **migration trends** have been greatly **impacted on** by the **economic situation** of the country. In times of **economic growth**, Ireland has experienced high levels of **net immigration** – along with high levels of **net emigration during economic recession**. Our migratory history dates back to the **Great Famine (1845–9)** in which **over 1 million people died** and **1 million people emigrated**. The Irish emigrated to countries such as the US, Canada, Britain and Australia, as these were English-speaking countries. The **majority** of emigrants at this time came from the **West of Ireland** and other **undeveloped rural areas**. This emigration had a major **impact** on **marriage and birth rates**: they **declined** greatly, as the majority of emigrants were young females. After the Famine, emigration continued. This, combined with older marriage ages and reduced birth rates, caused population decline.

🔺 **Fig. 3.6** Irish men and women emigrating from 1950s Ireland.

FACT

Over 58,000 people emigrated in 1958 alone: This was the worst year on record for emigration of Irish people.

Emigration: 1950s

Ireland experienced a deep economic recession throughout the 1950s, which led to roughly **408,000 people emigrating between 1951 and 1961**. The people who left during this period were economic migrants who left in search of work – particularly in **Britain and the US**, since both of those countries were experiencing **economic booms** at that time. By **1961,** the Republic **of** Ireland's **population** had fallen to **2.82 million** from a high of 6.5 million in 1841. As it was **mainly young people** from **rural Ireland** who were leaving, these areas became **severely depopulated** and developed **high dependency ratios.**

Immigration: 1960s and 1970s

This was a period of **economic prosperity**, as Ireland began to experience rapid economic development. As a result, **Ireland experienced a reversal in migration patterns: emigration** from Ireland **decreased** steadily, while **immigration increased**. This allowed Ireland to experience a slight **net immigration** for the **first time in over 120 years** as more job opportunities became available.

During this time, the then **Taoiseach – Sean Lemass –** launched several **programmes for economic expansion**, as **foreign direct investment** and **free trade** were **promoted** through attractive grants, newly built industrial estates and financial incentives, e.g. tax-free exports. As a result of this, **manufacturing jobs were created** through large MNCs who were attracted to Ireland. Outward migration decreased as there were large employment increases throughout the country with over **300 foreign companies** operating in Ireland by **1966.**

Further economic expansion occurred as a result of joining the **European Economic Community (EEC) in 1973.** The EEC provided **grants** to **develop further manufacturing** industry and led to an increase in employment. This increase in employment opportunities saw more than **104,000 Irish emigrants return** to live in Ireland throughout the 1970s. Between **1971 and 1981** there was a **population increase** in Ireland of **15.6 per cent** while the country's **standard of living increased** by **50 per cent**.

Emigration: 1980s

During the 1980s, a number of factors combined to create a very **difficult economic climate** caused by an increase in **government debt**. This debt was caused by a **global economic crisis** brought about by an **increase in oil prices**, causing many **MNCs to leave Ireland** while many **home-grown industries closed down**.

Once again, **emigration** began to **increase**. It was predominantly young, highly educated people who were emigrating, and this led to a **brain drain**. Between **1981 and 1991**, over **200,000 Irish people** emigrated in search of employment. Emigration levels **peaked** between **1988 and 1989**, during which **70,000 Irish people emigrated**.

Immigration: 1995–2007

This period is referred to as the **Celtic Tiger era**. The **Irish economy grew** rapidly, leading to **widespread employment opportunities** as demands for **skilled and unskilled labour increased** dramatically. Eventually, the rise in demand for workers led to a labour shortage.

This shortage was filled by **immigrants from other countries** as Ireland became a **multiracial society** due to high numbers of foreign nationals. This became particularly evident **after 2004**, when **Eastern European countries** joined the **EU**, leading to an increase of **migrants,** e.g. from Poland. Large **MNCs** such as **Dell and Google** invested in Ireland due to our **highly educated workforce** and high-quality transport and communications.

During this period, Ireland contained just **1 per cent of the EU population**, but achieved **20 per cent of inward investment** in Europe. Applications for **asylum in Ireland peaked in 2002** with **11,634 applicants**, up from **362 in 1994**.

Fig. 3.7 Ireland joined the European Economic Community (EEC) in 1973.

Fig. 3.8 The 1980s saw recession sweep through Ireland once again, causing over 200,000 Irish men and women to emigrate.

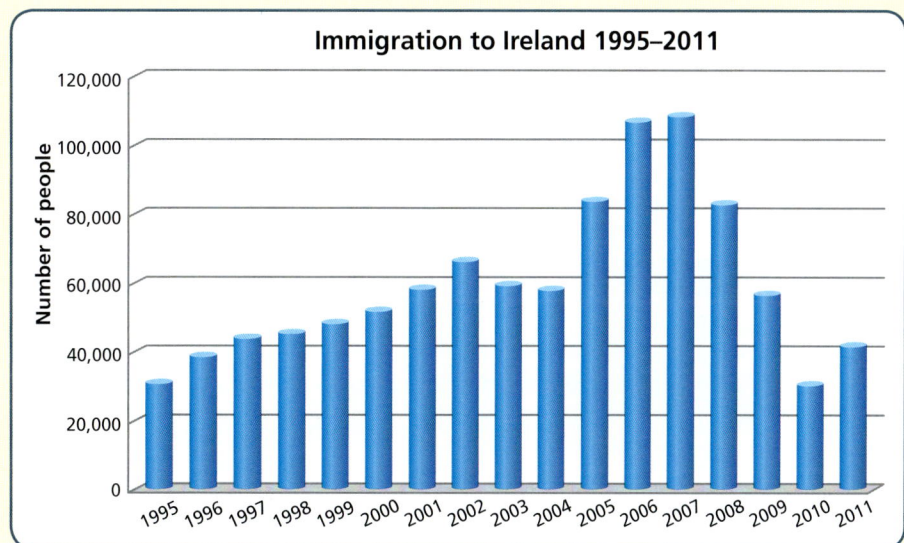

Fig. 3.9 The Celtic Tiger led to high levels of immigration into Ireland once again.

Immigration to Ireland 1995–2011

Emigration: 2008–13

Once again, Ireland experienced **economic recession** between **2008 and 2013**. Unemployment rates rose from **5 per cent in 2007** to its highest level of **15.1 per cent in 2012** as **uncontrolled lending of money by banks**, an inflated housing market and large amounts of **personal debt** led to the **collapse of** the **Celtic Tiger**. Government **debt** rose from **€38.5 billion in 2005** to **€84 billion by 2010**. This led to the Irish government receiving a **bailout from the Troika** – the **International Monetary Fund** (IMF), the **EU** and the **European Central Bank**. As a result of the 'Euro Crisis' the Troika required the Irish government to **cut its levels of public spending**, which led to a succession of **austerity budgets**.

Increased **taxes**, the introduction of a **Universal Social Charge** (USC) and a **rising cost of living** led to many **Irish and foreign nationals** emigrating in search of **better employment opportunities** and a **better standard of living**. The **collapse of the housing market** led to large-scale **losses** in the **construction industry**, with many builders and **skilled tradespeople emigrating** to countries such as Australia, which was experiencing a **construction boom**.

Immigration numbers **declined hugely** during this period, as migrants chose to move to EU countries that were not as badly affected by the Euro Crisis. For the first time since 1995, Ireland experienced net emigration **in 2009**. This was partly contributed to by **restrictions** put in place **by the government** regarding the number of immigrants allowed to enter the country.

2013 onwards

Despite showing **economic growth in December 2013** for the first time since 2008, **net emigration continues** with 21,400 more people leaving the country than entering it between April 2014 and April 2015. The majority of the 81,900 who left Ireland during this time were either young workers or students in the 18–30 years age bracket. If the **economy continues to grow**, Ireland should once again return to a **positive net migration**; however, there is still much concern regarding the economic stability of Ireland.

Fig. 3.10 Austerity protests in Ireland.

ACTIVE LEARNING

1. How does government policy impact on Ireland's migration patterns?
2. What factors led to net emigration between 2008 and 2013?

Note!

Despite Ireland's commitment to many years of austerity budgeting, a recent study by the International Monetary Fund (IMF) has found that austerity does not work.

GEO DICTIONARY

Net immigration: more people immigrating into an area than are emigrating from it
Net emigration: more people emigrating from an area than are migrating into it
Austerity: strict budget or cuts to spending

3.4 Irish Migration Policy

On 1 October 2014, the Irish government introduced the Employment Permits Act. This put in place much **stricter regulations** regarding **entry of workers** from **outside of the European Economic Area (EEA)**.

The Employment Permits Act focuses on **permitting people into the country**, if they possess the **skills** that are in **short supply**, e.g. doctors or midwives. There are four main types of employment permit available, along with a further five lesser permits available.

GEO DICTIONARY

European Economic Area (EEA): is the collective name given to the members of the EU and its trading partners of Iceland, Norway and Liechtenstein.

General Employment Permit

This permit was formally referred to as the 'Work Permit'. It is available to people with an **annual salary** of **above €30,000**. Only people considered 'exceptional cases' will be considered for jobs with a **lower annual salary**. A **labour means test** is required in order to ensure that a suitably skilled **Irish or EEA worker** is offered the employment opportunity. Should **no suitable candidate be found within Ireland** or the **EEA**, then the job can be **offered** to a **non-EEA national**.

Therefore, any vacancy that occurs must be advertised by the employer in the following ways:

- Advertised with the Department of Social Protection Employment Services / European Employment Services (EURES) employment network for at least 2 weeks
- Advertised in a national newspaper for at least 3 days
- Advertised in either a local newspaper or jobs website for at least 3 days.

Critical Skills Employment Permit

This permit was **formerly** referred to as the 'Green Card Permit'. This permit is generally available for **employment positions** with an **average salary** of **over €60,000**. The permit is also available for occupations with an annual salary of at least **€30,000** should it appear on the 'Highly Skilled Occupations List'. This list indicates that it is a skill which is highly required in Ireland or for which there is a **general labour deficit**.

Dependant/Partner/Spouse Employment Permit

This permit applies to **spouses**, **partners** and **dependants of holders of Critical Skills Employment Permits** or existing Green Card Permits. This permit also allows the spouse **to work in Ireland**.

Reactivation Employment Permit

This permit allows foreign nationals who entered the State on a **valid employment permit** but who **fell through the system** through no fault of their own, or who have been **badly treated or exploited** in the workplace, to work again.

Asylum Seekers

Asylum seekers have the **right to apply for refugee status** in Ireland. However, once in Ireland, they cannot work or leave the country. While here, they are entitled to **state accommodation, healthcare, education and welfare**. If they are granted refugee status, they become entitled to the same rights as any other Irish citizen. If refugee status is not granted, then the **asylum seeker is deported**. In 2003, the Irish government changed its policy regarding the granting of **citizenship to foreign-born parents** of children born in Ireland.

▶ **Fig. 3.11** Attitudes towards immigration in Ireland

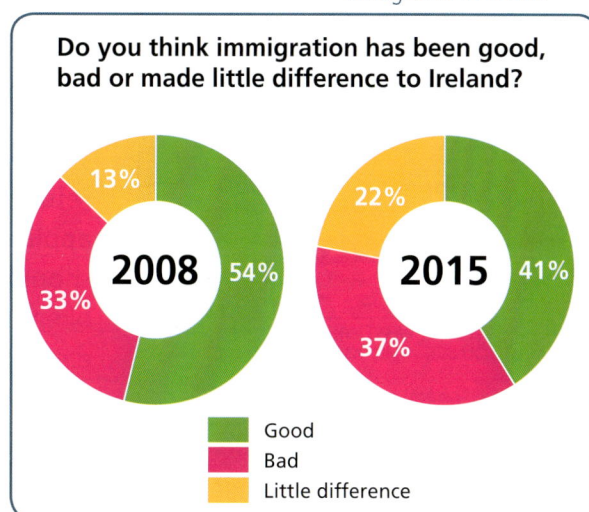

Do you think immigration has been good, bad or made little difference to Ireland?

2008: 54% / 33% / 13%
2015: 41% / 37% / 22%

- Good
- Bad
- Little difference

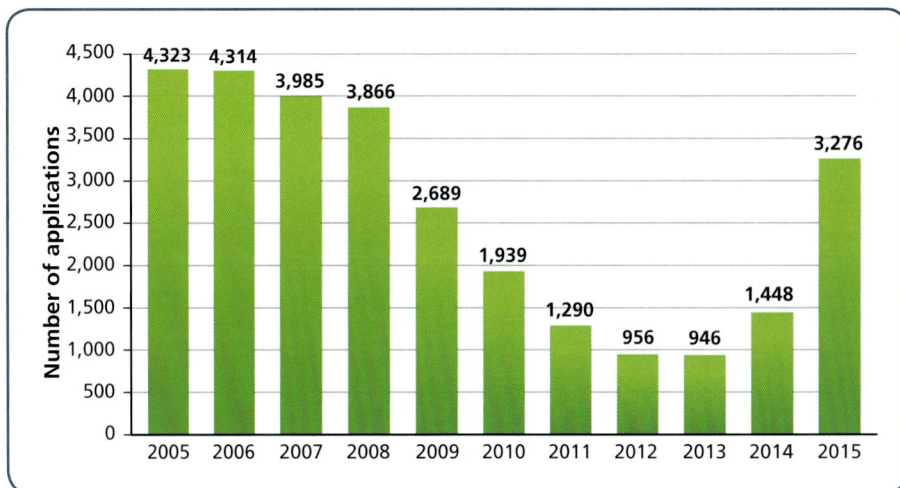

Fig. 3.12 Applications for asylum in Ireland between 2005 and 2015

Fig. 3.12 chart data:
- 2005: 4,323
- 2006: 4,314
- 2007: 3,985
- 2008: 3,866
- 2009: 2,689
- 2010: 1,939
- 2011: 1,290
- 2012: 956
- 2013: 946
- 2014: 1,448
- 2015: 3,276

(Y-axis: Number of applications)

ACTIVE LEARNING

1. What is the difference between a General Employment Permit and a Critical Skills Employment Permit?

2. What is meant by the term *asylum seeker*?

GEO DICTIONARY

Asylum shopping: term used to describe the practice of asylum seekers applying for asylum in several states or choosing a particular state to apply due to it being more desirable

---

WELCOME TO EUROPE! NO CLIMBING. NO FLYING! DON'T USE LADDERS!!!

POOR! PLEASE HELP!

EUROPE A FORTRESS? WHAT ARE YOU TALKING ABOUT?! CAN'T YOU SEE - THE DOOR IS OPEN WIDE!

Fig. 3.13 The UN has criticised the EU's response to the migration crisis.

Following a **referendum** held in June **2004**, there is no **automatic right to citizenship** for Irish-born children of non-national parents.

3.5 EU Migration Policy

Today, **foreign nationals** from **within the EU do not need a permit** to work in Ireland; **non-EU foreign nationals do** need a work permit. One of the key principles of the EU since it was founded with the Treaty of Rome has been the **freedom of movement** of workers within the EU. **Migrants are needed** in Europe, as the **majority of European countries** are in **Stage 4 or Stage 5** of the Demographic Transitional Model and have **low levels of birth rates**. As the populations of these developed countries age and decline, migrants are needed to **fill labour shortages** or bring skills that may be lacking in a country. For example, **many European countries lack** the **skills to fill job vacancies in research, IT and engineering**. It is estimated that by **2020**, the **EU** will need roughly **20 million immigrants** to **fill labour shortages**.

However, increased migration into the EU has seen a move towards a **common EU immigration policy**. A common policy would regulate immigration and ensure it is more evenly spread throughout the EU.

The Dublin System and FRONTEX

In 2003 the Dublin System (named after an EU meeting in Dublin) was introduced whereby the EU **country that refugees first entered** has to deal with their **asylum application**. The aim of this system is to **prevent 'asylum shopping'**. Asylum seekers are fingerprinted at their point of entry, with this information then being stored on a central database available to all EU member states.

The border control agency **FRONTEX** was **founded** by the EU in **2004** in order to **provide assistance** to member states who needed help in **securing their borders**. In particular, the agency provides assistance to countries along the **Mediterranean Sea** (e.g. Greece, Italy and Spain) who have become the main **gateway for migrants** fleeing from African and Asian countries. While these moves initially saw a **reduction** in the **number of migrants** entering the EU, civil war in countries such as Syria, Afghanistan and Iraq has once again put **enormous pressure on EU borders**.

The Schengen Agreement

The **Schengen Agreement** (1995) allowed for the **free movement of people between** most **member states** of the EU. Since this agreement was implemented, the EU has aimed to develop a set of common laws to regulate the levels of immigration and asylum seekers entering the EU. **Ireland** is **one of only six EU member states** who are **not part of the Schengen Agreement**. The justification for these laws are that they:

- **Prevent** the **readmission** of **immigrants** already refused by another EU member state
- Make it more straightforward for immigrants to obtain work permits and residency in the EU
- **Share** the **responsibility** of migration among all EU member states
- Help to **prevent illegal immigration** and fight against human trafficking of migrants into Europe for the purposes of slave labour or prostitution.

The EU Blue Card

In 2011 the EU Blue Card was introduced. It gives **work permits and residency to non-EU migrants**. In order to qualify for the card, the migrant must be offered a **salary 1.5 times the EU average** in their host country. By putting such a demand on migrants who wish to obtain the card, the EU hopes it will **attract migrants with the right skills** when they are needed.

Concerns Regarding Common EU Migration Policy

Although the common EU migration policy is seen as a positive move in **safeguarding the EU** from being flooded with migrants they cannot support, many argue that it creates a '**Fortress Europe**' which makes it extremely difficult for migrants to enter the EU. In turn, many fear that this will lead to xenophobic attitudes towards migrants as immigration laws are tightened. Some people believe this fear is well founded, given the **increased popularity of far-right political parties** who wish to **reduce immigration** in their countries. Laws now allow authorities to fine or imprison illegal immigrants and further punish those who provide them with shelter or other forms of assistance.

Another concern is the **loss of sovereignty** as more power is given to the EU regarding the migration laws of individual states. It is important that any future common policy is both cautious towards the safety of the EU and also humane towards potential immigrants.

> **AZ GEO DICTIONARY**
>
> **Fortress Europe:** an unofficial term used to describe the increasing difficulty for migrants to enter EU states
>
> **Far-right political parties:** political parties that are extremely nationalist and anti-immigration in outlook and that oppose social democracy

The Need for Migration Policy

Many argue that the **strict migration policies** implemented by the EU were **necessary** and justified given the **mass influx of migrants** fleeing into Europe from war-torn Syria and Afghanistan in 2015. Over half a million refugees arrived in EU member states, with the EU **struggling to control its borders** and cope with the overwhelming number of migrants. **FRONTEX recorded** over **100,000 migrants in 2015** for the first time since they began keeping records in 2008.

The majority of pressure has been placed on southern member states, in particular Greece, Hungary and Croatia, which are the first points of entry into the EU for migrants fleeing from Africa and Asia. Tensions have developed at these borders with the governments of some of these countries building barbed wire defences, using tear gas and deploying armed soldiers at their borders. The United Nations has criticised the methods used and have expressed the desire for orderly management of these countries' borders.

Fig. 3.15 A border at Macedonia is closed to refugees.

However, due to the **Dublin System**, many **southern states** now feel aggrieved and **abandoned by** the **EU** during this crisis.

The aggressive response by EU members has **frustrated and angered migrants** who are met with **border closures** and a lack of compassion. In late **August 2015**, **Macedonia** declared a **state of emergency** as it was unable to deal with the huge volume of migrants passing through its borders on a daily basis. This crisis soon reached other EU member countries and tensions continued to rise. In Germany, an incident involving the tearing up of a copy of the Koran led to riots in a refugee shelter during which 17 people were injured. It is estimated that Germany has taken in 40 per cent of the migrants arriving into the EU in recent years.

Future of EU Migration Laws

It is clear throughout the migration crisis of recent years that policies such as the **Dublin System** have **failed** to bring about stability and unity of immigration laws among EU member states. The **EU** now **needs to upgrade its migration laws** to deal with human rights, anti-discrimination, citizenship and family reunification. If this is not done, the EU faces the continuous risk of crises such as those experienced as a result of the Syrian war. The future of EU immigration policy, therefore, must stress the **importance of attracting skilled migrants** to its countries while also **providing compassionate assistance** for asylum seekers from developing or war-torn countries.

In **December 2015** the European Commission proposed **major changes to amend the Schengen Agreement**. While previously only non-EU travellers have had their details checked on police databases, the rule change now applies to migrants from within the EU also. Non-EU nationals typically did not experience ID checks once they had passed through the external borders.

However, since the French and Belgian terror attacks of 2015 and 2016, these checks have become much more common.

The 2016 decision of the UK to leave the EU has led to further complications regarding EU migration policy. The support for the decision to leave was heavily influenced by negative views towards immigration in Britain. However, EU migrants tend to be young and highly skilled and contribute greatly to public finances in the UK. These migrants are necessary in order to fill labour deficits and provide the necessary skills for a variety of industries. In order to ensure a sufficient workforce, the UK will need to come to agreement regarding the movement of EU workers.

> **FACT**
>
> More than 75 per cent of Syrian refugees are women and children.

> **FACT**
>
> Less than 1 per cent of Syria's refugees will be granted asylum in the EU.

ACTIVE **LEARNING**

1. Visit **www.bbc.com** and search for 'migration crisis in Europe' or 'EU Syria' for several reliable reports on the migration crisis in Europe.
2. What are the major concerns surrounding a common EU migration policy?
3. Why was the Dublin System considered a failure?
4. What changes were made to the Schengen Agreement in December 2015?
5. Do you think Ireland should grant asylum to refugees fleeing Syria? Discuss your views with your classmates. Go to **www.syrianrefugees.eu** for information on the Syrian migrant crisis in Europe.

3.6 Ethnic, Religious and Racial Issues of Migration

The most notable impact of migration is that it **mixes together people** of **different cultures**. Unfortunately, this mixing **does not always occur peacefully**: tensions may develop between **migrants and resident populations**. As **migrants** arrive from other countries, they **bring** their **culture with them**. Often these cultures are very different from the **cultures and traditions of the host country**. These **differences** have the **potential to cause conflict** between both groups.

Although migration has the **ability** to makes its **host country more multicultural**, some residents may feel **overwhelmed by the changes** to their society, while migrants must deal with the pressure of **learning a new language, customs and social interactions**. Therefore, the **potential for misunderstanding** is high. In order to **prevent issues arising**, both **education and tolerance are needed**. Different approaches may be taken to cultural difference. It has been observed that Ireland uses the '**melting pot**' approach, whereby **migrants are integrated** into Irish culture; while Britain uses the '**salad bowl**' or multicultural approach, where migrants **keep their own cultures and traditions**.

GEO **DICTIONARY**

Melting pot: a place where different people, cultures and traditions are mixed together and integrated

Salad bowl: people, cultures and traditions are mixed together but do not integrate into a single culture; each ethnic group keeps its own distinct qualities

Ethnic Issues

Ethnicity refers to a **state of belonging to a group of people** who share a **collective identity** through common culture or tradition within a larger population. An example of this would be the **Polish community** living in Ireland. Ethnicity can be defined according to place of **birth, religious belief and language**. Unfortunately, throughout history, people have experienced discrimination on the grounds of ethnicity.

Ethnic groups sometimes **struggle to gain employment** or progress through the **Irish education system**. The Irish government has attempted to address this issue through the **introduction of the languages spoken** by **major migrant populations** to the Leaving Certificate exam.

Racial Issues

Race refers to the **biological inheritance of a person**. In simpler terms, race is the division of humanity into groups based on their physical appearance, in particular skin colour. **Racism** is the belief that **people are inferior** as a **result of their physical appearance or ethnic group**. Racism ranges from **verbal to physical abuse** in which a racial community are stereotyped by the larger community. Ireland is not immune to racism, with racist attitudes being experienced by:

- Migrants from Eastern Europe
- African and other ethnic groups
- Muslim and Jewish communities
- The Travelling community.

In order to prevent racism from escalating in **Ireland**, a **national policy against racism** was developed between 2005 and 2008. Its main five aims were to:

- Help migrants to **participate fully in all areas of life**
- Raise **awareness of their identity** and educate others on how to accept them
- Include ethnic groups in all areas of **Irish economic and social life**
- **Protect migrants** with the same laws that protect Irish nationals
- Provide **all basic human needs**, such as shelter, food, education, health, etc.

Unfortunately, racist attitudes throughout a number of EU countries have been on the increase in recent years, mainly due to political and media bias.

A/Z GEO DICTIONARY

Race: the biological inheritance of a person

Stereotype: a generalised or widely held belief about a group of people; this view is normally oversimplified or insulting

Why?

During the Euro Crisis, governments or aspiring political parties channelled the anger of their populations towards anti-immigrant sentiment. During recession, some political parties try to exploit people's anger over increased debt, unemployment and poverty. Migrants become easy targets for blame, as a result of their cultural differences. This is further fuelled by actions committed in the name of religion by extremist groups, in which media reporting creates a sense of fear in relation to immigrants. For example, in the aftermath of the Paris attack in November 2015, many Irish tabloids ran headlines linking immigrants in Ireland to extremism and terrorism. These reports encourage racist attitudes in Ireland and the EU.

Conflict in France

Often, many migrants live together in one area of a city, which leads to the creation of a **ghetto.** This further **isolates migrants** from the wider community. Some migrants never leave the ghetto, meaning they do not learn the host country's language and are **unable to gain employment.** This leads to **high levels of poverty**, which can lead to frustration, anger and rioting in the ghettos of cities. An example of this was the **race riots** that took place in **France in 2005.** The rioting was mainly carried out by **French youths of North African descent**, whose families migrated to France in order to fill labour shortages. Many of these migrants **experienced discrimination** and were employed in **low-paying jobs.** These migrants settled in the **cheap accommodation along city suburbs**, which resulted in high-rise ghettos. People in these ghettos felt **isolated from French culture** and community, which led to **tension developing**.

In **November 2005**, **two French youths** of **North African descent** were accidentally **electrocuted** in a power station as they hid from police. **Rioting spread** throughout the ghettos of France, as a state of emergency was declared for over two weeks. The rioting caused **€200 million of damage** and the **death of one person**. The rioting **highlighted** the **need** for **proper integration** of migrants into French communities, as well as proper housing and employment opportunities. The French government **invested €30 billion in aid** to help create employment in ghetto regions.

Religious Issues

Religious issues arise as migrants of **different religious beliefs** are often viewed as being **incompatible** with the practices of the host country's culture. Such issues include:

- **Polygyny:** Some Muslim cultures recognise polygynous marriages (in which a man has more than one wife at the same time). Polygamy (more than one husband/wife at the same time) is **illegal in EU countries**, including Ireland. Although the law was challenged, polygamous marriage remains illegal in Ireland.

- **Clothing:** In 2010, the French government passed a law **banning the wearing of the**

⬆ **Fig. 3.16** A French ghetto

⬆ **Fig. 3.17** French riots in 2005

⬆ **Fig. 3.18** Areas of rioting in France in 2005

AZ GEO DICTIONARY

Polygamy: the practice of having more than one wife/husband at the same time

Fig. 3.19 An Educate Together school

niqab (facial veil). It is estimated that, of the 5 million Muslims living in France, only 2,000 women wore the niqab. Although the bill had overwhelming public support, many stated that the ban shows a **fear and intolerance** of those who are different.

- **Education:** Much of the Irish education system is under the **trusteeship of the Catholic Church**, which some view as an issue with regard to the integration of immigrant children into the Irish education system. The **Equal Status Act of 2000** allowed schools to offer **first preference** places to **children whose religions** were **in line with the school ethos**. As the State is legally obliged to provide education for all children under the age of 16, to date 81 **multi-denominational schools known as Educate Together schools** have been established in order to ensure that the future needs of Irish families are met.

ACTIVE LEARNING

1. Explain the following terms: *ethnicity*, *race*.

2. Explain how issues can arise for migrants of different ethnicities or race in their host country.

3. What is meant by the term *racism*?

4. What measures, do you think, should the Irish government take to prevent racist attitudes from developing?

GEO DICTIONARY

Niqab: a veil worn by some Muslim women in public, which covers all parts of the face except the eyes

Trusteeship: control or administration of a building or service

Ethos: a spirit or cultural belief that is shown through practices or community

Multi-denominational: multiple religions

Educate Together: schools where children are educated together, irrespective of their social, cultural or religious backgrounds

3.7 Rural–Urban Migration: Developed World

Rural–urban migration refers to the movement of people from the countryside to cities and towns. This has occurred in the developed world since the beginning of the Industrial Revolution in the eighteenth century, as people began to move to cities in large numbers in search of work.

Rural–urban migration has two main effects:

- Urban sprawl occurs as the population of cities increases
- 55 per cent of the world's population now live in urban areas.

Ireland

Traditionally the migration that has occurred in Ireland has been from **west to east**. This is due to a number of **push factors in the west** and a number of **pull factors in the east**.

Since the **1960s** the number of **people working in the agricultural sector has reduced by 75 per cent**, which has led to **population decline** in rural areas.. This has particularly impacted the population of the west, border areas and midlands, as their populations **moved to the larger towns of the east** in search of work. The increasing **mechanisation** of farming (e.g. tractors, combine harvesters and milking machines) has further **reduced the need for labour on farms**, with younger people moving to urban areas. The majority of manufacturing and industries are **located in urban areas**, which **attract rural migrants**. More often than not, workers choose to live close to the urban area for cheaper and shorter commutes.

In order to attend third-level education, young people move to cities. Often these young workers become employed in the city where they attended college and rarely return to their places of birth.

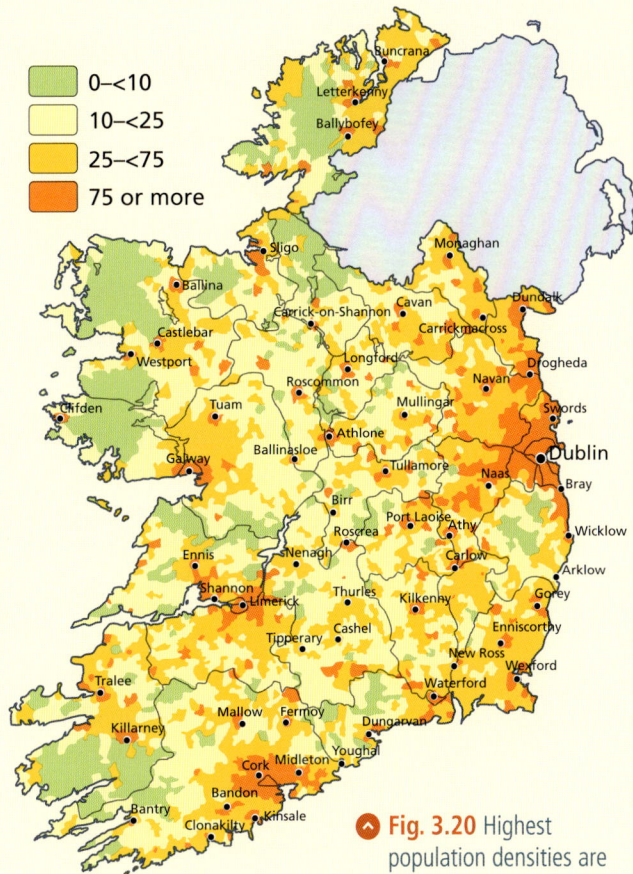

Map legend:
- 0–<10
- 10–<25
- 25–<75
- 75 or more

⌃ **Fig. 3.20** Highest population densities are found in urban areas.

Effects on Rural/Donor Region

Population Decline

Rural–urban migration typically affects **young adults aged 18–30**. Therefore, as young people **leave rural areas, marriage and birth rates decline** in rural communities. The remaining population grows older, which leads to the **greying of rural areas**, and gives rural areas a high dependency ratio. The counties of Ireland with the **highest dependency ratios** are all located in the **Northern and Western Region** in which one-third of their combined population declined during the Celtic Tiger era.

Gender Imbalance

Rural to urban migration has led to a **gender imbalance** within the rural communities of Ireland. **Traditionally**, **males** (especially the older son) **stayed at home** on the family farm. **Female siblings were educated** to a higher standard in order to obtain a living (e.g. nurses, teachers, doctors, receptionists). Once employed in towns and cities, women were not attracted to agriculture or living in a rural area. This explains the high number of unmarried older men living alone in remote parts of the West of Ireland.

Reduction of Services

As population **declines** in rural areas, so too does the **number of services** available. Major services such as **health and education** are **reduced** in areas with **low population densities**. As declining birth rates occur due to outward migration,, there is a **reduction in school enrolments**, leading to some schools

Fig. 3.21 Young protestors show their support for Roscommon Hospital.

being forced to amalgamate or close. Similarly, **24-hour A&E services and staff in hospitals** have also been **reduced**, e.g. **Ennis and Roscommon**. In times of **economic downturn**, many **rural services are the first to be reduced** due to **low population densities**, e.g. the **closure of Garda stations**, in which fewer guards now cover larger rural areas.

Socially, rural areas are finding it **increasingly difficult to get volunteers** or members for sports teams, youth clubs, etc. All of this has combined to create a **lack of choice** for those still living in rural areas. This has created a divide in Ireland, with many rural dwellers feeling isolated and resentful of the government, who oversee these closures.

Effects on Urban Areas/Host Region

Rural–urban migration can have both positive and negative effects on urban areas.

Increasingly Skilled Workforce

As mainly **young educated people** migrate to urban areas, they provide a **skilled workforce** which helps to attract **further investment from MNCs** and increase productivity. Due to high levels of industry, **transport links and infrastructure** are continually **upgraded** and improved to accommodate the new industries investing there.

Increased Demand for Goods/Services

As the population of a rural area increases, so too does the demand for its goods and services. Therefore, increased migration into a region causes further economic prosperity.

Urban Sprawl

With city populations increasing, the rate of **urban sprawl has increased rapidly**. **Dublin** has experienced the **highest rates of urban sprawl**, with the farmland surrounding its urban fringe being rezoned for housing estates to cater for its growing population. Urban sprawl has a **serious effect on the countryside** as **natural landscapes and wildlife are destroyed**. Dublin is now surrounded by several **'new' towns** such as Adamstown, while counties such as Kildare, Meath, Laois and Wicklow have become **commuter zones** for people working in the city. Outside of Dublin, other towns and cities are also increasing: the population of Galway has trebled in the last half century.

Unlike other European cities, Dublin does not have high-rise, high-density housing in its city centre. Instead, it is similar to American cities where low-rise, low-density housing exists.

Fig. 3.22 The City of Dublin spreads into surrounding counties

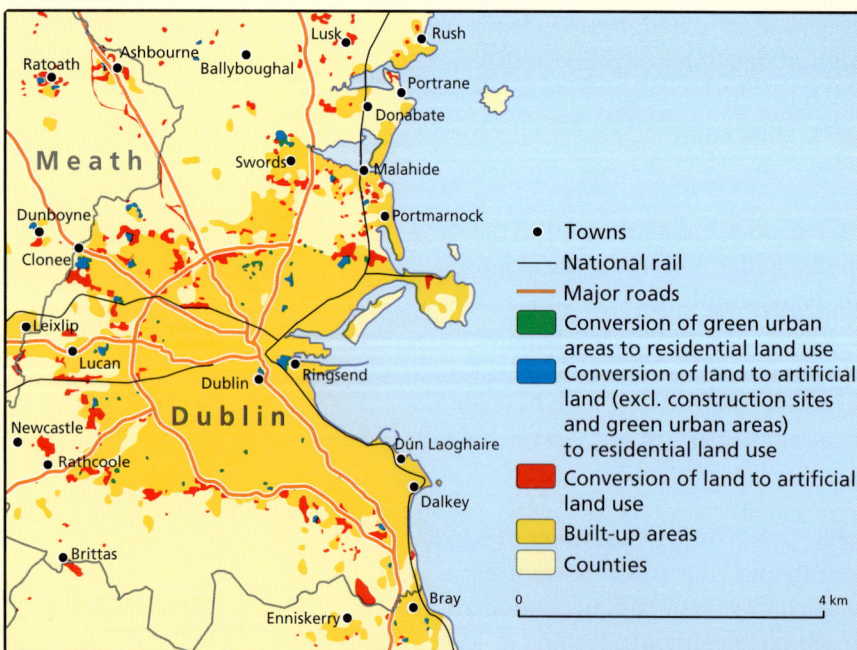

Towns
National rail
Major roads
Conversion of green urban areas to residential land use
Conversion of land to artificial land (excl. construction sites and green urban areas) to residential land use
Conversion of land to artificial land use
Built-up areas
Counties

0   4 km

Traffic Congestion

Rapid urban growth and **increased car ownership** has led to **traffic congestion**. The Irish government responded to the outdated transport infrastructure through **Transport 21**, which has since been **replaced with the Planned National Roads Network 2020**. **Transport 21** oversaw the **building of motorways** to increase access to the country's cities. However, motorways are shown to **increase urban sprawl** as workers are now choosing to **commute longer distances** to the cities. This has led to the growth of dormitory towns and major traffic congestion during rush hour. Traffic passing through **Dublin** city now has an **average speed of just 8 km/h** in those cities and towns that are not bypassed by motorways or ring roads. Traffic congestion is major problem. An example of this is **Galway City**, in which all traffic moving from the **west to the east of the county** must pass through the city. Public transport is limited in smaller towns, meaning people are **completely dependent on a car** as their only mode of transport.

ACTIVE LEARNING

1. Describe one positive and one negative impact of emigration in rural areas.
2. Describe the negative effects of immigration on Dublin.

GEO DICTIONARY

Dormitory towns: towns and villages in which people live and travel to work from

3.8 Rural–Urban Migration Developing World

The most **rapid rural–urban migration** is occurring in the **developing world.** By 2024 the world's urban population is predicted to reach 8 billion, with much of the expected growth to take place in developing countries. **Agriculture** is the basis of the economy for many **developing countries**, meaning that rural populations are high. **Increasing levels of mechanisation** on land or i**ncreased drought and poverty** had led to large numbers of young adults moving to cities in search of a better life. An example of this is seen in **Brazil**, which receives large numbers of migrants from the **Sertão** region in the north-east of the country.

CASE STUDY 📁

Brazil

Many cities of Brazil have seen their populations swell as a result of rural–urban migration. **São Paulo is a megacity** located on the eastern coast of Brazil. With a population of **23.3 million people**, it has grown rapidly as a result of rural–urban migration.

Push Factors

Many parts of Brazil suffer from **extreme poverty**. The poorest area is Sertão in the north-east, where the **life expectancy and rate of child mortality** are the **worst in**

⌃ **Fig. 3.23** Sertão region of Brazil

Brazil. The quality of life for people living in Sertão is similar to those living in the Sahel region of Africa, due to the climate, lack of resources, **lack of services** and **unfair land ownership**.

The Sertão experiences a **semi-arid climate** with a dry season that normally lasts from July to February and often much longer. With increased levels of drought, food **crops** suffer as yields become **unpredictable**. This has led to many people going hungry, as there is simply not enough food to go around. The **lack of food security** forces many people to migrate to cities in the hope of a better life.

There is a shortage of **land in the Sertão** for the poor, as much of it is **owned by landlords**. Much of the **land is left idle**, while large farms, known as *fazendas*, are used for the growing of **cash crops** such as **cocoa and cotton**. The number of **labourers needed** for these **fazendas** has been greatly **reduced by mechanisation**, meaning **those who depended on wages** earned from harvesting must **look elsewhere for work**.

While many parts of Brazil are rapidly developing, **services in the Sertão** are **almost non-existent**. There is a **low level of education** with **low literacy rates**, while **hospitals and policing are poorly funded**. This has led to **high levels of violence and crime** throughout the region. Therefore, poor people in the Sertão **move to the city of São Paulo** in **hopes of better housing**, services, **employment** opportunities and **safety**.

▲ **Fig. 3.24** The barren Sertão region

GEO DICTIONARY

Megacity: a large city with a population in excess of 10 million people.

▼ **Fig. 3.25** Favelas have developed in São Paulo as Brazil's government is unable to house the large number of immigrants.

Effects

Over **85 per cent of Brazil's population** now **live in cities** such as São Paulo, Belo Horizonte and Rio de Janeiro as a result of inward migration. As the **majority** of migrants are **young adults**, **child births are high**, which further increases urban populations.

Due to rapid increase in population, the government is **unable to provide adequate housing** for its inhabitants. This has led to the **formation of favelas** on the hillsides of cities, which house millions of people. In **São Paulo** alone, over **40 per cent of the inhabitants live in favelas**. Many of these favelas **lack basic services** such as **water and sanitation**, while **electricity and waste** collection are rare. This leads to the **rapid spread of disease** in favelas, while there is also a **high risk of fires** due to rubbish piles. **High levels of unemployment** mean that people are forced to earn money in other ways. This has given **rise to criminal gangs**, who sell drugs, often using teenagers as dealers. These gangs also force many young women into prostitution.

Overcoming Problems

In order to improve the quality of life for favela dwellers in Brazilian cities a number of incentives were used, such as:

Self-help Schemes

Residents of favelas are **given materials** by the local council to **improve their existing shelters**. **Community schemes** to improve education and medical services are also developed. Local authorities provide electricity, clean water and sewage disposal.

Site and Service Schemes

The government provides a **site and a small concrete hut** which has **basic services** such as water and electricity. The migrant has ownership rights to the hut but must finish the hut at their own expense.

ACTIVE **LEARNING**

1. What has been the common cause of rural–urban migration in both developed and developing countries?

2. Describe the push factors in the Sertão region.

3. Describe three ways in which the Brazilian government attempts to overcome problems in favelas.

EXAM QUESTIONS

ORDINARY LEVEL

1. (i) Explain the *push factors* associated with migration from rural to urban areas.

   (ii) Explain the *pull factors* associated with migration from rural to urban areas.

(i)
Push factor named	2m
Description: 6 SRPs @ 3m each	18m

(ii)
Pull factor named	2m
Description: 6 SRPs @ 3m each	18m

2016 Q10B 40M

2. 'Migration takes place due to push factors and pull factors.'

   (i) Name **one** push factor and **one** pull factor associated with migration.

   (ii) Describe and explain the positive impacts of migration on Ireland.

   (iii) Describe and explain the negative impacts of migration on Ireland.

(i)
Push factor named	2m
Pull factor named	2m

(ii)
Impact named	3m
Description and explanation: 5 SRPs @ 3m each	15m

(iii)
Impact named	3m
Description and explanation: 5 SRPs @ 3m each	15m

2015 Q10B 40M

Elective 5: Human   **CHAPTER 3**

3. (i)   State **two** reasons why people migrate from rural areas to urban areas.

    (ii) Describe and explain the effect of this migration on the urban areas that people migrate to.

    (iii) Describe and explain the effect of this migration on the rural areas they leave behind.

(i)	2 @ 2m	4m
(ii)	Examination: 6 SRPs @ 3m	18m
(iii)	Examination: 6 SRPs @ 3m	18m

2014 Q12B 40M

4. (i)   Describe the push factors which contribute to migration from rural to urban areas.

    (ii) Describe the pull factors which contribute to migration from rural to urban areas.

(i)

Push factor named	2m
Description: 6 SRPs @ 3m	18m

(ii)

Pull factor named	2m
Description: 6 SRPs @ 3m	18m

2013 Q10B 40M

1. Describe and explain changes in patterns of migration to and from Ireland over time.

15 SRPs @ 2m	30m

2016 Q11B 30M

2. Examine the impact of migration on a city in the developing world that you have studied.

Named developing world city	2m
Impact identified	2m
Examination: 13 SRPs @ 2m	26m

2015 Q11C 30M

HIGHER LEVEL

3. With reference to a developed region that you have studied, explain the impact of rural to urban migration on donor and receiver regions.

Named developed region	2m
Impact on donor region	2m
Impact on receiver region	2m
Examination: 12 SRPs @ 2m	24m

2014 Q10C 30M

4. Describe and explain changes in pattern of migration into and out of Ireland since the 1950s.

Changing patterns into Ireland	2m
Changing pattern out of Ireland	2m
13 SRPs @ 2m each	26m

2013 Q10C 30M

5. Examine how ethnic and religious issues can arise as a result of migration, with reference to examples you have studied.

Named example	2m
Religious issue identified	2m
Ethnic issue identified	2m
Examination: 12 SRPs @ 2m	24m

2013 Q11C 30M

HIGHER LEVEL

Questions on migration appear every year on both the Higher and Ordinary Level papers. The most commonly asked questions are (i) the changing migratory patterns of Ireland and (ii) the impacts of rural–urban migration in both the developed and developing world. Issues concerning migrants are also constantly covered in the media (e.g. newspapers, TV, social media) so there is a wealth of information outside of this book that you can use to build your knowledge. It is not uncommon to forget information you have studied for exam purposes, while remembering facts you heard or saw elsewhere. Therefore, independent knowledge through internet searches or a quick read of newspaper articles can provide additional SRPs.

In this section, we will look at the impact of rural–urban migration on both host and donor regions. Although the question is answered using a Higher Level marking scheme, this question has appeared on Ordinary Level papers also, so it is relevant to both.

HIGHER LEVEL

EXAM QUESTION

With reference to a developed region that you have studied, explain the impact of rural–urban migration on donor and receiver regions.

2014 Q10C 30M

Marking Scheme
Named developed region @ 2m
Impact on donor region @ 2m
Impact on receiver region @ 2m
Examination: 12 SRPs @ 2m

As always, it is important that you closely read the question. The Geography exam is one of the most intense exams on the Leaving Certificate with regard to timing, so an extra few moments analysing the question prevents mistakes and might well save time in the long run.

The potential for making a mistake with this question is in the word 'developed'. When looking for key words, it is possible to focus solely on the section of the question after the comma. However, if you had used the Brazilian case study to answer this question you would be awarded 0 marks (i.e. lose 6 per cent of the total Geography exam).

Although not specified in the marking scheme, the best way to answer this question is to divide it into two headings (i) impact on donor region and (ii) impact on receiver region. It is good to begin your answer with a *definition* of Rural–urban migration, in order to show the examiner that you understand the topic.

SAMPLE ANSWER

Rural-urban migration refers to the movement of people from the countryside to towns and cities [2m]. Rural-urban migration has occurred in Ireland since the beginning of the twentieth century as people migrate from the rural region of the West to Dublin City [2m].

Donor Region

The outward migration experienced in the rural west has led to population decline occurring [2m]. From the 1960s onwards, increasing levels of mechanisation led to a 75 per cent reduction in the number of people working in the agricultural sector [2m]. As a result, people were forced to move eastwards in search of work, with most migrating to Dublin, where there were pull factors such as employment opportunities and a higher standard of living [2m]. As it was mainly young adults aged 18-30 who left the West,

The answer is well structured and deals with all aspects separately. A definition is given, which shows understanding of the topic, while an impact on both donor and host regions is established and expanded on.

EXAM FOCUS

both marriage rates and birth rates declined, leaving the region with a 'greying' population and a high dependency ratio [2m]. These low levels of births have led to smaller school enrolments, which has caused many schools to close or amalgamate. Health services and the number of Garda stations have also been reduced [2m]. As a result of the loss of its young population, the region suffers from brain drain, as it is robbed of its skills and talents, making it unattractive for MNCs to locate in [2m]. This loss of population and services has left rural dwellers isolated and feeling abandoned due to a lack of government support [2m].

Host Region

The large number of immigrants from rural areas of the West has had positive effects for Dublin, such as an increasingly skilled workforce. However, it has also led to an increase in urban sprawl [2m]. Urban sprawl is the uncontrolled spread of cities into the surrounding countryside and has increased in Dublin as new houses are needed for those migrating to Dublin [2m]. Urban sprawl has a negative impact on the countryside, as natural landscapes and wildlife are destroyed [2m]. New towns such as Adamstown have been built to accommodate the growing population, while the city commuter belt has also increased [2m]. Increased car ownership in Ireland means that migrants are able to commute longer distances to the city for work. This means that counties surrounding Dublin have also experienced urban sprawl, e.g. Kildare, Wicklow and Meath [2m]. As Dublin planning does not allow for high-rise/high-density housing, the city must expand outwards rather than upwards [2m]. The high demand for housing means house prices are high close to the city, so young workers are willing to travel long distances via motorways to areas where property is cheaper [2m].

Marks Awarded
Named developed region @ 2m
Impact on donor region identified @ 2m
Impact on host region identified @ 2m
Best 12 SRPs @ 2m each
Total 30/30

TOPIC MAP

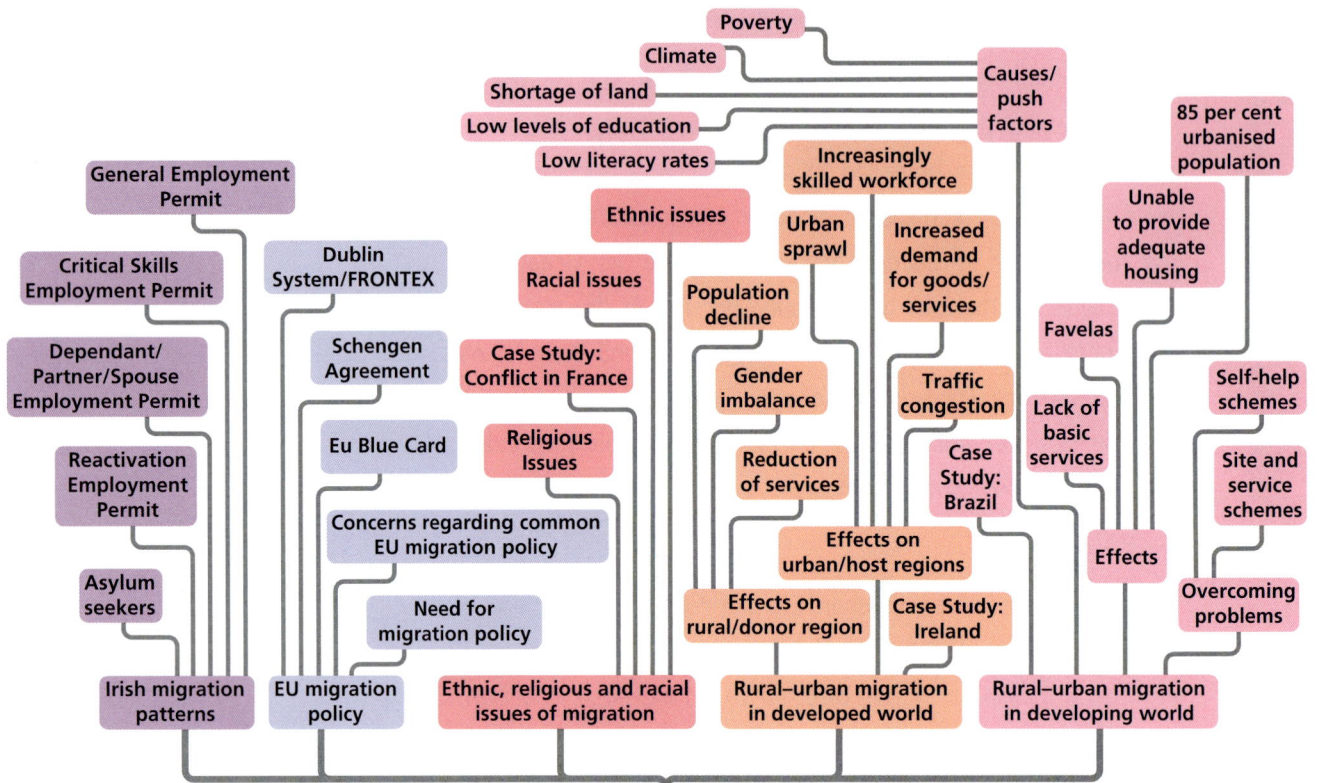

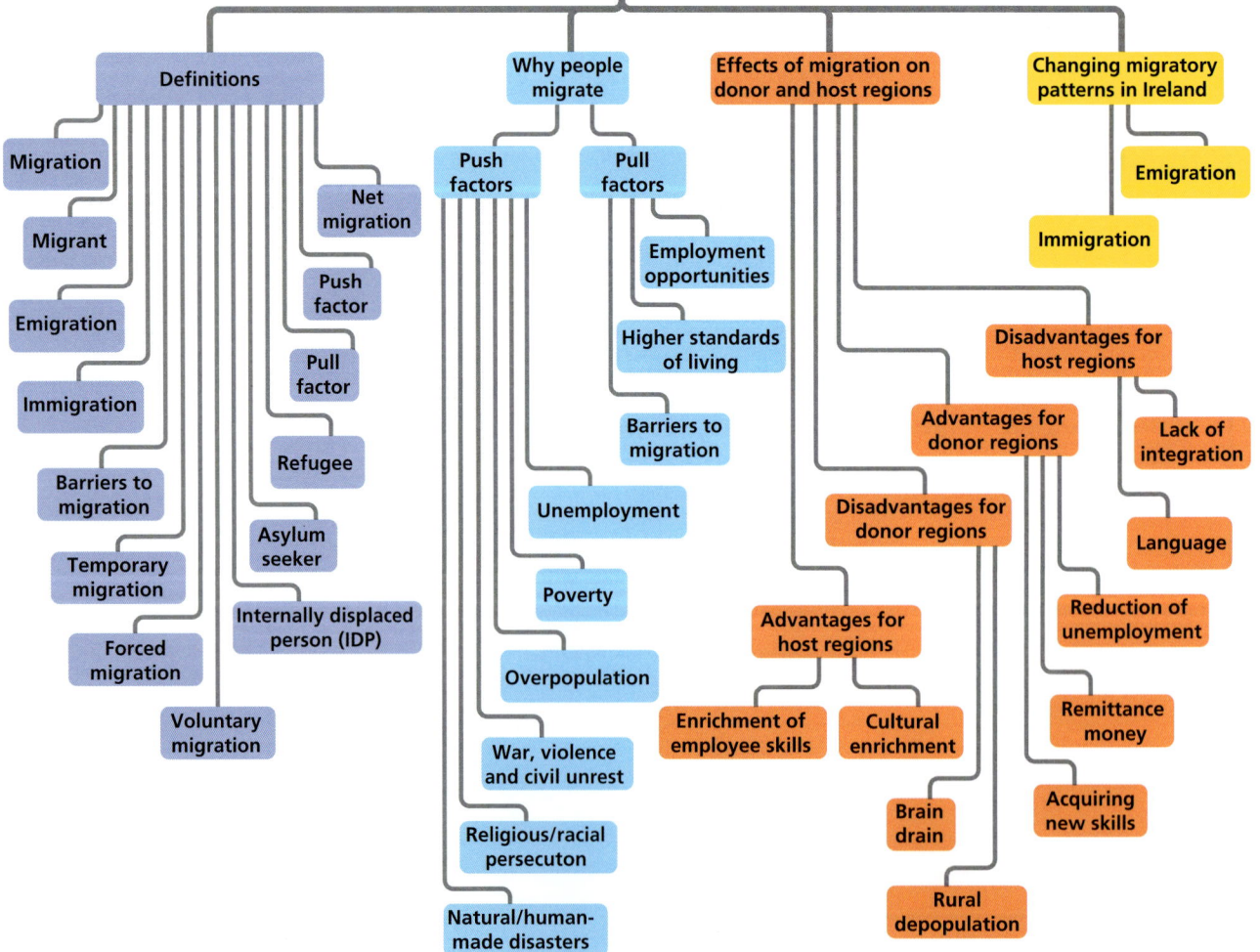

Settlement

So far, you have learned about the dynamics/movements of population in response to push and pull factors. In this chapter, we will examine the idea of settlement, i.e. where people live. We will begin by looking at the development of settlement and its changing functions as a result of that development. Throughout this chapter, Ordnance Survey Maps will be used to examine settlement in Ireland.

KEY WORDS 🔒

- Mesolithic
- Neolithic
- Bronze Age
- Celtic
- Viking
- Norman
- Plantation towns
- Settlement
- Site

- Situation
- Functions
- RICEPOTS
- Urban hierarchy
- Central Place Theory
- Range
- Threshold
- Hinterland
- Distribution

- Density
- Nucleated/dispersed
- Linear/ribboned
- Dispersed/scattered
- Absence
- County development plans
- National development plans

LEARNING OUTCOMES 🧠

What you MUST know
- How to identify evidence of prehistoric and historic settlement on OS maps
- How to describe the site, situation and functions of settlement
- How functions of settlement change over time
- Central Place Theory and urban hierarchy
- How to describe the density and distribution of settlement
- Rural settlement patterns
- Rural planning in Ireland

What you SHOULD know
- The Case Studies provided in this chapter can act as templates in preparing answers for your exams

What is USEFUL to know
- Up-to-date information regarding Ireland's rural planning laws and policies
- The Irish names for antiquities on OS maps (e.g. Dingle map, Fig. 4.35 on page 129)

Elective 5: Human   CHAPTER 4

Introduction

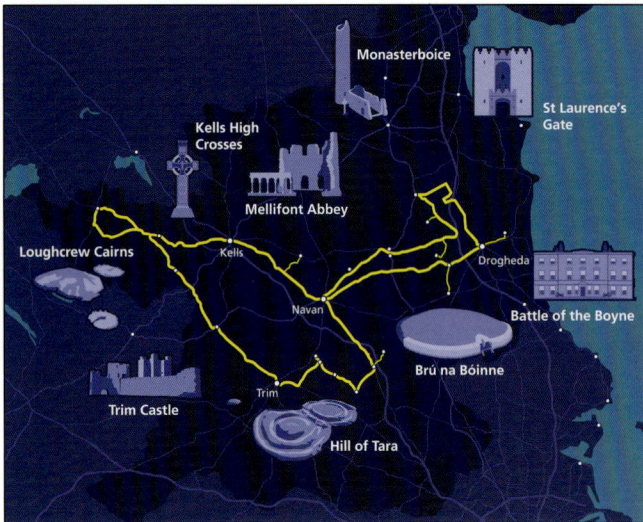

Fig. 4.1 The Boyne Valley in Co. Meath was the location of Ireland's first settlers and many other civilisations that followed.

Settlement refers to a **place where people live**. These settlements range in **size** from a **single house to a large city**. The development of settlements began in Ireland **9,000 years ago** when the first settlers arrived by crossing land bridges connecting Ireland with Britain. The **first settlers** chose the **Boyne Valley** in Co. Meath as their first site because of its **fertile land, fresh water and shelter**. Since then, the **functions of** Irish **settlements have changed several times** as a result of **several different civilisations** which eventually formed the **modern settlements of today**. In examining the evolution of settlements we will look at the following:

- Historic settlements of Ireland and their evidence on maps
- The site, situation and functions of settlements
- Central place theory
- Rural settlement patterns
- Rural planning in Ireland.

ACTIVE LEARNING

1. Why did the first settlers choose to settle in the Boyne Valley?
2. Group Work: Imagine you are the chieftain of a Celtic tribe arriving by boat into the area shown on the Dingle map, Fig. 4.35 on page 129. Choose a suitable location for a settlement and explain fully, using map evidence, three reasons for your choice of location.

4.1 Prehistoric and Historic Settlement

Fig. 4.2 Evidence of middens

The remains of **prehistoric and historic settlements** can be found in **almost all parts of Ireland**. In this section, we will look at each **civilisation** and we will examine information to help to identify these civilisations on Ordnance Survey maps.

Prehistoric

Mesolithic: 7000–3500 BCE

In general, there is **very little evidence** of Mesolithic (Old Stone Age) settlers in Ireland, as the people of this time were nomadic hunter-gatherers. The only significant evidence of this civilisation is **middens**, which are **old rubbish** heaps consisting of the bones and shells of food eaten. Middens tend to be located near water, which was used for drinking, cooking, food supply and transport. Middens may also be **located along hilltops** which were used for defence. People at the time used **stone weapons** and tools such as flint spearheads.

> ### GEO DICTIONARY
>
> **Prehistoric:** relates to a period before written records; or, in this context, it means primitive or basic
>
> **Flint:** a hard grey rock consisting of nearly pure silica
>
> **Civilisation:** stage of human development and organisation

Neolithic: 3500–2000 BCE

The **Neolithic people** were **Ireland's first farmers**, and also the **first civilisation** to **leave evidence** of their lives behind. At this time, the people of Ireland began **clearing** the **country's** vast **deciduous forests** in order to make room for farming. **No longer nomadic**, the farmers **settled in one place** and began **growing crops** and farming animals. Their **houses** were **constructed** with **wattle and daub**; therefore, these dwellings have not survived to today. Neolithic people chose **low-lying land** that was **close to a river** to build their settlements. **Rivers** provided **fertile alluvial soils** and **good drainage**.

⌃ **Fig. 4.3** Newgrange shows great engineering ability.

The **main evidence** of Neolithic civilisation found in Ireland today is **burial tombs**. Evidence includes megalithic tombs, passage tombs, portal dolmens and standing stones. These are typically found in **upland or hilly areas** – presumably a place of honour to remember the dead. Many of these tombs have **markings or carvings**, while many others were **aligned with the sun**, e.g. Newgrange has an inner chamber that is lit up by the sun on the shortest day of each year, the winter solstice. This **shows Neolithic knowledge of the position of the sun, awareness of seasons, and a greater level of engineering** than Mesolithic ancestors.

Bronze Age: 2000–600 BCE

Bronze Age settlers **moved from using stone tools** and weapons **to metals** such as **copper and tin.** Evidence of their settlement can be found in **Mount Gabriel, Co. Cork** where there is an ancient copper mine. Most Bronze Age **settlements** appear to have been **built next to their resources**, e.g. tombs were built alongside copper mines. As copper is a soft metal, it was mixed

⌃ **Fig. 4.4** Gleninsheen Gorget (bronze) from 800–700 BCE

1. Name three towns or townlands in your county beginning with Lios (Lis), Dun or Caher.

2. Try to find the meaning of the name of your local town/townland. Note: you may have to translate the name into Irish in order to find its meaning.

with tin to **form the alloy bronze**. This shows an **increased technological advancement**. The Bronze Age people left much **smaller tombs** than the Neolithic people. Bronze Age settlers buried their people in **wedge tombs, stone chambers** and **small burrows**.

Celtic Settlement: 600 BCE–500 CE

The Celts came to Ireland from mainland Europe and **brought new technology**, such as **iron weapons**. The Celts were an **aggressive and warlike** people who lived in a **structured society** that was divided into **kingdoms called** tuaths. Within each tuath, Celts lived in **isolated dwellings** that were scattered throughout the countryside. The Celts typically chose areas that were **easy to defend**, such as **elevated sites, cliff-edges** or near **marsh lakes**. Defensive sites were encircled with walls to offer **further protection**.

A settlement known as a crannóg was common. Crannógs were **constructed in lakes** and had a series of **hidden steps for access**. There is an abundance of evidence of Celtic settlement scattered throughout Ireland, e.g. **ring fort, hill fort, promontory fort, crannóg, togher, souterrain, fulacht fiadh** and **ogham stones**. A former Celtic **tuath can also be identified by place-names such as rath, Lios/Lis, Dun, Caisel, Cahir** or **Caher**.

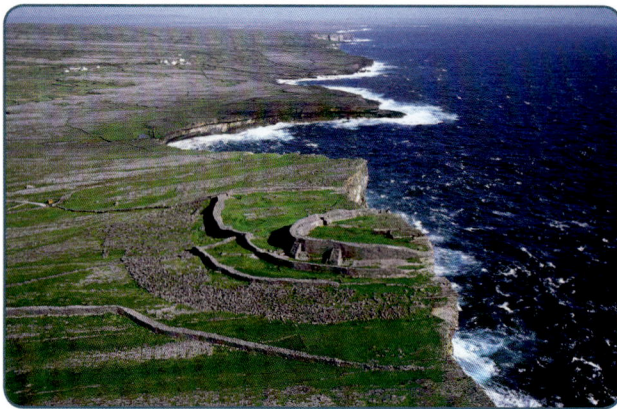

🔺 **Fig. 4.5** Dun Aengus promontory fort

🔺 **Fig. 4.6** Ring fort

Note!

OS map evidence:
- Ring fort
- Hill fort
- Promontory fort
- Crannóg
- Togher
- Souterrain
- Fulacht fiadh
- Ogham stones
- Place-names that include: *Rath, Lios/Lis, Dun, Caisel, Cahir* or *Caher*.

GEO DICTIONARY

Tuath: a Celtic kingdom

Crannóg: an ancient fortified dwelling made of wattle and daub, often built in a lake or an area of marsh land

Promontory fort: a fort built on a point of high land that juts out into the sea

Togher: a road or track across bogland

Souterrain: an underground chamber or passage

Fulacht fiadh: burnt mound thought to be a Celtic cooking/washing area

Ogham stone: an upright stone used to mark the boundary of a túath; ogham stones have carvings/markings of the ancient alphabet called ogham

Historic Era

Early Christian Settlement 500–800 CE

The first early Christian settlers lived in **isolated and scenic areas** such as Glendalough in Co. Wicklow. These **isolated locations** allowed for **peaceful prayer** and **undistracted devotion**, while also providing defence. Many monasteries became the **sites of the first towns** in Ireland, e.g. **Kells in Co. Meath** or **Skellig Michael in Co. Kerry**. Churches were often built **close to** an **important site** such as a **well**. The **houses** of the **early Christians** were constructed from **wattle and daub** and surrounded by a circular fence. As with Celtic settlement, there is an abundance of evidence of Early Christian settlement throughout Ireland.

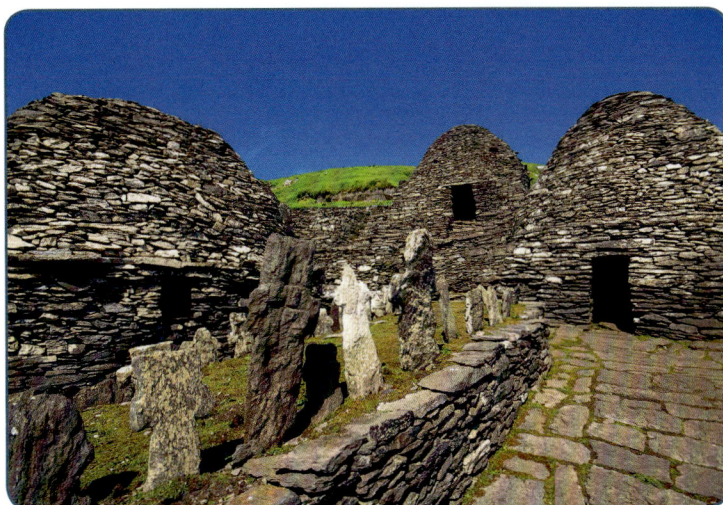

Fig. 4.7 Beehive huts on Skellig Michael (Sceilig Mhichíl) are evidence of Early Christian settlement.

Viking Settlement: 800–1169 CE

The **Vikings** arrived in Ireland from Scandinavia in the **late eighth century**. They **raided monastic sites** along coastal areas before moving inland by river. **Until** the **Vikings** arrived, **no towns really existed in Ireland**. As Vikings had **trading links throughout Europe**, they built towns at **sheltered mouths of rivers** – mainly along the **east and south-east** of the country. The **ports** were also **located in areas** which were **easy to defend** against the native Irish.

Very **little evidence** of Viking settlements has survived, as Viking settlements were wooden structures. However, the **radial layout of the original street patterns** has survived in town centres, e.g. **Dublin** (*Dubh linn*: Blackpool). As well as building settlements for trade and defence, Vikings also chose to build on sites which were a **dry point**.

Viking settlements can be identified mainly by **place-names** ending in *ford* or *low*, e.g. **Arklow, Wexford, Waterford**. Viking towns also have a **radial street pattern**.

Note!

OS map evidence:
- Holy wells
- Cross-inscribed stones
- Round towers
- High crosses
- Monasteries
- Churches
- Graveyards

GEO DICTIONARY

Dry point: land above tide level or the flood level of rivers

Note!

OS map evidence:
- Place-names ending in *ford* or *low*

Fig. 4.8 Viking settlements in Ireland

Norman Settlement: 1169 CE

The Normans were originally from Scandinavia but settled in Normandy in France. They **travelled to Ireland from Britain** and **conquered or captured Viking settlements**. The Normans were castle builders, with **defence and control** being important factors. The majority of Norman **towns developed around castles** as the settlements took on both **military and dwelling functions**. Castles were typically **built on sites** that were **easier to defend**, such as on **elevated ground** or on the **bend of a river**.

Bridging points of **rivers and fertile land** also influenced settlement choices of Norman settlers, with many castles being found on low-lying areas where water and farmland were available. **Town walls and gates** were built to **protect the town** further from attack, and also as a means of **controlling trade and disease**.

The Normans were **Christians** and had **close links** with the **Cistercian and Franciscan** religious orders. As a result, **priories or abbeys** are found near castles.

Fig. 4.9 Kilmallock in Co. Limerick is an example of a Norman town, as evidenced from the remnants of its town gate.

Note!

OS map evidence:
- Castles
- Motte
- Moat
- Bailey
- Town walls
- Town gates
- Abbeys
- Priories
- Place-names with *Bally* (derived from *baile*) indicate Norman origins

Plantation Town Settlements: 1500–1700 CE

Plantation towns were created during the **sixteenth and seventeenth centuries** when land was granted to **English and Scottish planters** who were **loyal to the English crown**. Many of these plantation towns have **fortified buildings or defensive walls**, as **attacks** from the displaced native Irish population were **common**. Most of the plantation towns have a **main street and a market square/diamond**, where **weekly trades** or **fairs took place**. Plantation towns were planned and had wide streets with two- or three-storey buildings. These towns were located near a **large landlord estate**, known as a **demesne**, which was divided into **small plots of land** called **lotts**. As the towns developed, so too did **road and canal networks**. Examples of **plantation towns in Ireland** are Charleville, **Co. Cork**; Adare, Co. Limerick; Birr, Co. Offaly; Maynooth, Co. Kildare; Donegal Town, Co. Donegal.

Note!

OS map evidence:
- Fortified houses
- Market square/ diamond
- Demesne
- Canals
- Grid-patterned streets
- Ornamental gardens

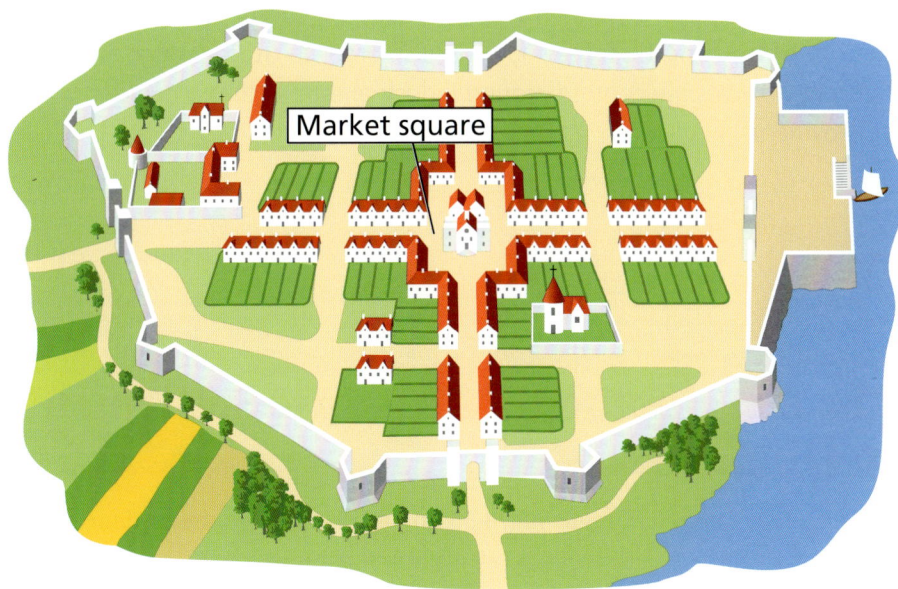

◀ **Fig. 4.10** A typical plantation town in Ireland

Market square

New Towns: 1960 CE and onwards

New towns were created from the **1960s onwards** and laid in a way to address **urban planning** issues. Towns such as **Tallaght** were developed by planners, turning them from **smaller villages to larger urban areas** in order to contain the **urban sprawl from Dublin**. These towns are sited around **transport links, factories** or **modern infrastructure**. For example, **Shannon in Co. Clare** was built in the 1960s to accommodate workers from the airport and the then newly built Shannon Industrial Estate.

GEO DICTIONARY

Urban planning: designing and organising urban space and activities

Urban sprawl: the uncontrolled spread of cities into the surrounding countryside

ACTIVE LEARNING

1. Using the OS map of Westport, Fig. 4.28 on page 119 identify all historic civilisations evident.

2. Give a six-figure grid reference for each historic settlement present.

3. Describe the settlements of (a) the Celts and (b) the Early Christians. Refer to the map of Westport, Fig. 4.28 on page 119, to aid your answer.

◀ **Fig. 4.11** Adamstown in Dublin is an example of a new town.

Adamstown in Dublin is the newest town in the country. It has a **higher density of housing** than previous towns in order to **utilise space fully**. Many new towns are centred around industrial estates that provide employment.

CASE STUDY 📁

The Development of Historic Settlement in Dingle

The OS map extract of Dingle, Fig. 4.35 on page 129, shows the evidence of historic civilisations. This evidence is discussed below.

Neolithic: New Stone Age

The earliest settlers of which there is evidence on the OS map of Dingle are the **Neolithic people**. These were Ireland's first farmers and lived from **3500–2000 BCE**. Evidence of Neolithic settlement can be seen through the several **gallans** (*gallan*: standing stone) dotted throughout the area. Examples include those at **V 527 992, Q 491 025 and Q 526 029**. Standing stones were used to mark burial sites or to mark the positions of the sun and stars. At **Q 478 008** a **standing stone** exists on low-lying land. Neolithic people often chose these sites as the **land was fertile** and **soils** were **easily worked** for agriculture. Added to this, it is less than **500 m from the Garfinny River**, which provided the settlers with **fresh water** and **transport**.

Megalithic tombs are located at **Q 525 994 and Q 527 997**, in an area of **200 m above sea level**. **Megalithic tombs** were typically built on **elevated sites and marked graves** of the dead. The tombs were constructed with large stones called megaliths (*mega* = large, *lith* = stones).

Celtic Settlement

Evidence of **Celtic settlement** can be seen throughout the Dingle area, with **ring forts, fulacht fiadhs, ogham stones** and a number of **promontory forts** visible on the OS extract. The Celts arrived in Ireland around **500 BCE** and quickly set up **kingdoms, called tuaths,** throughout Ireland. The Celts were an aggressive and warlike people, preferring to live in tribes of small numbers. The Celts built ring forts to protect themselves from attack from native Irish or other Celts. Often, these ring forts were located on elevated sites that offered protection and a bird's-eye view of the surrounding countryside. Evidence of **ring forts** can be seen **Q 423 043 and V 513 983**.

Other Celtic evidence seen on the map includes **ogham stones** (*cloch ogham*), which can be seen at **V 496 994**; and **fulacht fiadhs**, which can be found **at Q 469 001**. Ogham stones marked the **territorial boundaries** of tuaths,, with lines out in the stone indicating the particular tribe. Fulacht fiadhs were the cooking places of Celts. Fulacht fiadhs were holes in the ground which were filled with water. Hot stones were inserted into the water, which heated it. Meat was then boiled in this water.

Along the coastline of Dingle, there is evidence of several **promontory forts**, such as those located at **V 529 985 and V 478 986**. These forts were built along **cliff edges**, as they were **easier to defend**.

> ### Note!
> In order to answer questions on historic settlement, it is useful to remember the acronym **IDLE**. These letters stand for **I**dentify, **D**escribe, **L**ocate and **E**xplain. This means that you must identify the civilisation, describe their settlement habits, locate evidence of their settlement on the OS map and explain why they would have settled at that location. For a 30-mark question, it is recommended you do this for three different settlements. Note that this Case Study is written in exam-answer style.

Early Christian

Early Christian settlement is also evident on the map. In Ireland, Christian settlement dates back to **500 CE**. As the Irish were converted to Christianity, **churches were built**, such as that located at **Q 514 013 (Eaglais)**. Often these churches were built on low-lying land close to water. For example, this church is located less than **40 m above sea level** and **less than 500 m from the river Owenalondrig**. Sites of churches grew into towns as people settled near them in hopes of receiving education, protection and alms. Early Christians often **converted significant sites into Christian symbols**, such as the erecting of a **high cross** (Lathair Luathre Chriostai at **Q 063 426**). They also converted important sites, such as wells into 'holy wells'.

Section 4.2 Settlement Site and Situation

In this section, we will look at site and situation of settlements.

Site

Site refers to the **land or area on which the settlement is built**. In describing site, we look at the **main physical characteristics** of an area. These characteristics explain why settlers were attracted to the area. There are several reasons:

- **Nearby water:** Settlements chose to locate close to rivers as they were a **source of fresh water,** a mode of transport for trade and a bridging point which was a natural meeting point.

- **Relief and altitude:** Settlements are usually built on flat land as it is much easier to access and build on. The **altitude** of an area also determines its **suitability for settlement**. Areas of land below 200 m are usually more favourable as they are easier to build on and access and they allow for easier communication. Added to this, lowland areas are not as exposed to winds, meaning they have a more favourable climate than upland areas.

- **Aspect:** Aspect refers to the direction a slope faces. As **south-facing slopes** receive **more sunshine** than north-facing slopes, they are preferable sites for settlement.

- **Flooding:** Dry points are **suitable for settlement** as they are **above** the **flood level** of rivers and are usually **well drained and gently sloping**.

- **Coastal areas:** Many of Ireland's **largest settlements** are located **alongside river mouths** or sheltered bays which develop into **centres of economic activities**, e.g. fishing, trade, shipping.

⊘ **Fig. 4.12** What site advantages do each of these settlements have?

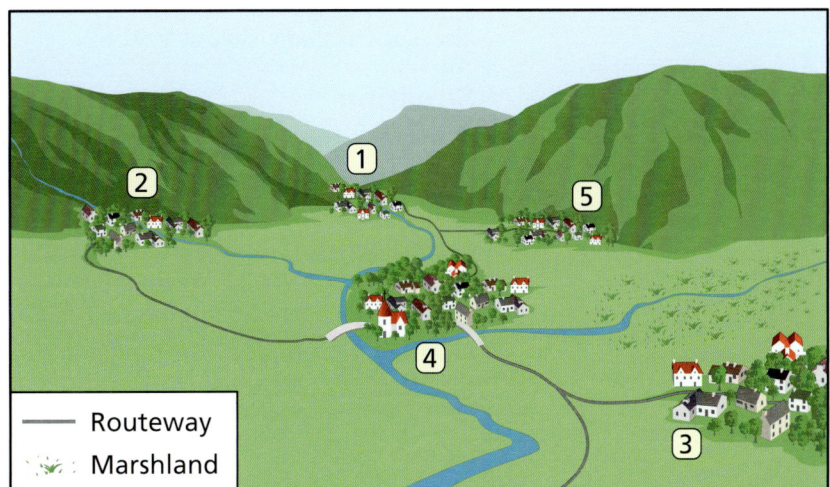

Legend:
— Routeway
⁂ Marshland

Situation

Situation refers to the location of the settlement in relation to the surrounding area and other towns. **Modern growth** and **expansion** of settlements depend on their situation in relation to:

- **Natural routeways:** These are naturally formed landscapes which allow for the construction of communications. These natural features include **gaps and valleys** created by **rivers** and glaciers, which first attracted settlers.

- **Developed routeways:** These refer to **transport lines** which have developed over time as the **settlement expanded**, e.g. **motorways**, **railway lines**.

CASE STUDY 📁

The Site and Situation of Kenmare

In this Case Study we will look at the **physical factors** that have impacted the site of Kenmare and its situation in relation to access to the settlement.

Site

From the **OS map of Kenmare** (Fig. 4.29 on page 120), we can see that the town developed on **gently sloping lowland of under 50 m**, as seen by the **widely spaced contour lines**. To the north and south of Kenmare, upland **regions above 200 m** are **unsuitable for settlement**. Kenmare is built on the northern bank of the **Kenmare River**, which would have been chosen by early settlers due to the **fertile alluvial soils** which were formed by annual winter floods. These **soils** are **fertile** and **easily worked**, making the site a perfect location for growing food.

The **river** could also be used as a **mode of transport** and for trade with surrounding areas, while also providing a **source of food and fresh water**. The flat land allows for the **easy construction of housing** and **communication links**. The **gentle relief** has also allowed for the **town to expand along the riverbank**, with evidence of settlement developing along the southern bank also, such as that visible at **V 91 69**.

Situation

Kenmare is a **route centre** for many **roads**, both **major and minor**. These include the national routes (N70 and N71), the regional routes **R569 and R571** and a network of third-class primary roads. Therefore, Kenmare could develop as a market town for its agricultural hinterland, making it a nodal point. The **pier** at **V 906 701** suggests that the town has a fishing industry or boating activities for the tourist industry. The **V 911 706 hostel** suggests that the town has a **tourist function**. The mountains to the north and south of Kenmare mean that it is **sheltered from strong winds**.

Fig. 4.13 Site and situation of Kenmare

Section 4.3 Functions of Settlement

Residential
Industrial
Commercial
Educational
Port
Open space and recreational
Tourism
Services

Function refers to the main economic and social activities of a settlement. As a settlement develops, its functions change over time. Today, most towns are multifunctional, meaning they provide many different functions at the same time. The most important functions of towns can be remembered by the acronym **RICEPOTS**.

Identifying Functions on Aerial Photographs/OS Maps

- **Religious:** also known as *ecclesiastical* functions, can be identified by churches, cathedrals and graveyards, mosques
- **Residential:** housing estates, apartment blocks
- **Industrial:** factories, port facilities, industrial estates
- **Commercial:** shop fronts, market square, shopping centres
- **Communications:** refers to transport – road networks, railway stations, canal, ferry terminals, ports
- **Educational:** schools, colleges, universities
- **Port:** harbours, quays, piers, marinas, warehouses, large ships
- **Open space:** car parks, picnic areas, walking trails, nature reserves, national parks
- **Recreational:** swimming pool, tennis courts, golf course, race course, marina, football pitches
- **Tourism:** tourist information offices, hostels, camping/caravan sites, viewpoints, antiquities
- **Services:** hospitals, Garda stations, fire stations, post offices

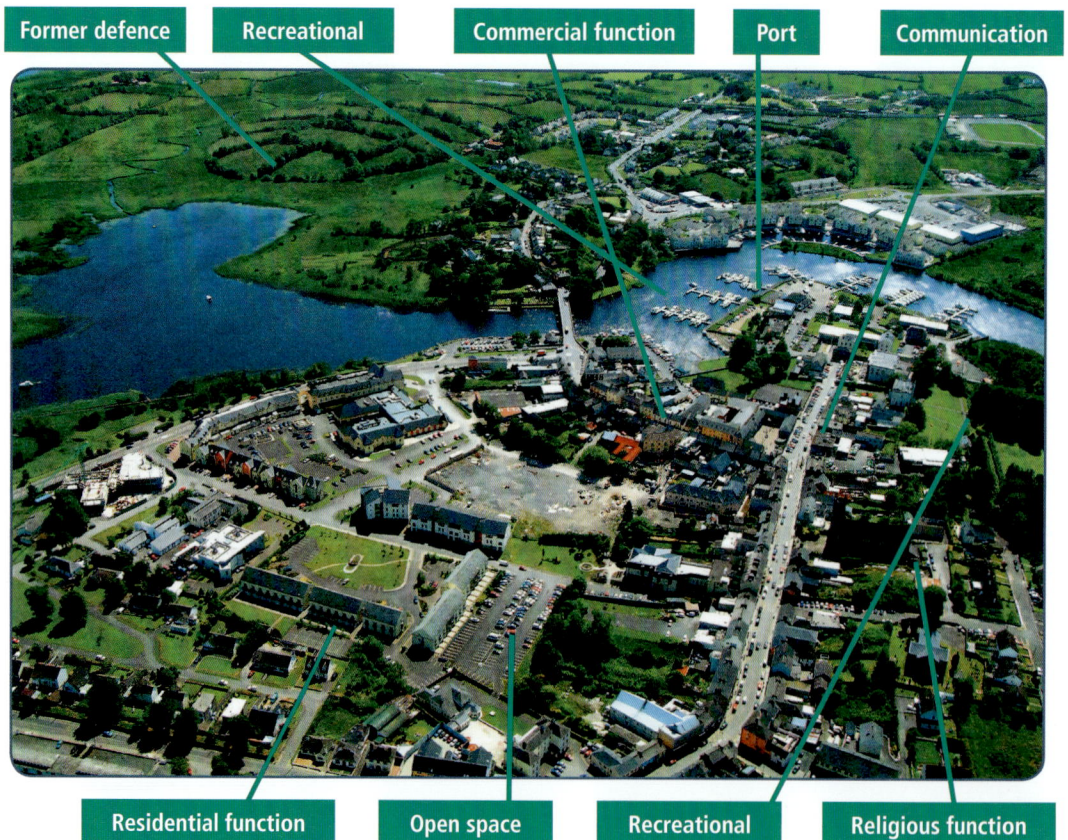

> **Fig. 4.14** Functions of Carrick-on-Shannon

Former defence · Recreational · Commercial function · Port · Communication

Residential function · Open space · Recreational · Religious function

Galway

Galway is the **fourth largest city** in Ireland and is the **main urban centre** of the West of Ireland. It is located **north of Galway Bay** on the **River Corrib**. Now approximately **53 km²** in **area**, the city has grown outwards to the east and west along its flat land. Today, the city is home to over **75,000 people** and has a **variety of functions** in order to meet their needs.

Port Function

Galway (Fig. 4.15 on page 108) prospered as a **port city**, with **14 families** (or tribes) dominating commercial trade in the city throughout **medieval times**. The city's **commercial life developed** around the **port**, with ships **exporting wool, fish and leather** to France. In turn, **textiles, wines** and other foods were **imported from the French**. The **port** can be seen at **M 301 246**.

Over time, the city became a centre of **distribution for imported goods**, which in turn **developed routes to and from the city**, making it a route focus. **Bridges were built across the River Corrib**, while ports were expanded to accommodate larger ships. In the **aftermath of the Famine** (1845–9), in which thousands died or emigrated, **port functions declined** in the city as **Dublin's, Cork's and Waterford's ports** became **centres of trade**.

Education

Galway has an **educational function**, with a number of schools and a university located there. A **school** can be found at **M 293 253**, a **college** at **M 329 258** and the **university** at **M 294 259**. Galway became a **university city in 1845** as it was chosen as the location for one of the Queen's colleges in Ireland, which gave it **important educational status**. The university, now known as **NUIG** helped the city to grow as **accommodation**, **shops** and other services for **students and staff** grew over time. Galway is also home to the **Galway-Mayo Institute of Technology** (GMIT), while the **university regional hospital** teaches medical students and nurses from NUIG.

Manufacturing

Galway has become the leading **manufacturing centre** in the west region of Ireland. In recent decades it has become the **location of multinational companies**, especially American-owned **medical device companies**. They are attracted to the city due to the **highly educated workforce** provided by NUIG and GMIT, its **ease of access** and its well-developed communication links. The city provides services and facilities for these companies such as newly built **industrial estates, e.g. M 325 275**.

Other functions of Galway include **transport**, with the **M6 motorway** connecting Galway to the capital, while the city also has a **railway terminal**. Galway also has an important **tourist function** and is known as the **cultural capital of Ireland**. The city is a **gateway to Connemara**, which is a popular destination for tourists.

Fig. 4.15 Functions of Galway City

Fig. 4.15 Functions of Galway City

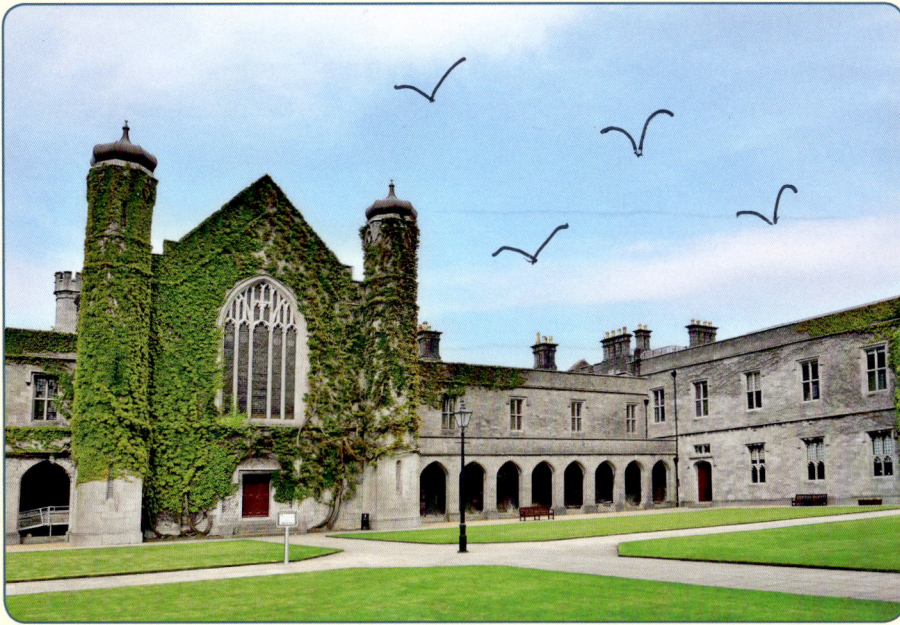

4.4 Central Place Theory and Urban Hierarchy

Central Place Theory was devised by a German geographer, Walter Christaller in 1933. His theory tries to explain the **size and distribution of settlements** across a countryside. Christaller devised his theory while studying the distribution of settlements in southern Germany in which he concluded that settlements are part of a **system of central places**. The term *central place* is used to describe an **urban centre**, which **provides goods and services to a much larger area** known as its hinterland. In other words, a central place is a market centre, where the population of its hinterland will go to buy goods and use services. A central place can **vary in size from a small village to a large city**. Central Place Theory shows how **settlements** are **spaced in a manner** so that they **do not compete** for the same customers. The main parts of Christaller's theory are:

- Range
- Hierarchy of goods
- Threshold
- Urban hierarchy
- Hinterland.

Fig. 4.17 Walter Christaller devised the theories of central theory and urban hierarchy.

Range

Range refers to the **distance that people are prepared to travel** for certain goods or services. These can be divided into two sections:

- **Small range:** people are **not prepared to travel as far for goods or services** that they need frequently, e.g. **milk, fuel and newspapers**
- **Large range:** people are **willing to travel greater distances** to purchase 'one-off goods', e.g. **cars** and furniture.

GEO DICTIONARY

Central place: an urban centre that provides goods and services to a much larger area known as its hinterland

Hierarchy of Goods

Goods and services can be further divided into three categories, depending on the importance of the product and the willingness of people to obtain them:

- **Lower order goods and services:** these are goods that are **widely available** to people; therefore, they have a **low range** and a **low threshold**, e.g. milk, bread, fuel.

- **Middle order goods and services:** people will **travel further for these goods** and services as they are needed less frequently, e.g. supermarkets, clothes shops, doctors.

- **Higher order goods and services:** people will **travel even longer distances** for these goods and services, which are **not frequently bought**. Examples include **new cars, engagement rings, laptops, furniture and mortgages**.

🔺 **Fig. 4.18** Urban hierarchy

Threshold

Threshold is the **minimum number of customers that a business needs** in order to maintain its service. **Local grocery shops** need only a **small number of customers** to stay in business, as they provide a **small range of goods** which are **bought frequently**. Therefore, they have a **low threshold**, since **people from the area buy goods** from the shop **several times a week**. In **contrast** with this, people shop in a **computer store** or pharmacy **far less frequently** than they shop for local groceries. Therefore, a **large pool of customers is needed** in order to stay in business: these businesses need a **high threshold** in order to survive. This explains why **jewellers** and **computer stores** are **found in towns rather than in small villages**.

Urban Hierarchy

Urban hierarchy is the **ranking of the importance of urban centres** in relation to each other. The hierarchy of a country's urban system is **arranged like a pyramid**, with a small number of cities at the top and a large number of villages and hamlets at the bottom. In Ireland, **Dublin is at the top of the pyramid** as the country's primate city, with the **highest number of high, middle and low order goods** and **services** provided to its customers. Below Dublin are smaller cities such as Cork, Galway and Limerick. Below these cities are larger towns such as Portlaoise, Ennis and Letterkenny. Below these are small towns such as Kilmallock; and below this, villages and hamlets.

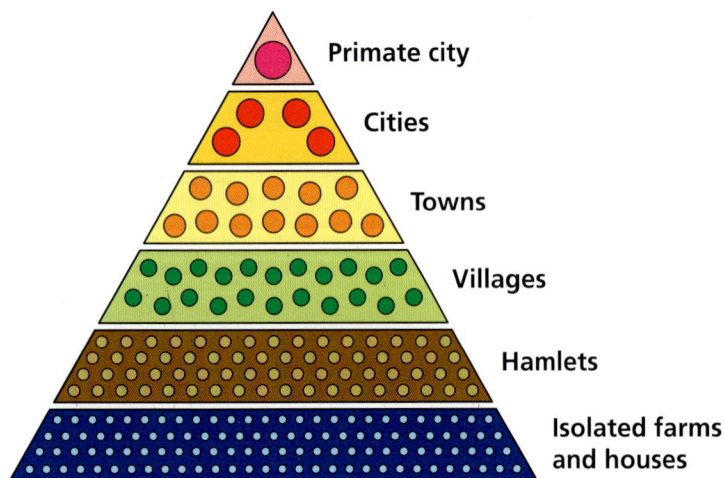

🔺 **Fig. 4.19** Urban hierarchy

Hinterland

The **hinterland** is the **area surrounding an urban centre where customers live**. It is also referred to as the **market area**. For Christaller, these hinterlands had to be

Central Place Theory

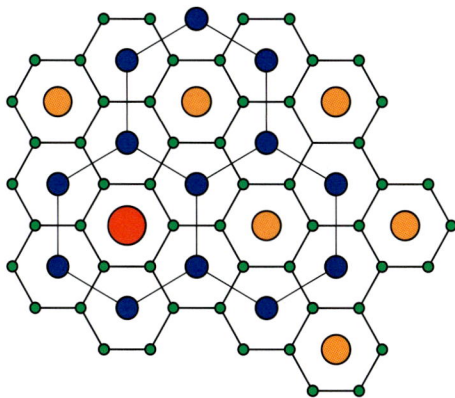

Fig. 4.20 Hexagonal hinterlands fit together perfectly with no area unserved or overlapping

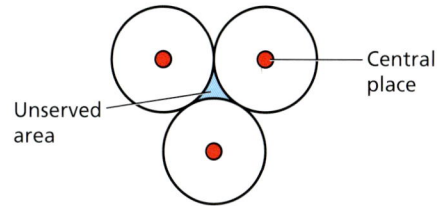

Key

- 🔴 City
- 🟠 Town
- 🔵 Market town
- 🟢 Village
- ▭ Boundaries

Fig. 4.21 Circular hinterlands do not serve all areas.

hexagonal in shape so there were **no overlapping** or **missed hinterlands** of **urban centres**. Hinterlands with **circular shapes** are **not satisfactory**, as some **areas between the circles are not served**, or there is an overlap if the circles intertwine. The size of a hinterland is **partly dependent on its size and functions** of its **central place** (town) and the **population density of the area**. Central places located in areas with **low population density** tend to have **larger hinterland**, as **people travel larger distances** for **lower order goods and services**.

GEO **DICTIONARY**

Range: the distance people are willing to travel for a good or service

Urban hierarchy: ranking of importance of urban centres

Hinterland: area surrounding an urban centre where customers live

---

Note!

A question on central place appears almost every year on the Higher Level paper. The question either asks you to explain the theory **or** to apply it to the main urban area visible on the OS map provided. On the next page, there is a useful Case Study of Carrick-on-Suir.

Criticisms and Weaknesses of the Theory

Christaller **explained** his **theory** on the **basis that the population is evenly distributed** over a **flat area** where the **transport links** to **market centres** are the same and that people will always travel to the **nearest central place** for their needs. However, in real life there are several factors that impact on people's behaviour:

- **Physical factors** such as **mountains, marshes** and **bogland** prevent settlement from being distributed evenly.

- **Modern transport facilities** give the **advantage to larger settlements**. This can be seen in the downgrading and closures of regional hospitals in favour of the establishment of medical centres of excellence in the HSE.

- People **do not always behave rationally** when they are buying goods and services. People today are far more mobile than when the theory was devised. Most people now have cars and are prepared to travel further for better choice and cheaper prices.

- **Local resources** also impact on the **development of central places**, e.g. **mines** or **tourist amenities**.

ACTIVE **LEARNING**

1. What is a central place?
2. What is meant by the term *threshold*?
3. What are the limitations of Christaller's theory?
4. Using the OS map of Dungarvan, Fig. 4.30 on page 122, explain the town's role as a central place.

Central Place of Carrick-on-Suir

The town of Carrick-on-Suir serves as a central place for the surrounding hinterland, as can be seen in the OS map extract (Fig. 4.34 on page 128).

🔺 **Fig. 4.22** Carrick-on-Suir acts as a central place to the surrounding hinterland.

A Route Focus

Carrick-on-Suir is a **route focus**. It has **national route ways** such as the **N24**, which connects the town to its hinterland. **Regional roads** such as the **R697, R696 and R680** also **focus on the town**. A railway serves the town, with a **station** located at **S 407 220. Several third-class roads link the town to its hinterland.** All these **routes converge in Carrick**, making it the **central place** for the area. Therefore, Carrick-on-Suir is a **nodal point**, providing easy **access to the town** for the **people living in the hinterland**. The **railway is a high order service** which enables people to travel well beyond the town.

Hierarchy of Goods

Carrick-on-Suir has a high **population** and occupies an **area** of more than **3 km²**. There are many people living in the hinterland who also avail of services in the town. The town has services including s**chools, Garda station, churches, fire stations**, and **tourist information offices**. It is also likely too that the number of services in the town will increase as the town is served by national routeways. **Services and jobs are available** to the people of the hinterland.

Note!

This Case Study is written in the format used to answer an exam question on central place, while using an OS map.

Range of Threshold of Services

Carrick-on-Suir has a relatively high population and it offers a wide variety of goods and services. These services vary **from low order services** such as **groceries** to **middle order services** such as **schools** at **S 404 221** and **S 411 223**. There are **only three other schools** on the map, which are most likely small **rural primary schools**. The schools in Carrick must therefore be large, as they are providing education to a very large hinterland. With a population of over 5,000 people, the town has the **potential for the development of high order goods** with a high threshold in the town.

4.5 Distribution and Density of Settlement

From studying the various factors that affect site and situation of settlements, we can **also determine** the **reasons for population density and distribution** in areas. Many **social and economic factors affect** where people choose to live. **Physical factors** must also be considered. **Lowland areas** with **fertile land** and **developed services** are **attractive for settlement,** whereas **harsh, steep and isolated upland areas** have **low population densities.**

The Distribution and Density of Settlement in Dungarvan

From examining the density of population in **Dungarvan** (see Fig. 4.30 on page 122), some areas appear to have **higher populations** than others. Population appears to be **lower in areas** with **poor physical characteristics.**

- **Low population density** is seen **north of northing 97.** This **decrease in population** is due to the **increase in altitude beyond this point.** The **poor quality of the soil** is also evident by the presence of an area of **coniferous forest at X 27 99.** Coniferous trees are often **planted in upland areas** with **poor soil** and are **not suitable for farming.**

- **High population density** in the region is highest in the **lowland areas** around the **mouth of the Colligan River.** This is as a result of the **low-lying land under 20 m,** which allows for **easy construction of buildings and communication** lines.

◀ **Fig. 4.23** Upland areas surrounding Dungarvan have low population densities compared to the lowlands.

Dungarvan is the **focus of routes** in the area, such as **N25** and the **regional routes (R675 and R672).** These routes helped to **promote services in the town,** which has a **higher population density per km²** than anywhere else on the map.

Section 4.6 Rural Settlement Patterns

In rural areas, **individual houses make up a settlement pattern**. There are **four types of rural settlement patterns** found in the countryside. These are:

- Nucleated settlement
- Linear settlement
- Dispersed settlement
- Absence of settlement.

Nucleated Settlement/Clustered Settlement

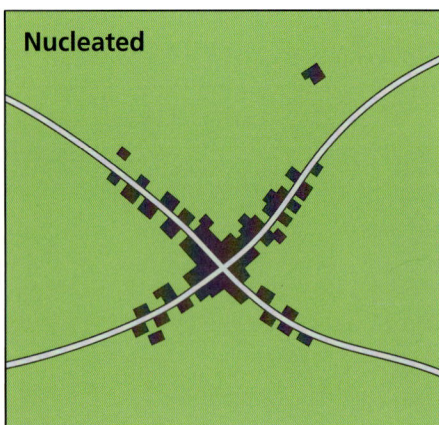

Nucleated settlement, also referred to as clustered settlement, consists of **houses located in groups**, often in **housing estates**, or at the **focal point of roads**, e.g. the **bridging point of rivers**. Businesses (e.g. shops and pubs) and services (e.g. schools and churches) are frequently located at such meeting points – often forming the nuclei of villages. Some older nucleated settlements **formed around old landlord estates. Older nucleated settlements** developed **close to castles or monasteries** which provided people with protection or charity. Some small nucleated settlements in the West of Ireland are **remnants of an ancient farming system** called **the Rundale system,** in which the farming families lived in small clusters.

Fig. 4.24 Nucleated settlement

Linear Settlement/Ribboned Settlement

Linear settlement, also referred to as ribboned settlement, consists of **houses built in a line along roads** due to ease of **access to communications**. Such settlements **became** very **common** in Ireland between the **1960s and 1990s,** as a number of factors combined to encourage this type of development.

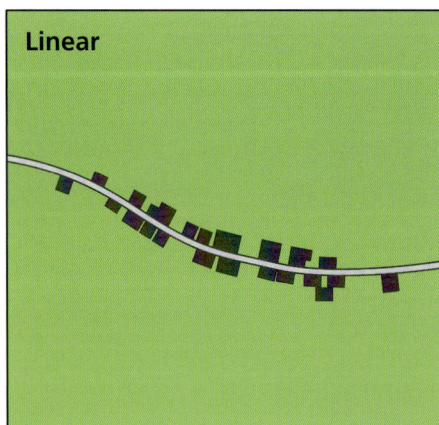

At this time, many roads were **connected with electricity and telephone lines** and also with **water and sewage mains**. People wished to **build houses where these services were widely available,** meaning houses with 'road frontage' became popular. Also, it was convenient for people to live along roads to towns and villages where more services and facilities are located. **Linear settlement** can also occur along coastlines, especially in **scenic areas** where people build houses along **seafronts** with scenic views.

Fig. 4.25 Linear settlement

Dispersed Settlement

Dispersed settlement refers to **'one-off' isolated dwellings** that are **dotted over a wide countryside area**. Dispersed settlements are typically **farmhouses** surrounded by their own farmland. Dispersed settlements are generally **located near local and third-class roads** or at the **end of long driveways**.

Prior to the **eighteenth century** there was an **open-field system** of farming called 'common land' on which all animals grazed, which was surrounded by a central settlement. After the **Agricultural Revolution** in the eighteenth century, **land ownership changed**. The former common land was **divided up and enclosed** by individual farmers who worked their own land. **Farmers built individual houses** on their own land, leading to dispersed settlement. These houses can be very **widely spaced** in the east and south of the country where farms are large.

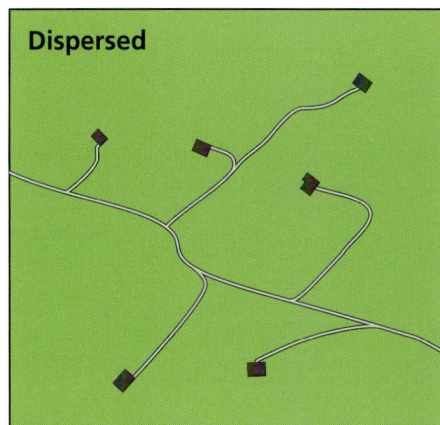

Dispersed

⌃ **Fig. 4.26** Dispersed settlement

Absence of Settlement

If there is no settlement, it generally means that the **area** is **unsuitable for settlement**. Examples of these areas are **bogs, marsh, highland areas** and areas **prone to flooding**. It can also occur due to outward migration, particularly along the **west coast of Ireland**. **Steep slopes** make the **building of houses** and **roads both difficult and expensive**. Settlement may also be absent from **flat low-lying floodplains**, which are **prone to flooding**.

GEO **DICTIONARY**

Nucleated settlement: houses located in groups, e.g. housing estates, focal point of roads and villages

Linear settlement: houses built in a line along roads or seafronts/scenic areas

Dispersed settlement: one-off, isolated dwellings dotted along the countryside

Absence of settlement: no evidence of settlement, usually due to areas being unsuitable, e.g. mountainous, bog, marsh, prone to flooding

Rundale system: the division of land into plots which were rented and farmed by a number of tenants

ACTIVE **LEARNING**

1. What are the benefits of building a house along a road?

2. What sort of roads typically lead to a dispersed settlement?

3. What physical factors may lead to an absence of settlement in an area?

4.7 Rural Planning

Rural planners in Ireland are given the responsibility of **whether to allow development** of the countryside areas within a county, while also **ensuring** that **uniqueness, biodiversity and heritage** are **not destroyed** in the process. One of the **biggest issues** facing rural planners in Ireland is the issue of **one-off housing**.

Rural Planning

While **rural depopulation** has occurred in Ireland for several generations, it is also true that since the **1960s, one-off housing** in rural areas has become **increasingly popular** as a result of **counter urbanisation**. Counter urbanisation occurs when people who **work** in **towns and cities** choose to **live in the countryside**. Therefore, they commute to the nearby town for work. This trend led to an **increase in linear settlement** along the **exit routes of towns** and **cities** in Ireland. Irish **planning authorities felt** that this was **unsustainable** as these areas have experienced **rapid population growth** and **demands on services**. Since the recession, one-off housing has declined while **planning laws aim to protect the rural landscape**.

> **Fig. 4.27** One-off housing is strictly controlled by rural planners.

County Development Plans

Each county council now produces a **County Development Plan** as a response to the unprecedented increase in housing during the Celtic Tiger era. These plans aim to **protect the distinctiveness** of rural areas and **reduce the impact of suburbanisation**. In order to do this, **strict planning laws** are included in all County Development Plans. As part of these plans, there is a **limit to the number of housing developments** allowed each year. In order to qualify for housing, there is a list of criteria which must be taken into account, e.g. being a **native of the county**, showing a **need for** housing and limitations on building heights and the building materials. The main concerns of the planning authorities are:

- The reduction in scenic quality of areas
- A constantly expanding commuter-belt because of a lack of jobs in rural areas
- The provision of adequate services to areas
- Traffic management and pollution of local water supplies due to unsatisfactory septic tanks.

These concerns are to the fore of all County Development Plans, along with the strategies on how to deal with these issues. These plans are revised and updated every five years and are of vital importance to managing development for current and future generations.

National Development Plans

The National Development Plan (NDP) 2007–13 and the introduction of the Commission for the Economic Development of Rural Areas (CEDRA) 2012 have both helped to develop planning strategies that will protect the rural environment of Ireland. The latest areas of NDP investment were:

- Preservation of scenic areas, development and maintenance of farmlands
- Social inclusion through the provision of improved rural amenities and services – especially for the inclusion of the elderly
- Improved infrastructure to link rural areas to urban centres
- Education and training schemes in rural areas.

ORDINARY LEVEL

Use Fig. 4.28 and Fig. 4.29 to answer these questions.

1. Examine the 1:50,000 Ordnance Survey map of Westport and legend accompanying this paper.

    (i) Name **three** different rural settlement patterns evident on the Ordnance Survey map **and** give a six-figure grid reference for the location of an example each.

    (ii) Explain each of the **three** rural settlement patterns named in part (i) above.

    (i)

3 settlement patterns @ 3m each	9m
3 six-figure grid references @ 3m/2m/2m	7m

    (ii)

8 SRPs @ 3m each	24m

    2016 Q12C 40M

2. Examine the 1:50,000 Ordnance Survey map and legend of Kenmare accompanying this paper.

    Explain **three** reasons why the town of Kenmare developed at this location, using evidence from the Ordnance Survey map to support each reason.

3 reasons @ 10m each	30m
For each reason: Map evidence: 1m Explanation: 3 SRPs @ 3m	

    2015 Q10C 30M

3. Examine the 1:50,000 Ordnance Survey map of Kenmare and legend accompanying this paper. Draw a sketch map of the area shown on the Ordnance Survey map.

    On it **show** and **name** the following:

    - The built-up area of Kenmare
    - **Four different** examples of historic settlement evident on the map.

Sketch outline Limits/frame: 1m Proportions: 2m (2/0) Overall impression: 2m	5m
Five items shown @ 3m each	15m
Five items named @ 2m each	10m

    2015 Q11A 30M

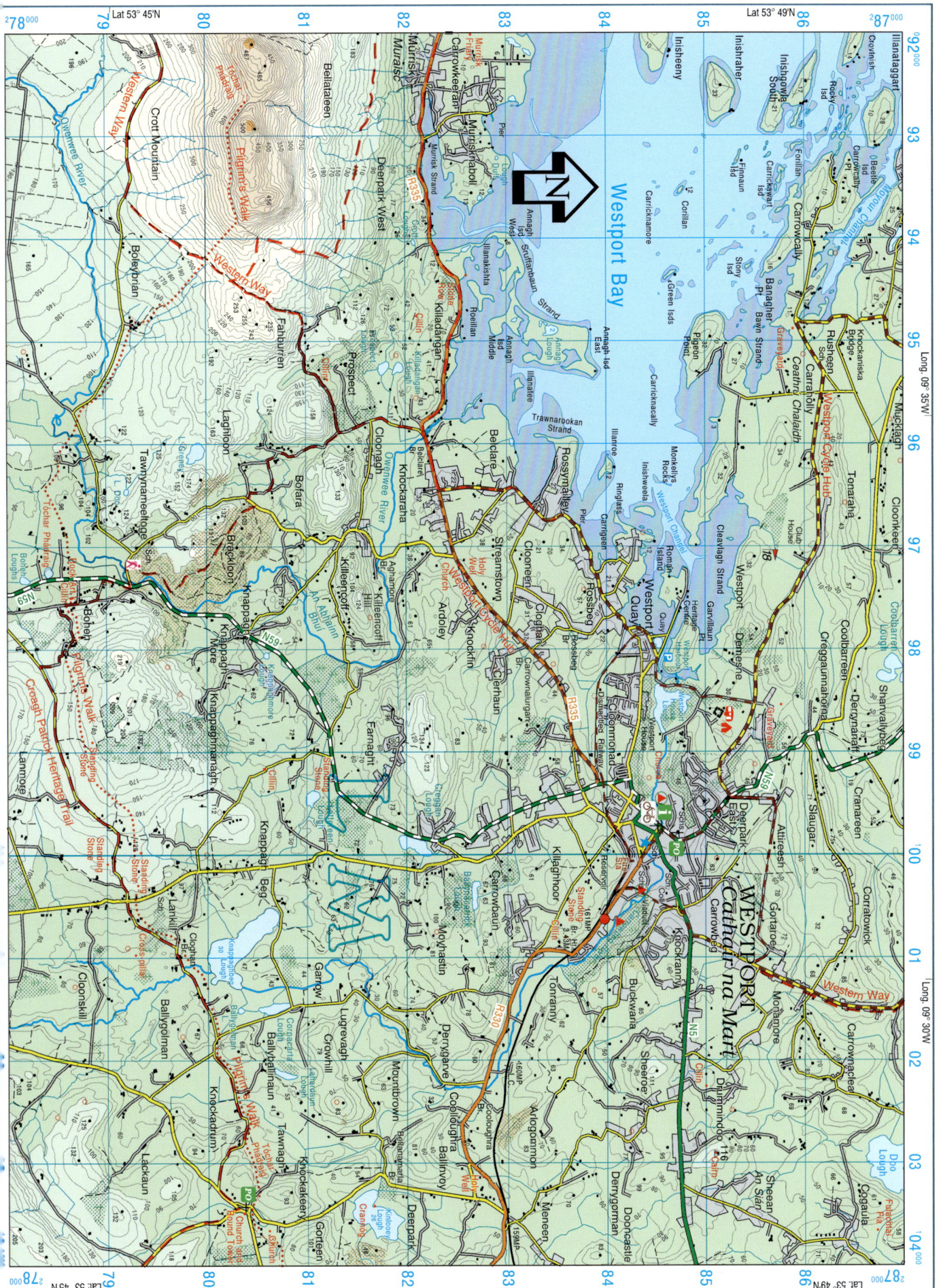

Fig. 4.28 OS map of Westport

Fig. 4.29 OS map of Kenmare

EXAM QUESTIONS

ORDINARY LEVEL

Use Fig. 4.30 and Fig. 4.31 to answer these questions.

4. Examine the 1:50,000 Ordnance Survey map of Dungarvan and legend accompanying this paper.

(i) Name and locate, using a six-figure grid reference, **three** examples of historic settlement evident on the Ordnance Survey map.

(ii) Describe and explain each of the examples of historic settlement named in part **(i)** above.

(i)

3 settlements named @ 2m each	6m
3 settlements located @ 2m each	6m

(ii)

Settlement 1 explanation: 2 SRPs @ 3m each	6m
Settlement 2 explanation: 2 SRPs @ 3m each	6m
Settlement 3 explanation: 2 SRPs @ 3m each	6m

2014 Q11B 30M

5. Examine the aerial photograph of Dungarvan accompanying this paper.
Using evidence from the aerial photograph, explain three reasons why the town of Dungarvan developed at its present location

Aerial photograph evidence	3m
Reason 1: 3 SRPs @ 3 marks each	9m
Reason 2: 3 SRPs @ 3 marks each	9m
Reason 3: 3 SRPs @ 3 marks each	9m

2014 Q12C 30M

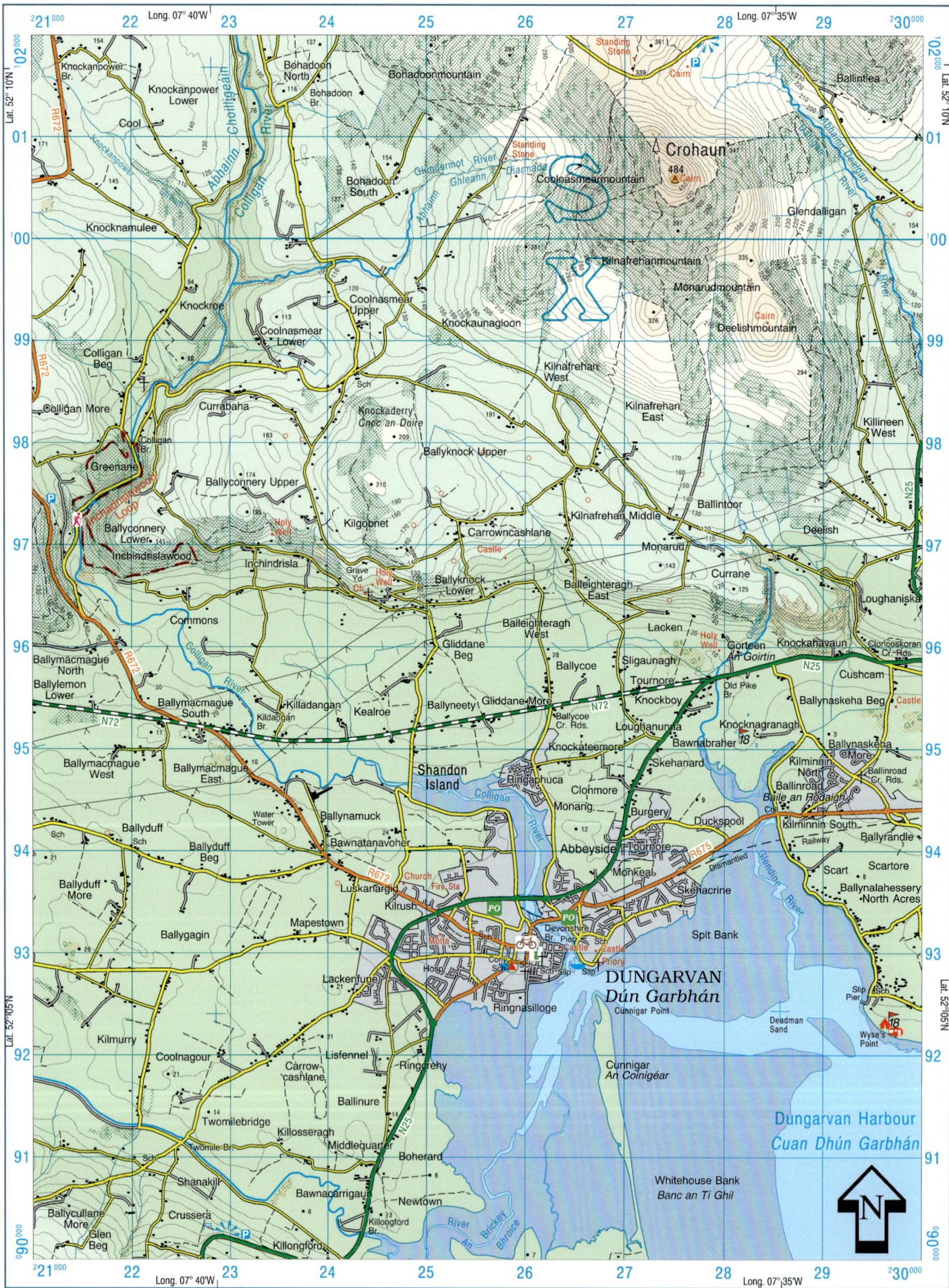

Fig. 4.30 OS map of Dungarvan

Fig. 4.31 Aerial photograph of Dungarvan

Use Fig. 4.29, Fig. 4.30 and Fig. 4.32 to answer these questions.

1. Examine the 1:50,000 Ordnance Survey map of Kenmare and legend accompanying this paper and answer each of the following questions.

    (i) Name **three different** phases of historical settlement evident on the Ordnance Survey map.

    (ii) Name and locate, using six-figure grid references, examples of each of the **three** phases of historical settlement named above.

    (iii) Explain briefly each of the three phases of historical settlements named above.

(i)	Three historical phases named: 3 @ 2m each	6m
(ii)	Examples of each phase named: 3 @ 2m each	6m
	Location/grid for each example 3 @ 2m each	6m
(iii)	Explanation of each phase: 3 @ 4m each (2m + 2m)	12m

2015 Q12C 30M

2. Explain the importance of hierarchy and hinterland in Central Place Theory.

Explanation: 15 SRPs @ 2m each	30m

2014 Q11C 30M

3. Examine the 1:50,000 Ordnance Survey map of Dungarvan and legend accompanying this paper. Explain **three** reasons why the area north of northing 97 is less attractive to human settlement, using evidence from the Ordnance Survey map to support each reason.

3 reasons @ 10m each For each reason: Reasons stated: 2m Map evidence: 2m Explanation: 3 SRPs @ 2m each	30m

2014 Q11B 30M

4. With reference to the 1:50,000 Ordnance Survey map of Enniscorthy accompanying this paper, describe and explain **three** rural settlement patterns evident on the map.

3 patterns @ 10m each For each pattern: Pattern named: 2m Map evidence: 2m Explanation: 3 SRPs @ 2m each	30m

2013 Q10B 30M

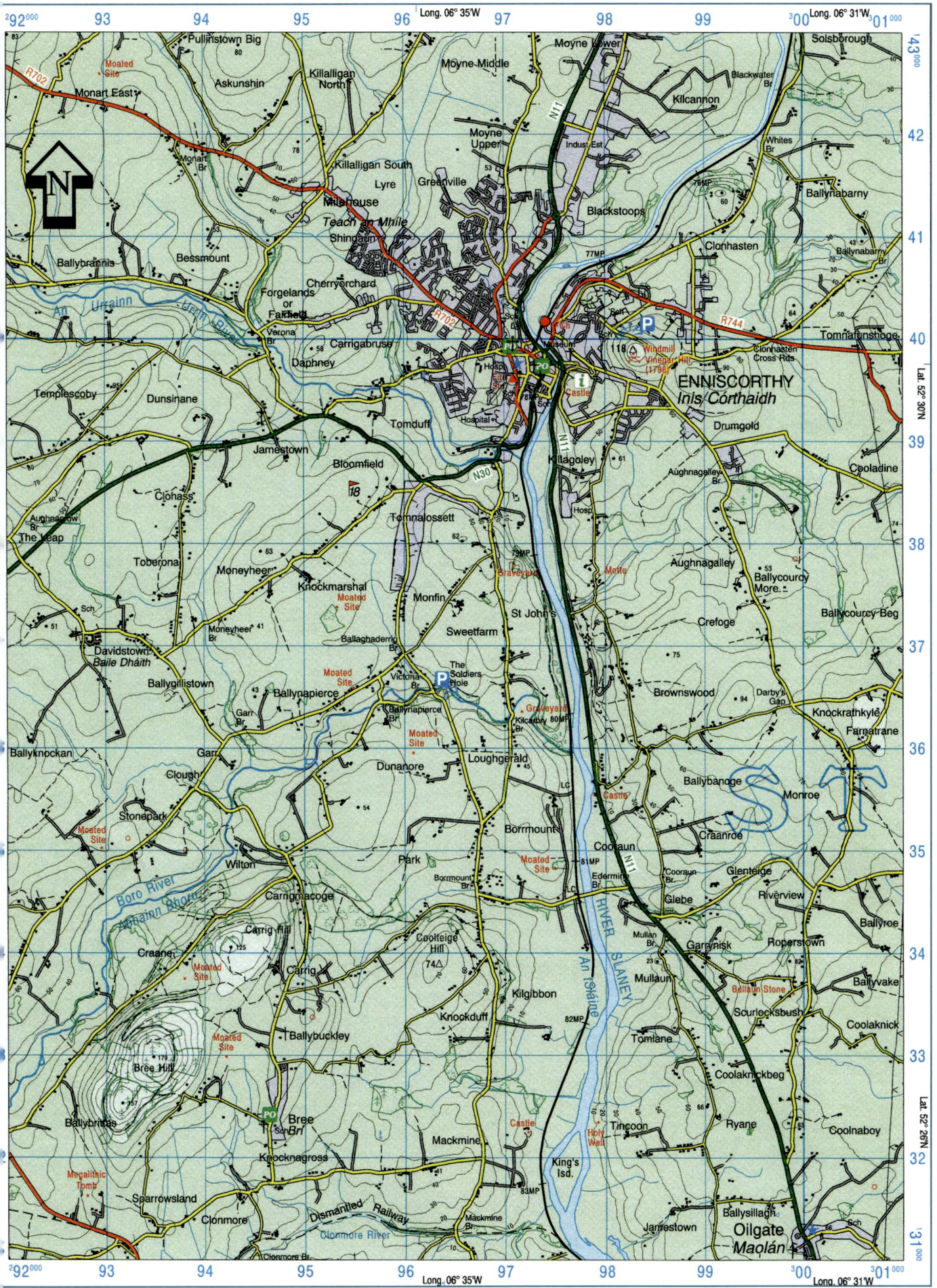

Fig. 4.32 OS map of Enniscorthy

EXAM QUESTIONS

HIGHER LEVEL

Use Fig. 4.33 and Fig. 4.35 to answer these questions.

5. Study the aerial photograph of Carrick-on-Shannon accompanying this paper.

Examine any **three** different functions of Carrick-on-Shannon, using evidence from the aerial photograph to support your answer.

3 functions @ 10 marks each For each function: Function named: 2m Location of evidence on the aerial photograph: 2m Explanation: 3 SRPs @ 2m each	30m

2012 Q11B 30M

6. Examine the 1:50,000 Ordnance Survey map of Dingle and legend accompanying this paper. Explain, using evidence from the map, why the area east of easting 44 and north of northing 03 has such a low population density.

OS map evidence	2m
Reason identified	2m
Explanation: 13 SRPs @ 2m each	26m

2011 Q11C 30M

Fig. 4.33 Aerial photograph of Carrick-on-Shannon

Fig. 4.34 OS map of Carrick-on-Suir

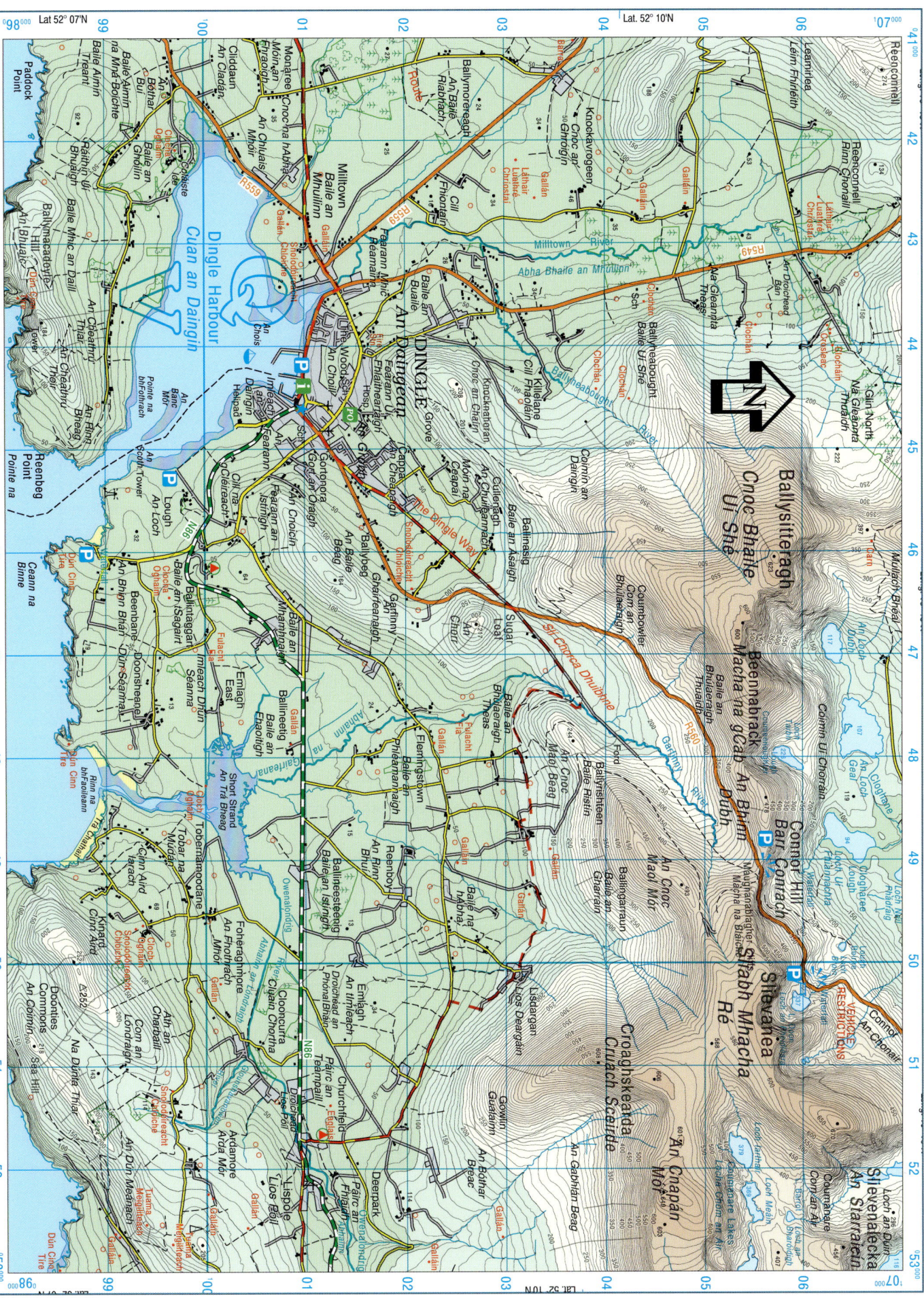

Fig. 4.35 OS map of Dingle

In this section, we will look at Q11C from the 2011 Higher Level paper, which asks the student to explain the reasons for the low population density in the north-eastern section of the map.

EXAM QUESTION

Examine the 1:50 000 Ordnance Survey map and legend of Dingle (Fig. 4.35 on page 129) accompanying this paper. Explain, using evidence from the map, why the area east of easting 44 and north of northing 03 has such a low population density.

Marking Scheme
OS map evidence @ 2m
Reason identified @ 2m
Explanation: 13 SRPs @ 2m each

From looking at the question, you are not given a set amount of reasons to give in your answer, nor are you limited to grid-reference evidence only. My advice is that you should try to find three reasons, as it allows you to divide your answer into three separate sections and you can apply the IDLE method of answering the question. These answers require you to think about what exactly makes the region unsuitable for land, as there is no such thing as a 'one answer fits all' for this topic. While the factors discussed are general reasons for an absence of settlement or low population density, it is up to you to find evidence on the map and explain why you think it is relevant.

SAMPLE ANSWER

From examining the Ordnance Survey map of Dingle, there are three main reasons for the low population density experienced in this area.

Reason 1

The upland relief and poor drainage make the area unattractive for settlement [2m]. The majority of the region is over 200 m above sea level, with some mountain peaks in access of 600 m, e.g. Ballysitteragh's peak of 623 m is seen at Q 461 057 [2m]. The closely packed contour lines, such as those seen in Q 45 06, indicate that the slopes in this area are very steep and would be very difficult and expensive to build houses on [2m].

Instead, humans would be far more attracted to settle in the lowland areas further south, where construction would be much easier [2m]. The upland region here would be much wetter due to relief rain, while the land is also exposed to winds, making it much colder [2m]. The lowland areas here might have been ideal for settlement but for the poor drainage evident from the marsh lakes at Q 47 06 and Q 48 06 [2m].

Reason 2

This area has an absence of communications, making it difficult to access and somewhat isolated [2m]. There is only one road, the R560, which passes through a valley carved out by Garfinny River [2m]. Settlements need communication links for day-to-day life, such as commuting to work or school, while developed transport links also allow for more efficient trade and access to markets [2m]. During the winter months, the R560 would be more prone to ice and snow, as temperatures would be lower in upland regions. This, combined with the steep profile of the road, would make journeys dangerous [2m]. Linear settlement typically develops along main roadways; however, there is an abrupt decline of settlement north of northing 03 as the road passes through a narrow valley which does not provide ideal sites for building [2m].

Reason 3

The soil in this area of the map is unproductive for agriculture [2m]. Ireland's first settlers were farmers who chose low-lying fertile soils to build their first settlements. Heavy relief rainfall in the upland areas means the soil is heavily leached and unproductive for agriculture [2m]. There is evidence of coniferous forestry at Q 44 06, which is typically planted in unproductive agricultural soil [2m]. In the areas with higher altitude, there are no forestry plantations as the land is too thin and temperatures are too cold. Therefore, the land is commercially useless and not suitable for settlement [2m]. On the steepest slopes, such as at Q 50 05, there is a potential hazard as mudslides and landslides could be triggered by heavy rainfall [2m].

The answer selects three specific reasons for the low population density in that area of the map. All of these reasons are linked by a single factor: the upland relief of the region. Evidence given from the map shows grid-referencing skills and also an awareness of the functions of settlement. Evidence from the map is also explained in a common-sense manner, which shows an ability to use evidence to form conclusions regarding the settlement.

Marks Awarded
OS map evidence @ 2m
Reason identified @ 2m
Explanation: Best 13 SRPs @ 2m each
Total 30/30

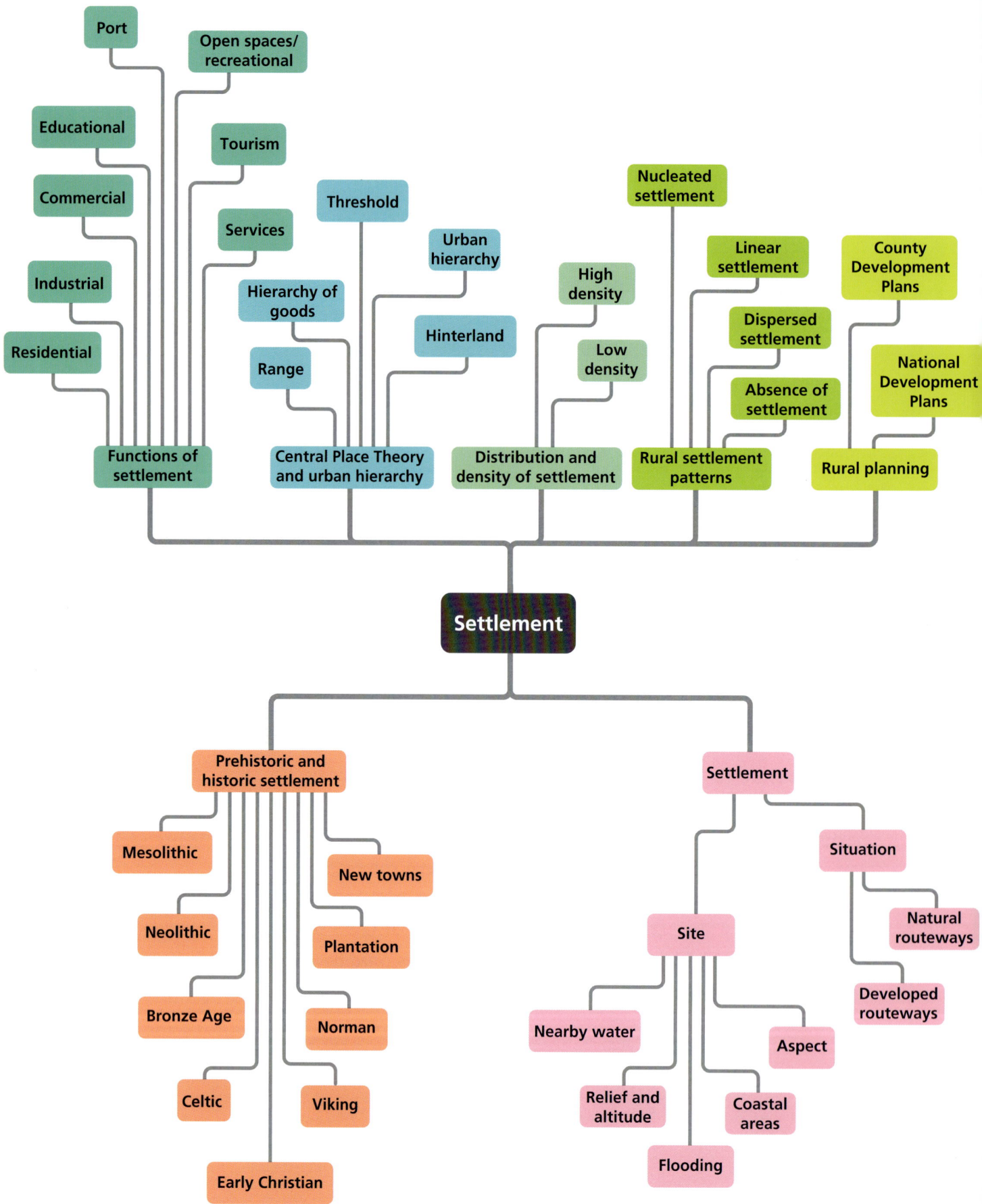

TOPIC MAP

Settlement

Functions of settlement
- Port
- Open spaces/recreational
- Educational
- Tourism
- Commercial
- Services
- Industrial
- Residential

Central Place Theory and urban hierarchy
- Threshold
- Hierarchy of goods
- Range

Distribution and density of settlement
- Urban hierarchy
- Hinterland
- High density
- Low density

Rural settlement patterns
- Nucleated settlement
- Linear settlement
- Dispersed settlement
- Absence of settlement

Rural planning
- County Development Plans
- National Development Plans

Prehistoric and historic settlement
- Mesolithic
- Neolithic
- Bronze Age
- Celtic
- Early Christian
- New towns
- Plantation
- Norman
- Viking

Settlement
- Site
  - Nearby water
  - Relief and altitude
  - Flooding
  - Coastal areas
  - Aspect
- Situation
  - Natural routeways
  - Developed routeways

CHAPTER 5

Urban Land Use and Planning

In Chapter 4, you learned how settlements develop and about the functions they provide.
In this chapter, we will look at the structures of urban settlements and how they have changed over time.
There is a particular focus on Dublin in this chapter, as it is the primate city of Ireland.

KEY WORDS 🔑

- Commercial
- Industrial
- Residential
- Transport
- Recreational
- Zoning/rezoning
- Central Business District
- Suburb
- Social stratification
- Open space
- Absence of community
- Concentric zone model
- Sector model
- Multiple nuclei model
- Zone of transition
- Dormitory town
- Greenbelt
- Commuter zone
- Urban renewal
- Urban redevelopment

LEARNING OUTCOMES 🧠

What you MUST know
- The different land uses in cities
- Urban land use theories: concentric zone model, sector model and multiple nuclei model
- Social stratification and its impacts on Dublin
- Changes in urban land use and the Dublin Docklands
- Land values in cities and how they vary
- Pressures on rural areas, caused by urban expansion

What you SHOULD know
- Urban land uses in Dublin City
- Multiple nuclei theory in Dublin

What is USEFUL to know
- Additional information from relevant Case Studies
- Information on urban development studied in the regional Geography section can be used as additional Case Studies, where relevant

Introduction

By 2030, more than 60 per cent of the world's population will live in urban areas, with most of the world's population growth over the next 15 years being absorbed by cities and towns in developing countries. This increasing pressure on land use has led to increased difficulty in urban planning and has put further strain on local and national government.

Fig. 5.1 Central Business Districts have multi-storey buildings to maximise space.

5.1 Urban Land Use

Modern cities are divided into districts used for specific needs and activities. These typical districts are:

- Commercial
- Industrial
- Residential
- Transport
- Recreational.

Sometimes local authorities may decide to **rezone** land within cities, thereby changing its original land use. Examples include the Dublin Docklands or the Georgian houses that are now used for offices.

In order to **prevent free-for-all developments** within a city, local authorities must devise **long-term plans** that **control the zoning of land** for specific **social and economic activities**. *Zoning* of land means that local authorities have designated the land for specific use, e.g. land can be zoned for residential use.

Effective planning and zoning ensures that **cities develop in a logical manner**. For example, effective zoning should prevent a sewage treatment facility being built in residential areas.

Examples of logical zoning would be:

- The building of **residential areas close to recreational areas** such as parks and playgrounds
- The building of **industrial areas** with high volumes of traffic near to well-developed transport links.

Commercial

Commercial land use in cities refers to **retail shops, offices, banks and a wide range of personal services**, e.g. beauticians and hairdressers. The most important commercial zone in any urban area is the **Central Business District (CBD)**, which occupies the central position of the city/town.

The CBD can be identified by **general characteristics**:

- The CBD is typically located in the **centre of the urban area** where all **major roads converge**.

- **Space is limited** in the CBD, meaning **buildings are mainly multi-storey**. Due to the high demand for office/ business space, rents are high.

- Typically, businesses with a **high customer threshold** locate here, as it is easily accessible.

- The commercial areas of modern cities can be **stretched out along streets and roads** called **commercial ribbons**. These commercial ribbons can contain **commercial centres**, such as **shopping centres**. Shopping centres are **multi-retail outlets** that usually locate on the outskirts of urban areas where **land prices are cheaper** and there is room for parking, facilities and future expansion.

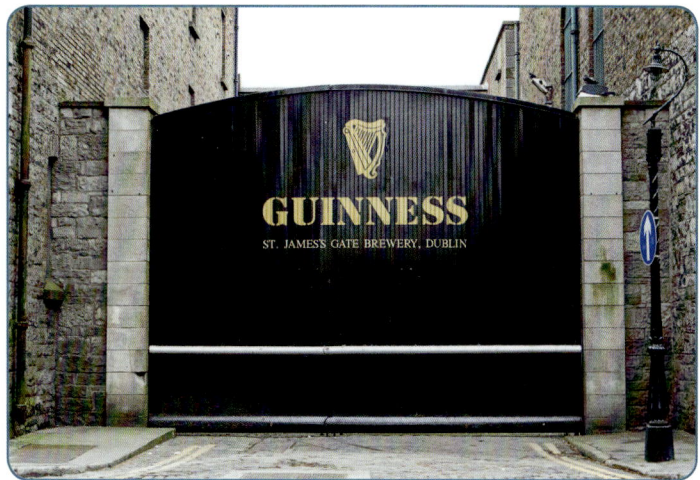

Fig. 5.2 The Guinness Brewery in St James's Gate is an example of a traditional inner city industry.

In the past, industries **located close to the CBD** near **railway links and canals**. However, modern industries now locate in industrial estates on the **outskirts of towns** where **land prices are cheaper** and there is easy access.

Industrial

From the beginning of the **Industrial Revolution in 1750**, factories were built **close to railway links and canals**. These factories became the **centre of economic activity** in cities, with **residential areas being built around them**, close enough for workers to walk to work. Today most **modern industries** locate on the **perimeters of cities**, where **land is cheaper**, where **ring roads and motorways** provide easy access and where there is **room for expansion**. Heavy industries such as **oil refineries, petrochemicals, steelworks** and **cement plants** locate in parts of the city where **bulky goods can be exported** and **raw materials** can be **imported**, e.g. **Aughinish Alumina** is located along the Shannon Estuary.

Fig. 5.3 Aughinish Alumina is located on the outskirts of Limerick City.

Large industries that move from the city centre leave behind **brownfield sites**, which are targeted by urban planners for **urban redevelopment**. Modern industrial estates also offer the opportunity to **create industrial links** with other industries.

Residential

As **population densities are high** in cities and towns, **residential** land use is **one of the largest functions** in an urban area. Residential housing **varies greatly in density** throughout urban areas due to two main contributing factors:

- Cost of land
- Age of area.

GEO DICTIONARY

Brownfield site: land that was previously used for industrial activity, which has now been abandoned for more favourable locations elsewhere in the city

● **Fig. 5.4** Inner city Dublin has experienced decay.

GEO DICTIONARY

Urban fringes: the outer boundaries of a city

Areas **close to the city centre** have the **highest land values**; therefore, the housing density also increases. High-density housing such as **multi-storey apartments** and **terraced housing** is built close to the CBD to **maximise land use**. Low-density **housing** tends to be located further from the city centre, in the **suburbs and urban fringes** where **land prices are lower**. These houses are mainly **detached or semi-detached** and are more spacious. As cities expand outwards into the surrounding land, it makes sense that **housing close to the city centre is older**, while newer residential areas are located close to the urban fringes.

Therefore, the **further you move from the city**, the **younger the residential areas** will be. Initially, residential areas were built close to the CBD to allow people to commute to work in the city's industries. However, from the **1950s onwards, car ownership** became **more commonplace**, which allowed workers to **commute longer distances**. As a result, **residents began to live in areas further from the congested city centre**, creating **commuter zones** along the edges of cities.

Transport

Transport land-use zones **consist of roads, railway lines, airports, navigable rivers/canals, car parks, railway stations and bus lanes.** Transport links occupy **large amounts of space** in cities but are necessary, as **well-developed transport** allows for the **efficient movement of people** in and out of a city. Many European cities **originated during medieval times**, meaning many of the streets close to these city centres are narrow, e.g. **Galway City**. As a result, many cities have **ring roads** around them to **avoid congestion**. More modern cities, such as those in the US, have much wider streets that are capable of accommodating **higher volumes of traffic**.

● **Fig. 5.5** Transport links in Dublin

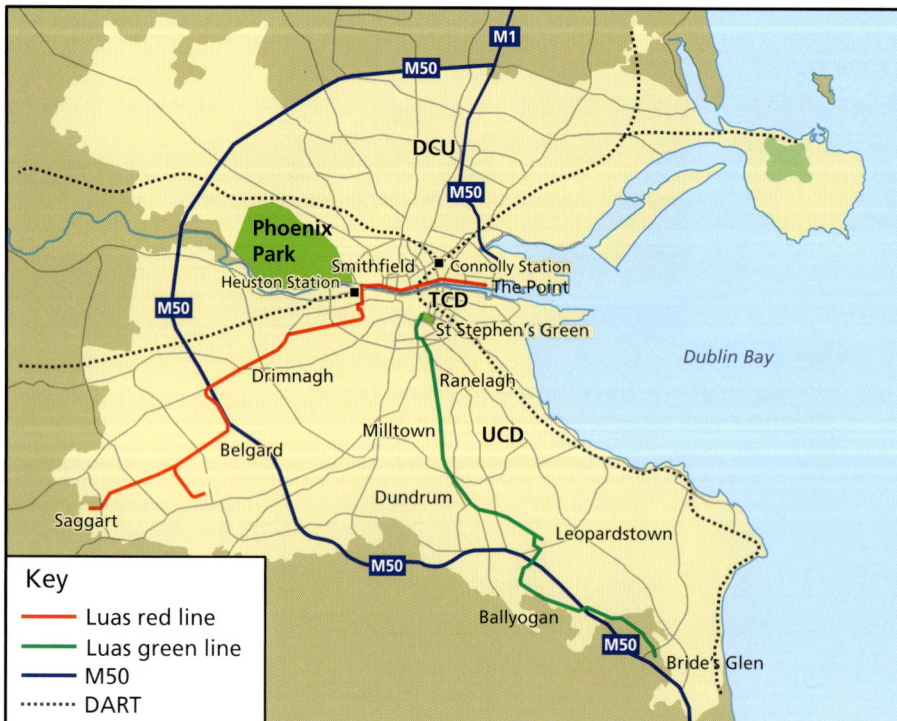

Key
— Luas red line
— Luas green line
— M50
······ DART

Recreational

Recreational areas are a **vital land use** in all urban areas for the health and wellbeing of residents. Today a **proportion of land used** in all development plans of cities must be used for **recreational facilities**. These facilities include **parks**, smaller greens, woodlands, walkways, sports fields, **playgrounds** and ornamental gardens. These areas are referred to as 'greenbelts' and they cannot be rezoned for any other use. **Phoenix Park** in Dublin is one of the **largest urban parks** in Europe at just over 7 km². Central Park in New York is another example of an important recreational park.

GEO DICTIONARY

Greenbelts: an area of land surrounding a city in which building is restricted

ACTIVE LEARNING

1. Explain how the location of industrial land use has changed in cities since the beginning of the Industrial Revolution.
2. Where would commercial land uses be expected to locate in cities?
3. How has residential land use changed over the past 50 years?

◀ **Fig. 5.6** Aerial view of Central Park

CASE STUDY 📁

Land Use Zones in Dublin City

CBD

Dublin's **CBD** is concentrated around **Grafton Street, O'Connell Street and Henry Street**, as they contain the majority of the city's retail businesses and services. **Rents** in the **CBD** currently average **€520 per m²** for office space, due to **high demand**. The CBD is made up of **multi-storey buildings**, with **space maximised** to the point that even **basements are used** for extra shop space. **Insurance companies and offices** are located on the **upper floors** of these buildings, where **rents are more affordable**. Due to urban redevelopments, Dublin's CBD has extended to the Docklands with the **International Financial Services Centre** (IFSC), restaurants and hotels locating along the River Liffey.

▲ **Fig. 5.7** Grafton Street, Dublin

Industrial Area

Some of Dublin's older, more **traditional industries** remain in the **city centre**, e.g. the **Guinness Brewery** at St James's Gate. However, the **majority of industries** moved away from the city centre to **newly built industrial estates** along the **urban fringes**. They did so to **avail of cheaper land, space for future development** and the **modern transport links** that service the estates, e.g. the **M50**. These motorways allow for the **quick and efficient distribution of goods** throughout the country, which also reduces costs and travel time.

Residential Land Use

Social stratification occurs among Dublin's residential areas. Many **middle- and higher-income earners** live in the **east of the city** near the coast (e.g. **Blackrock, Dalkey, Sandymount, Clontarf** and **Portmarnock**) or north of the city in areas such as Swords. **Lower-income workers** tend to locate along the west of the city (e.g. Tallaght, Clondalkin, Lucan, Blanchardstown and Ballymun). However, it is important to note that there are obvious exceptions to this on both sides of the divide.

As a result of **increasing housing prices** during the **Celtic Tiger**, many young workers chose to live in **more affordable areas** along the **urban fringes**. As a result, Dublin's **commuter belt expanded** greatly during this time, with many workers choosing to **live in towns and villages** of counties in the Greater Dublin Area. In order to facilitate the large number of people living in these **dormitory towns**, shopping centres and other **services and facilities have developed**.

Open Space

In order for people to **escape the stresses of daily life**, a number of small open spaces are dotted throughout the city. Large open spaces are located close to the city centre, e.g. **Phoenix Park and St Stephen's Green**. These greenbelt areas are maintained by the local council. These spaces provide **respite from the built-up areas** of the city and offer people a place to relax and exercise.

Ornamental gardens also exist close to the city centre and are remnants of walled gardens formerly owned by the wealthy landlords during the eighteenth and nineteenth centuries. An example is **Merrion Square**.

◀ **Fig. 5.8** St Stephen's Green, Dublin

5.2 Urban Land Use Theories

In order to explain the layout of the world's cities, geographers have developed different models to **show how different land uses are located within different areas or zones**. In this section, we will look at the three main theories of urban land use:

- **Concentric zone model**, devised by Ernest Burgess in 1925
- **Sector model**, devised by Homer Hoyt in 1939
- **Multiple nuclei model**, devised by Chauncy Harris and Edward Ullman in 1945.

Theory 1: Concentric Zone Model

Ernest Burgess was an American sociologist who devised the concentric zone model in 1925. His theory was **one of the earliest theoretical models** to explain the **social structures of urban areas**. His theory aimed to explain how **social groups are distributed** and land is used in different parts of urban areas. He **based** his theory **on the city of Chicago** and observed that **land use was organised into a series of concentric circles** around the Central Business District (CBD).

Burgess's theory is based on the idea that **land values are highest at the city centre** of a town or city. Burgess highlighted that the **outer fringe of the CBD is constantly changing** and expanding. As it expands, the land at its fringe is redeveloped for use in the CBD. Burgess referred to this area as the **zone of transition**.

It is important to note that, at the time, **society was particularly class-conscious**, with **residential zones divided strictly according to income and class**. Two particular observations made by Burgess were that:

- **Socio-economic status increased** with **distance from the city** centre, as the wealthy lived away from the city centre in suburbs
- The **density of housing is highest closer to the city centre** and decreases with distance from the CBD.

In total, Burgess identifies **five concentric zones** of land use in his theory:

- **Zone one:** This is the CBD and the **commercial heart of the city**. **Buildings** here are **tall and land is expensive**, leading to a higher density of buildings as all available space is utilised to its maximum potential.
- **Zone two:** This is known as the **zone of transition** and has a **mix of residential and commercial uses**. Although there is some industry here, it mainly **consists of high-density and low-quality housing**. Many of these **houses** are **filled by migrants** who avail of cheaper rent prices.
- **Zone three:** This zone is dominated by **lower-income residential housing**. **Working class people** live in this zone, which mainly comprises

Fig. 5.9 Concentric zone model

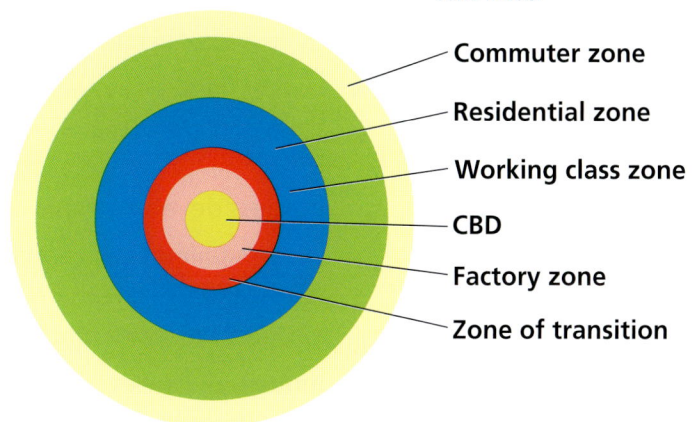

- Commuter zone
- Residential zone
- Working class zone
- CBD
- Factory zone
- Zone of transition

GEO DICTIONARY

Zone of transition: an area surrounding the CBD of a city, where functions and land uses regularly change

terraced housing. These residents are better off than those who live in zone of transition. Population **densities are high** in zone three, with many of the people here working in zone two.

- **Zone Four:** This is a **middle-class residential zone** comprising **detached or semi-detached houses** with their own gardens. The residents here are middle to higher class.

- **Zone Five:** This zone is a **commuter zone** made up of **towns and villages on the outskirts** of the city. These are **high-class residential areas**, with many of the residents of this zone travelling to the CBD for work.

Limitations of Burgess's Model

- The Burgess model is **old and outdated** and is not relevant to many of today's cities. It was **based on the cities of 1920s America**, where many **migrants had settled in the poorer inner city** areas. This had led to **social stratification**, whereby people with similar incomes settled in the same areas, therefore **dividing the city according to class**.

- Furthermore, an **increase in car ownership**, along with **advances in transport** mean that **many people now live outside of the city** and then commute to work. This way of living was **not considered when Burgess developed this theory**.

- Burgess **failed to take into account the impact that physical landscape** has on urban development. In real life, rivers, hills and valleys all affect the development of land.

- **Industrial estates, business parks and shopping centres did not exist** when Burgess developed his model, but have since become important features of modern urban development.

- The **wealth of urban dwellers does not always increase with distance from city centres**. Redevelopment can mean that inner city areas are renovated into expensive apartments, while low-income local authority housing estates can be found on the urban fringes of cities.

Theory 2: Sector Model

Homer Hoyt developed this model in 1939 after studying **rents paid for housing** by people in many cities. He believed that, by mapping rent values, a pattern of different types of land use could be seen in urban areas. Hoyt's model was **based on Burgess's model**; however, Hoyt also took into account the **impact of transport links** of land use. Hoyt's theory shows that **cities develop along major transport routes** that extend out from the city, such as roads, railway lines and canals. As a result of this, Hoyt's model shows that **towns have grown in sectors or wedges** that radiate out from the CBD, with **each sector reflecting a different zone of land use** and income.

As with Burgess's theory, **income and status divided the society of cities** at the time, meaning people of **different**

Fig. 5.10 Sector model

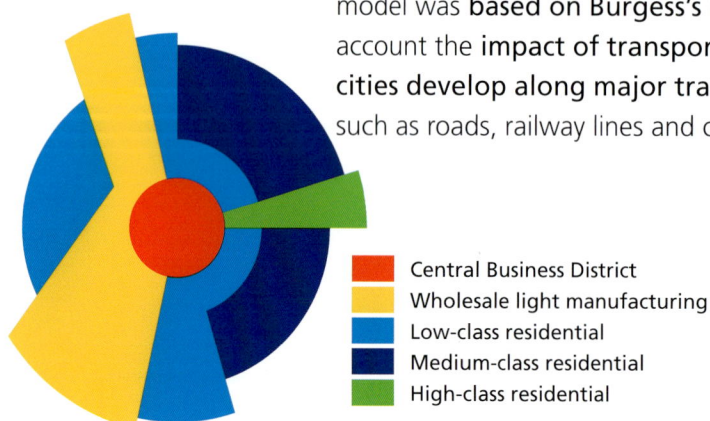

- Central Business District
- Wholesale light manufacturing
- Low-class residential
- Medium-class residential
- High-class residential

incomes did not live close to or mix with each other socially. This is referred to as **social stratification**. Like Burgess, Hoyt divided cities into five zones of land use.

- **Zone One:** This zone consists of the CBD and is the **commercial heart of the city**. Land **values** and density of buildings are **highest in the CBD**.

- **Zone Two:** This zone **follows railway lines or navigable waterways** such as canals. This sector contains **factories and manufacturing land use**, as the availability of railway or canals may lead to the **construction of warehouses and industrial areas** along the route. **Low-quality housing developments** are built here and may be confined to one side of the town, usually close to the industrial area.

- **Zone Three:** This zone contains **mainly low-income housing**, which is occupied by **slightly wealthier people**. Many of these residents **work in the industries of zone two**. Zone three has **high levels of noise and air pollution** from traffic and nearby industries.

- **Zone Four:** This is a zone of **middle-income residential housing** and is located on the side of the town that is **away from the poor areas**, due to social stratification.

- **Zone Five:** This sector consists of **high-income residents** and is the **most desirable part of the city** as it is the **furthest distance from factories and manufacturing** activity. Zone five can **extend a long distance** for the **rich inhabitants** who can afford to **commute relatively long distances** to work.

In **1964**, Hoyt **altered his model** to take into account the **greater levels of car ownership** by stating that commuter villages outside of the city have the highest rents.

Limitations of Hoyt's Theory

- Geographers feel that Hoyt's model is **too generalised and unrealistic** for modern-day cities. While Hoyt used 142 cities in devising his theory (compared to Burgess, who used just one city), the theory is outdated.

- Hoyt **believed that residential areas would remain segregated** due to their income levels. However, today the renovation of older inner city buildings to include modern apartments with high rents proves this belief to be incorrect.

- Another limitation is that Hoyt **studied US cities only**, meaning he did not take into consideration the layout of European cities.

Theory 3: Multiple Nuclei Model

The multiple nuclei model was developed by Chauncy Harris and Edward Ullman in 1945, as they suggested that **modern cities have a much more complex structure** than those outlined by either Burgess or Hoyt. They suggest that urban areas grow up around **multiple business districts** (multiple nuclei), **rather than around a single CBD**.

Harris and Ullman believed that it was possible to have **more than one business district** in an urban area, and that **certain activities attract each**

ACTIVE **LEARNING**

1. Describe the five different zones outlined by Burgess in the concentric zone model.

2. What are the limitations of Burgess's theory?

3. Describe the sector model.

4. What is the main difference between multiple nuclei theory and the two theories which came before it?

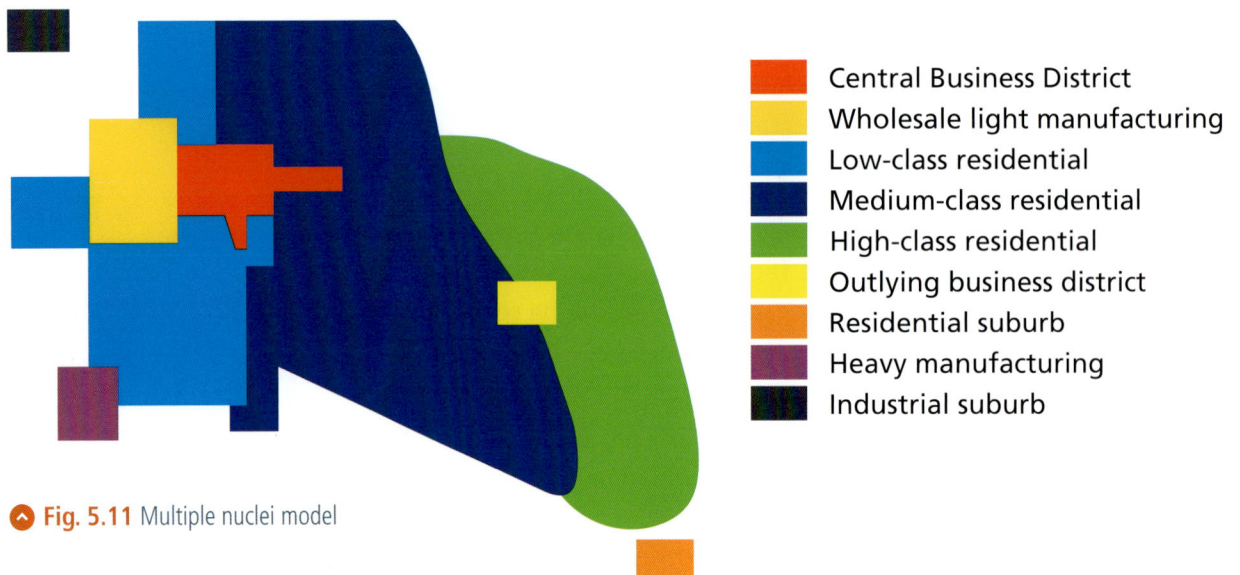

Central Business District
Wholesale light manufacturing
Low-class residential
Medium-class residential
High-class residential
Outlying business district
Residential suburb
Heavy manufacturing
Industrial suburb

Fig. 5.11 Multiple nuclei model

other. For example, many **factories locate together in an industrial estate** or **near a port**, while business districts may develop alongside a residential area. Similarly, **other activities repel each other**, e.g. **industrial areas repel residential areas**.

Therefore, the theory suggests that **urban areas can have more than one business district**, with each business centre attracting growth and becoming the focus for further development.

- The theory suggests that the **CBD is located in the city centre**, where access is good. However, as the city grows, other **districts grow to meet the different functions** and economic needs of the city's population.

- The location of **each type of land use reflects its economic need**, e.g. **heavy industry locates near a port**, **high-income housing** develops on or **close to a scenic site**, while **commercial retail** tends to locate **along busy route centres**.

- These **nuclei attract growth** as activities of a similar kind attract each other. For example, **manufacturing industries** will be **attracted to industrial estates** located on the **outskirts of the city** in the hopes of forming links with other industries there.

- **Social stratification is also evident** in this theory, with **separate lower-, middle- and upper-class areas. Higher-class residential areas** are located **away from heavy manufacturing**, with business and commercial districts nearby.

Limitations of the Multiple Nuclei Model

The multiple nuclei theory **does not fit all towns and cities perfectly**, as there are many factors that can alter the characteristics of urban areas in different parts of the world. However, **many large urban areas** and conurbations do **fit into this model (e.g. Dublin City)**, which we will examine in detail in the next section.

Multiple Nuclei Theory in Dublin

As already mentioned, **Dublin fits into the multiple nuclei theory** in several ways. Over the **past number of decades**, there has been much **movement and change** to the **industrial, residential and commercial areas** of Dublin's landscape.

Central Business District

Dublin's CBD stretches across the main shopping areas of **Grafton Street to O'Connell Street** and **Henry Street**, with commercial areas such as **banks and insurance offices** located at **Dame Street and College Green**. The city centre is accessible, since **all major transport routes** meet here. Dublin's CBD is the main **commercial and financial centre** of the entire Greater Dublin Area. The **International Financial Services Centre (IFSC)** is located along the **redeveloped Docklands**. Lower-class residential areas are located close to the CBD.

Multiple Nuclei

The Dublin region has **multiple nuclei** which have developed as the **city expanded into nearby towns and villages**, each with their **own business districts** and **retail areas**. Towns on the outskirts of Dublin had their own **business districts** and **retail areas** before they were **absorbed as the city expanded**, e.g. **Swords, Dundrum and Lucan**. **New towns** such as **Adamstown, Tallaght and Blanchardstown** were built with their own **business districts and services for residents living in the area**. These **nuclei** are now **self-sufficient** with a combination of **residential, economic, industrial and social services** and facilities.

> **Fig. 5.12** Urban land use in Dublin

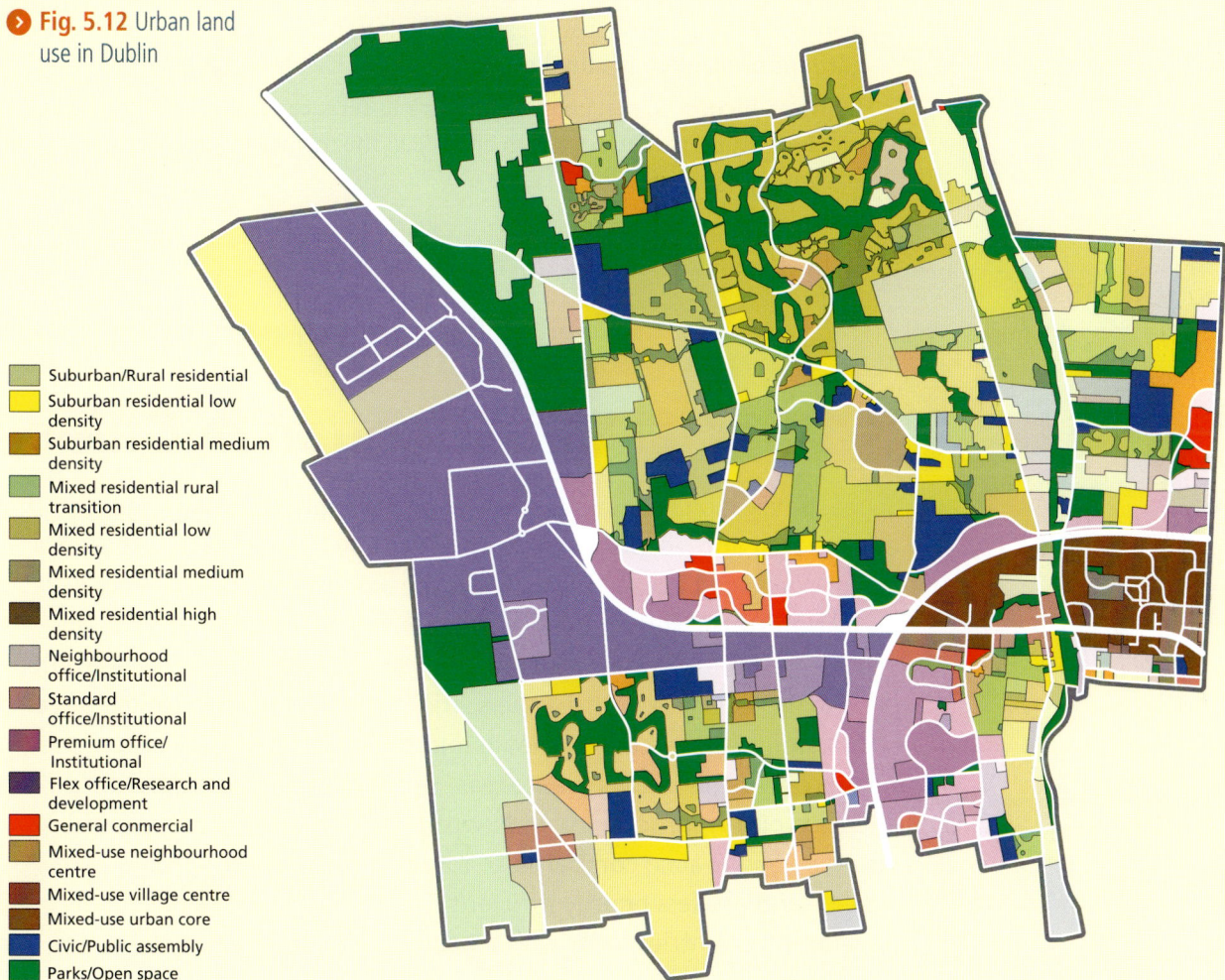

Legend:
- Suburban/Rural residential
- Suburban residential low density
- Suburban residential medium density
- Mixed residential rural transition
- Mixed residential low density
- Mixed residential medium density
- Mixed residential high density
- Neighbourhood office/Institutional
- Standard office/Institutional
- Premium office/ Institutional
- Flex office/Research and development
- General commercial
- Mixed-use neighbourhood centre
- Mixed-use village centre
- Mixed-use urban core
- Civic/Public assembly
- Parks/Open space

Location of Services

According to the theory, similar activities attract each other. This is evident in Dublin, which has distinct economic districts:

- **Several medical consultants** have located along **Fitzwilliam Square**, because of its **proximity to the city's hospitals**.
- **Manufacturers** are attracted to the same areas, which can be **seen along Dublin Port** and in industrial estates along the **M50, e.g. Sandyford Industrial Estate** on the south side of the city and **Airside Industrial Estate** on the north side of the city. These industrial estates have developed along the **outskirts** where they can take **advantage of cheaper land** and **property prices**.

Social Stratification

The **multiple nuclei theory** states that **social stratification** exists in **modern cities**, with **separate lower-, middle- and upper-class** areas developing. Social stratification occurs in Dublin, as residential areas can be divided into **two general zones** by dividing the city into east and west. In general terms, residents of the **east of Dublin** have a **higher level of income** than the residents of the west, who have a **low to middle income**.

Differences in the types of housing in different parts of Dublin City can reflect social stratification:

- Houses in **higher-income areas** of the city are typically **detached with large gardens**, e.g. Foxrock.
- In **middle-income areas**, houses are **detached or semi-detached** and **grouped together** in housing estates. Typically, these houses have **small gardens or large communal green areas**, e.g. Deansgrange.
- In **lower-income areas**, people often live in **terraced houses or apartment blocks** with no gardens or green areas, e.g. the former tower blocks in Ballymun.

Note!

Social stratification in Dublin is discussed in more detail in the next section.

5.3 Social Stratification in Cities

Social stratification describes the tendency of **people of similar age, educational and economic backgrounds to live in the same areas of a city**. It is repeatedly seen in cities across the world that people of a **similar education status and earning power** live in similar areas of the city. It is because of this that certain **parts of cities are considered more desirable** or are more sought-after than others. This is generally reflected in the **price of housing** in these areas. Homes in **middle- and upper-class areas** have **higher prices than lower-class areas**. **Housing** in upper- and middle-class areas is **typically larger and made with higher-quality materials** such as insulation and heating **compared to lower-class housing**, which is typically **smaller and are less energy efficient**. Social stratification is evident in **developing countries** today with the presence of **shanty towns/favelas**.

GEO DICTIONARY

Favelas: makeshift shelters used by the city's poor for shelter

Social Stratification in Dublin

As already mentioned, social stratification is **evident in Dublin**, which can be divided into two very **broad, generalised zones** by dividing the city into east and west. In general, the **wealthiest people of Dublin** live to the east of this line, in **middle-class and upper-class areas**. West of this line, residential areas are **generally** either **working class or middle class**. The inner city areas are mainly working class. **Ballymun**, which is located on the **edge of the city** , is also a working-class area.

The Celtic Tiger era changed the **dynamic of social stratification** somewhat, as **increased wealth led to some working-class** areas becoming **middle class**. Working-class children got the **opportunity to attend third-level education** and became **middle class**. As a result, many **former council-owned residential developments** are now privately owned. However, access to **third-level education** in Ireland is becoming **more expensive** and can be used as an **indicator of socio-economic stratification**. Children from **middle- and upper-class families** are seven times **more likely to go on to third-level education** than children from **less wealthy backgrounds**. The **Dublin Docklands** were once considered a **working-class area**, but are now a **mixture of both working-class and middle-class** housing as a result of urban renewal.

Age-Based Social Stratification

Social stratification can also be **age-based**, as people of **similar age groups** live in **certain areas of the city**. An example of this is seen in the **distribution of college students** in cities, with large student populations living in rented accommodation close to **colleges and universities**. Newer housing estates on the **urban fringes** are usually sold to **first-time buyers** and **young couples** with children, e.g. Tallaght. More elderly residents are **usually found in older parts** of urban areas **(e.g. Terenure)**.

A Five-Class Model

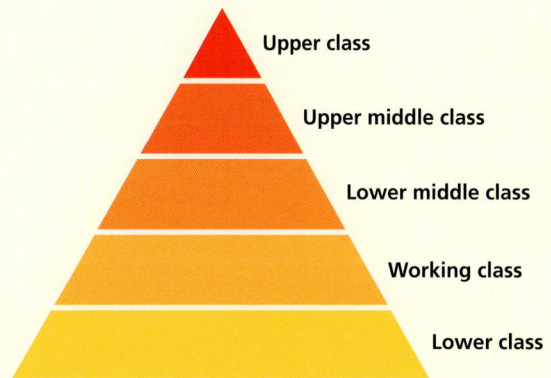

⌃ **Fig. 5.13** Model of social stratification

ACTIVE LEARNING

1. Why does social stratification occur?
2. Describe how social stratification has developed in Dublin.

5.4 Changes in Land Use and Planning Issues

GEO DICTIONARY

Urban renewal: the refurbishment or updating of an area without changing its original function

As you learned in Chapter 4, as an **urban area grows**, its **functions may change**. This leads to changes in how land in the area is used, e.g. former residential areas can be converted into industrial areas. Greater **demands for services** can lead to **industrial and commercial development**, which **spreads into residential areas**, replacing older housing with offices and shops.

Older parts of the city decay over time as **older factories are closed** in favour of more modern facilities in **industrial estates on the outskirts** of urban areas. These **purpose-built industrial estates** are also **linked to modern transport** links such as motorways. **Port** areas also **go into decline** as **modern ships** are much **larger** and can **no longer** be **accommodated** in **older port facilities**. Therefore, **newer port facilities** are built **further downstream** or along the coast where more **modern dockyards are built**. This leads to **unemployment in inner city** areas, causing many people to move out of their homes.

As a result of this, **homes and factories** become **derelict** and are often used by **squatters for shelter**. Old **derelict factories** are referred to as **brownfield sites**, due to the rusting of their **old machinery** and **galvanised roofs**. These derelict sites create a **negative impression** of an area, leading it to becoming run down. The solution to this decay is **urban renewal/ regeneration**, which changes or **modernises** the **land use** of the area.

CASE STUDY 📁

Dublin Docklands

History

Note!
This Case Study can also be used to answer a question on how urban land uses change over time.

Throughout the **nineteenth century**, Dublin's **port** was the **main point of export** of goods to the British Empire. **Canal and rail links** meant that it also became a **centre of distribution** for goods imported through the port. The port had **large coal yards**, **warehouses** and **cattle yards**, while a number of **industries chose to locate nearby**. Examples included **Boland's Mills** and the **textile factories** that used the **port to import raw materials** and **export finished products**. Many people **lived and worked** in the **docklands** as it grew into the **commercial hub** of the **city** due to its **high levels of industry** and **employment**.

🔺 **Fig. 5.14** Before and after: Dublin Docklands

Decline

Technological advance was the prime **cause of decline** in the **Dublin Docklands**, which **occurred rapidly** from the **1950s onwards**. The introduction of **heavy cranes** and **roll-on roll-off containers** reduced the **need for manual labour** for **loading and unloading ships**. **Coal imports** also **decreased** as **oil and gas** became **more popular sources of power** for industries, which further **reduced the need for labour** in the docklands. The **port moved downriver** to more modern facilities and as a result, many **jobs**

were lost. This led to a **spike in unemployment** in **residential areas around the port**, such as **Sheriff Street**. **Crime rates increased** as people became **more desperate to earn money**, leading to a **social and economic crisis** in the area.

Government Intervention

In **1987** the **government invested** in the **development of the IFSC**, which transformed **derelict warehouses** located in the Docklands into modern **high-rise offices**. In total over **450 companies** engaged in **banking**, **financial trading** and **financial services** set up there, making the intervention an overwhelming success. The success of the **IFSC encouraged the government** to **invest further** and in 1997, the **Dublin Docklands Development Authority** (DDDA) was set up to **renew** the **docklands** both **socially and economically**. The authority **manages 520 hectares of land** north and south of the Liffey and is **responsible** for the **regeneration** of **brownfield sites** and **derelict buildings** into a well-developed inner city area with access to **modern services**, **education**, **employment opportunities** and **amenities**.

The Dublin Docklands now has several modern and diverse buildings:

- 3Arena
- National Convention Centre
- National College of Ireland
- Grand Canal Theatre
- Samuel Beckett Bridge
- A range of modern restaurants and hotels.

While the DDDA was formally dissolved in 2015, it is hoped that the development of **modern apartments** and **housing** will be able to **repopulate the docklands** with a target of 45,000 people. The **2011 census** showed that the **population** is steadily **rising**, with **young professionals** moving into the area, leading to **gentrification**. **Community training schemes** have also been **put in place** to **upskill** the **local people** in the hope of **reducing unemployment**. Overall, the project aims to create over **40,000 jobs** and **11,000 new homes**. **Social integration** will be achieved by ensuring that **20 per cent of new homes** are provided as **social housing**.

Modern **transport links**, such as the **extended Luas line** and the **Port Tunnel,** have led to a **decrease in traffic congestion** around the docklands, which has created a **cleaner and quieter environment** for people to live in.

GEO **DICTIONARY**

Derelict: in a very poor condition as a result of not being used or being neglected

Gentrification: renovate or improve housing to attract middle-class residents

Social housing: housing provided by the government to low-income earners or people with particular needs

Urban decay: an area that falls into disrepair as a result of changing land uses within a city

ACTIVE **LEARNING**

1. Why does urban decay occur?
2. Describe the role of the DDDA in redeveloping the Dublin Docklands.
3. Visit **www.dublindocklands.ie** for more information on the latest developments in the area.

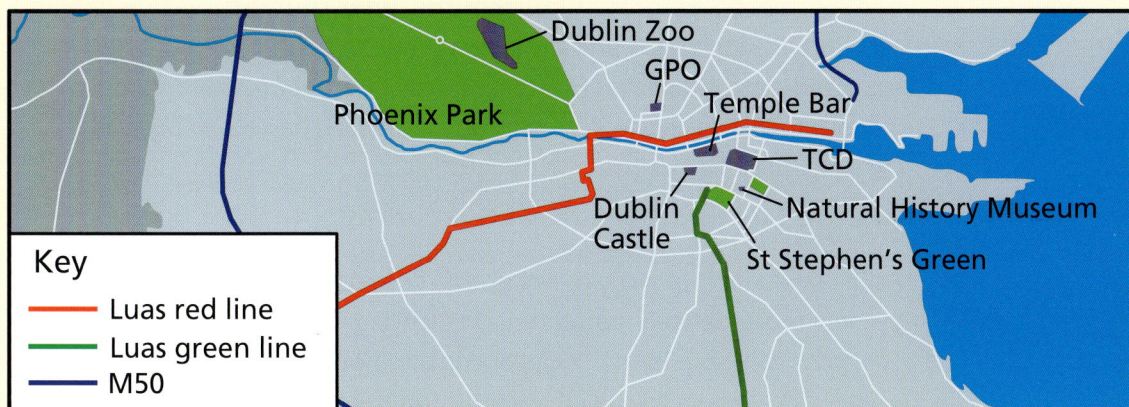

🔺 **Fig. 5.15** Luas lines of Dublin

Key
— Luas red line
— Luas green line
— M50

5.5 Land Values in Cities

Land values in cities vary greatly. Land closest to the CBD is the most expensive as it is the economic heart of the city. The value of land decreases with distance from the CBD. Land values in cities are based on the prices people/businesses are willing to pay for land – this is known as bid rent. Bid rents are highest in the CBD as land is in short supply and all major transport routes converge there, making it accessible.

Bid Rent Curve

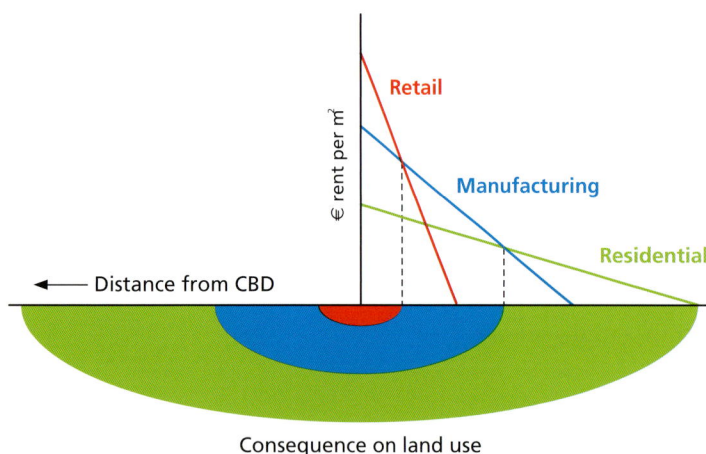

Retail

€ rent per m²

Manufacturing

Residential

← Distance from CBD

Consequence on land use

▲ **Fig. 5.16** Bid rents in urban areas

ACTIVE LEARNING

1. Why are land values in the CBD so high?

GEO DICTIONARY

Bid rents: prices of rent of a property are decided by the demand for property

Peak Land Value Intersection: land that has the greatest commercial value

Shops

The most valuable site within the CBD is known as the Peak Land Value Intersection (PLVI). It is typically filled with large department stores and other large shops, as the area is highly accessible and these shops experience a high volume of passing trade. Many of these department stores are multi-storey in order to maximise space. Shops tend to decrease in size with distance from the CBD as they are not as accessible and, therefore, do not experience the same volumes of trade. As a result, bid rents further from the CBD are lower.

Offices

Offices do not rely on passing trade to the same level that shops do, and therefore cannot afford to pay the highest rent prices. Many offices are often found on the upper floors and on the edges of the CBD, e.g. law firms, accountants and doctors.

Industry

In the past, manufacturing industries located on the fringes of the CBD but these are now located on the outskirts of the city, where urban land is cheapest. Most modern factories require large sites, which are more readily available and affordable on the outskirts of the city. Factories also benefit from being located far from the inner city traffic congestion, and close to ring roads and motorways on the edges of the cities, e.g. Sandyford Industrial Estate in the south of the city. In some cases, manufacturers will locate in areas of the city which have been renewed, e.g. the Dublin Docklands.

Suburbs

As the population of a city grows, so too does its suburbs. As suburbs become more densely populated, the value of land here also increases. The most valuable land is located where major transport links meet, as they offer access to the city centre. Independent commercial areas (multiple nuclei) have developed in these suburban areas to accommodate the needs of a growing population. Examples of these can be seen in

Blanchardstown and **Liffey Valley**. The increasing number of **skilled workers** living in the suburbs has made these areas **more attractive for industry**, resulting in the development of **modern industrial estates** such as Sandyford and Santry.

5.6 Expanding Cities and the Pressures on Rural Land Use

As cities **grow outwards**, **countryside** is lost to new developments. If left uncontrolled, urban sprawl can **destroy rural land** and put **high pressure** on rural services. Since the **nineteenth century**, Dublin's surface area has grown from **45 km²** to **150 km²**. This growth has come at a **terrible cost to** the **natural landscape** surrounding it.

There are numerous factors that cause cities to expand:

- **Rural to urban migration**
- **New residential developments** on urban **fringes to accommodate** growing populations
- Modern transport links that **encourage commuters** to travel longer distances to work, which causes the commuter belt to grow.

This has negatively impacted on the surrounding landscape:

- It has caused **former villages and towns** to become built-up **dormitory towns** (e.g. **Tallaght** and Dundrum). As a result of rapid growth, these towns lose their independent identity and become just another part of the city.
- **Traffic congestion increases** as existing roadways are unable to deal with the **rapid increase in traffic volume** using the roads.
- **Agricultural land** is **split by motorways** and other transport arteries, often into unusable sections or areas **too small for modern machinery**.
- The building of **new housing developments** on river **floodplains** has led to increased levels of flooding, e.g. the building of houses on floodplains of the River Shannon in Athlone.

In order to prevent further destruction to rural areas, **greenbelts** have been designated around cities. Greenbelts are areas of open land surrounding a city in which building is not allowed. Greenbelts **help to contain urban sprawl** by **preventing further expansion** of the city into agricultural land or small villages. Trees are often planted in greenbelts, since trees improve the overall air quality as they absorb harmful gasses and emit oxygen. **Greenbelts** can also help to prevent flooding, as they **reduce the lag time** in the aftermath of heavy rainfall.

> **Fig. 5.17** The impacts of urban sprawl

OLD MACDONALD HAD A FARM

Note!
The causes of, effects of and solutions to urban sprawl are covered in more detail in Chapter 6.

GEO DICTIONARY

Lag time: the time it takes for rainwater to soak through the soil

ACTIVE LEARNING

1. What are the main pressures caused by expanding cities?

1. (i) Name **one** urban area that you have studied and name any **two** functions of this urban area.

    (ii) Describe and explain how the functions of this urban area have changed over time.

(i)

Urban area named	3m
2 functions @ 3m each	6m

(ii)

7 SRPs @ 3m each	21m

2016 Q10C 30M

2. Describe and explain how the functions and services of urban areas change over time, with references to examples you have studied.

Example	3m
9 SRPs @ 3m each	27m

2014 Q10B 30M

3.

Examine the aerial photograph of Enniscorthy above. Draw a sketch map of the area shown on the aerial photograph. On it **show** and **name** the following:

- The Central Business District (CBD)
- An industrial area
- A residential area
- A religious building
- A river.

Limits/frame	1m
Proportions	2m
Overall impression	2m
Showing items: 5 @ 3m each	15m
Naming items: 5 @ 2m each	10m

2013 Q10A 30M

ORDINARY LEVEL

4.

Examine the aerial photograph of Carrick-on-Shannon above. Draw a sketch map of the area shown on the aerial photograph. On it **show** and **name** the following:

- An unfinished building
- A row of modern apartments
- A main shopping street
- A church
- A recreational (leisure) area.

Limits/frame	1m
Proportions (landscape)	2m
Overall impression	2m
Showing items: 5 @ 3m each	15m
Naming items: 5 @ 2m each	10m

2012 Q11A 30M

1.

Name, locate (using accepted notation) and explain **three** different urban functions evident on the aerial photograph of Westport above.

3 functions named @ 2m each	6m
3 functions located @ 2m each	6m
3 explanations: 9 SRPs @ 2m each	18m

2016 Q10B 30M

2. Examine the impact of urban planning strategies with reference to example(s) that you have studied.

Impact identified	2m
Example	2m
Explanation: 13 SRPs @ 2m each	26m

2015 Q12B 30M

3. Examine the 1:50,000 Ordnance Survey map of Dungarvan and legend (Fig. 4.30 on page 122). Draw a sketch map of the area shown to half scale. On it correctly **show** and **label** each of the following:
- The built-up area of Dungarvan
- An area of linear/ribbon rural settlement
- An area of dispersed rural settlement
- An area of clustered rural settlement.

Sketch outline	4m
4 features @ 4m each: shown 3m and named 1m	16m

2014 Q10A 20M

HIGHER LEVEL

4. Examine how the functions of urban centres can change over time, with reference to Irish example(s).

Function identified: 2m + 2m	4m
Example	2m
Explanation: 12 SRPs @ 2m each	24m

2014 Q10B 30M

EXAM FOCUS

HIGHER LEVEL

This chapter lends itself to several potential questions; however, the most common questions asked are (i) the sketching of aerial photographs and OS maps or (ii) how the functions of a town have changed over time. In this section, we will look at the sketch map question from the 2014 Higher Level paper.

EXAM QUESTION

Examine the 1:50,000 Ordnance Survey Map map of Dungarvan and legend (Fig. 4.30 on page 122). Draw a sketch map of the area shown to half scale. On it correctly **show** and **label** each of the following:

- The built-up area of Dungarvan
- An area of linear/ribbon rural settlement
- An area of dispersed rural settlement
- An area of clustered rural settlement.

Marking Scheme
Sketch outline @ 4m
4 features @ 4m each: shown 3m and named 1m

2014 Q10A 20M

SAMPLE **ANSWER**

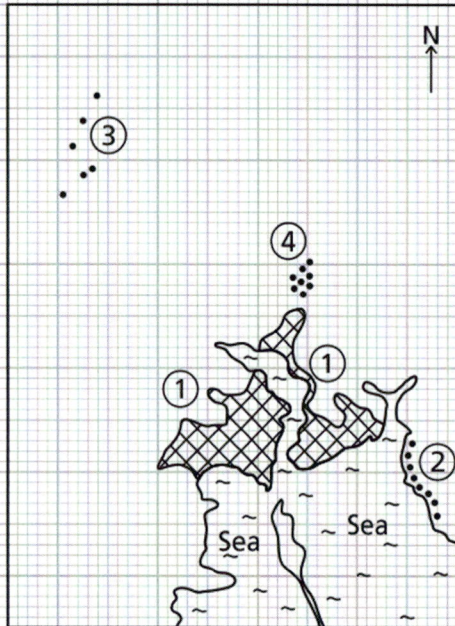

Sketch map showing settlement patterns in Dungarvan area

Key

1. Built-up area of Dungarvan
2. Linear rural settlement
3. Dispersed rural settlement
4. Clustered rural settlement

⌐~ ~⌐ Sea

The map is clearly drawn to scale using graph paper. A ruler has been used and care has been taken to ensure the sketch has the correct orientation and proportion. Each feature has been inserted and clearly labelled.

Note!

The sketch map at half scale should measure 9 cm (horizontal axis) and 12 cm (vertical axis).

Marks Awarded
Sketch outline @ 4m
4 features @ 4m each Shown 4 @ 3m each Labelled 4 @ 1m each
Total 20/20

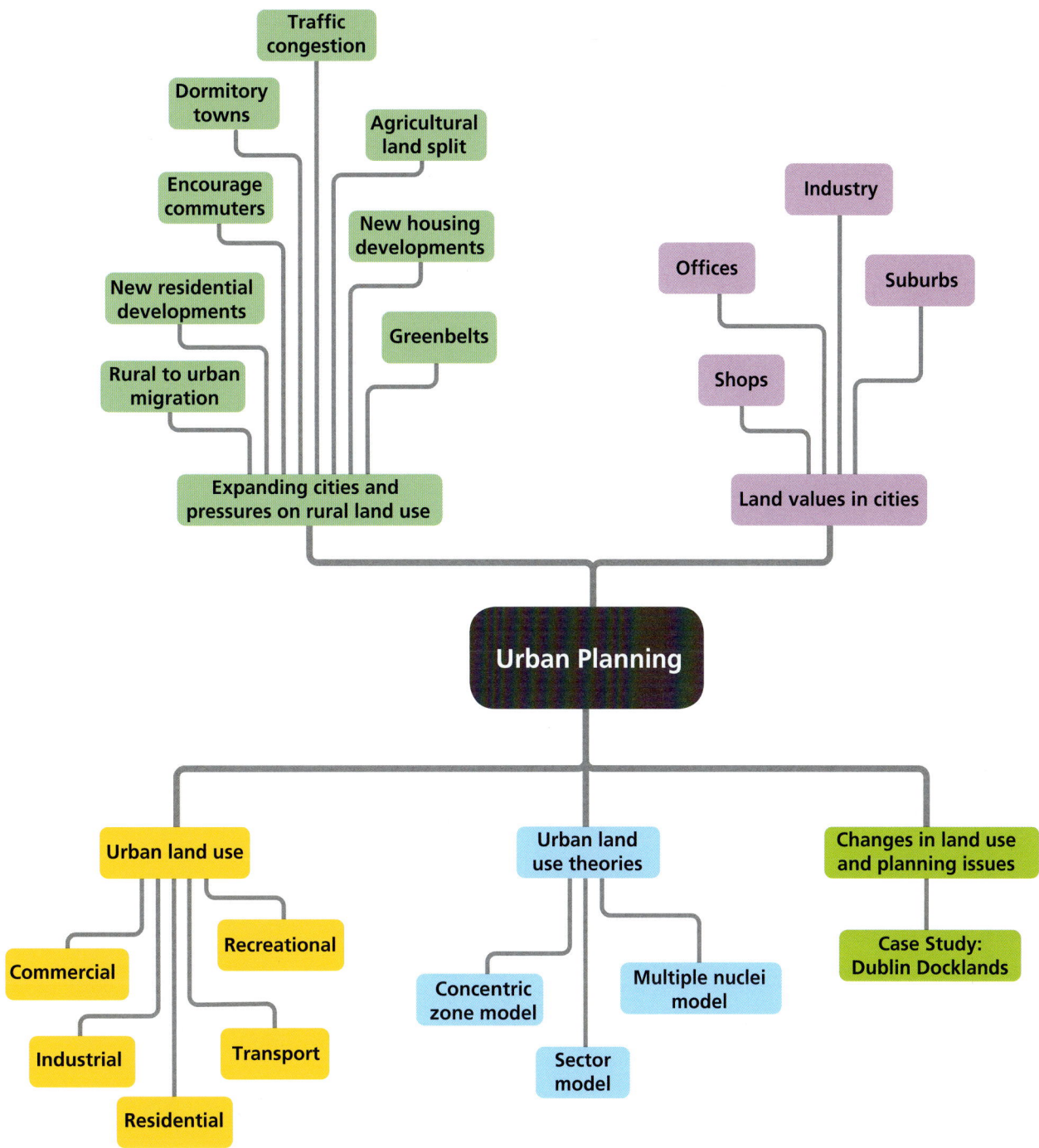

TOPIC MAP

Traffic congestion

Dormitory towns

Agricultural land split

Encourage commuters

New housing developments

New residential developments

Greenbelts

Rural to urban migration

Expanding cities and pressures on rural land use

Industry

Offices

Suburbs

Shops

Land values in cities

Urban Planning

Urban land use

Urban land use theories

Changes in land use and planning issues

Commercial

Recreational

Concentric zone model

Multiple nuclei model

Case Study: Dublin Docklands

Industrial

Transport

Sector model

Residential

CHAPTER 6

Urban Problems

In Chapter 5, you learned how urban land is used and structured through planning. A number of issues regarding urbanisation were also mentioned, such as urban sprawl and traffic congestion. In this chapter, you will learn about these and other issues in detail. You will also learn how some of these issues can be addressed, as well what our cities of the future will be like.

KEY WORDS 🔒

- Urban sprawl
- Traffic congestion
- Urban decay
- Social stratification
- Absence of community
- Urban renewal
- Urban development
- Heritage issues
- Environmental damage
- Urban planning
- Urban renewal
- São Paulo
- Favelas
- Sustainable cities

LEARNING OUTCOMES 🧠

What you MUST know
- Causes of and solutions to urban sprawl
- Causes of and solutions to traffic congestion
- Causes of and solutions to urban decay
- Impact of urban areas on the environment
- Problems caused by urbanisation in the developing world

What you SHOULD know
- Heritage issues caused by urban development
- Case Study on Chinese air pollution

What is USEFUL to know
- Up-to-date information regarding environmental policy in Ireland, the EU and São Paulo

Introduction

Urban problems are a major concern to countries at both national and international levels. Cities consume **75 per cent of all energy generated** in the world. This **energy** is **needed for transport, industrial and commercial activities, infrastructure, water supply** and **food production.** As well as consuming three-quarters of the world's energy, cities are also **responsible** for roughly **60 per cent of the world's greenhouse gases,** meaning that cities are highly polluted. This impacts on the environment – **locally and globally** – and also impacts on the **daily lives** of the people who live in cities. Through **new planning methods** and **new technologies,** some of these issues are being addressed. However, with the world becoming more and more **urbanised,** these problems are likely to continue. This chapter focuses on problems such as:

> **Fig. 6.1** Air pollution is a major issue in China's cities.

- Urban sprawl
- Traffic congestion
- Urban decay
- Heritage issues
- Environmental damage: namely air and water pollution.

Solutions to some urban problems are also discussed in this chapter:

- Urban planning
- Urban renewal
- Sustainable cities of the future.

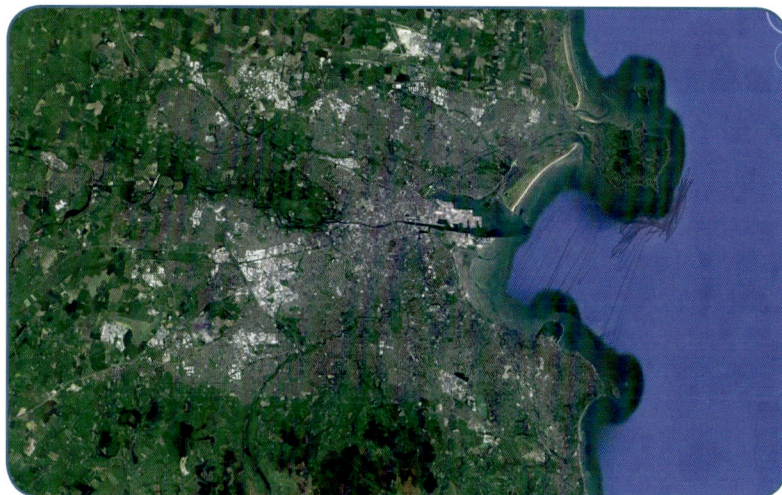

> **Fig. 6.2** Aerial view of Dublin City shows its impact on the surrounding countryside

6.1 Problem 1: Urban Sprawl

Urban sprawl refers to the **uncontrolled spread of cities** into the surrounding countryside. This is caused by the **rapidly growing populations** of the cities, who are **housed in the suburbs** along the **fringes of cities.** The **more rapidly a city's population grows,** the **more rapidly urban sprawl occurs.** Urban sprawl is a problem that is being **experienced by all Irish urban areas,** especially **Cork and Dublin.** In these cities, **housing and industry** are spreading into **greenbelts** of neighbouring counties. In **2006** the **European Environmental Agency** stated that the city of Dublin was a '**worst-case scenario of urban planning'** as **high-rise or high-density accommodation** is **not used,** meaning the city grows **outwards rather than upwards.**

Increased car ownership in Ireland means that people are able to live **longer distances from the CBD** and commute to work each day. This has resulted in **large areas of land** being **rezoned** for **residential housing,**

> **GEO DICTIONARY**
>
> **European Environmental Agency:** agency responsible for providing independent advice on the environment to the EU

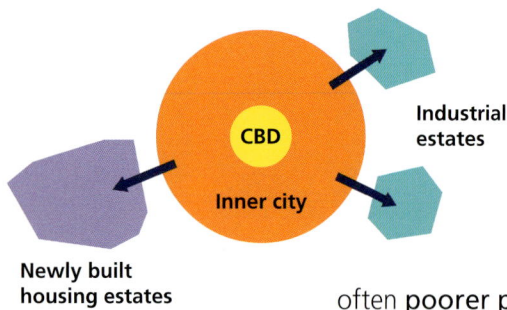

Fig. 6.3 The doughnut effect empties the inner city of residents and factories, as they move to the urban fringes.

causing the **cities to expand further outwards** into the countryside. When urban sprawl occurs, many **people leave their homes** in the inner city and move to the suburbs. This leads to what is known as the **doughnut effect**, as the **areas surrounding the CBD** are emptied. Those who remain in the **inner city areas** are **typically older people** who have lived in the area all their lives, or often **poorer people**. As the **wealthier population leaves**, the **city centre experiences** inner city decline, with **migrants** moving to **residential areas abandoned** by the wealthier population.

Cultural and Environmental Issues Associated with Urban Sprawl

There are a number of both **cultural** and **environmental issues** associated with urban sprawl.

Cultural Issues

- The **names** given to **new developments** are often completely **unrelated to the area** in which these developments are built. This is done for **advertising purposes**, as housing estates are given names that make them **sound more appealing**. However, this has a **negative cultural impact** when traditional place-names are lost.

Fig. 6.4 Ruins of Carrickmines Castle

- Often, **new roads and developments damage ancient monuments** or historically valuable sites. An example of this was the destruction of **Carrickmines Castle** during the building of the **M50 motorway**.

- **New dormitory towns** and housing estates **lack a sense of community**, as most of their residents commute to and from the city each day for work. This leaves **very little time for participation in community events.**

Environmental Issues

- Increased **air pollution** and **noise pollution** are caused by car owners **commuting** to and from work.

- As a **city grows outwards**, **natural habitats** are **destroyed**. As natural land is cleared for **construction**, the **habitats of wildlife** are destroyed.

- Poor planning can lead to some **property developments** being built on **river floodplains**. Examples of this can be seen all over Ireland, e.g. many houses built on the floodplains of the **River Shannon** were destroyed by flooding in the aftermath of **Storm Desmond in 2015.**

FACT

As of 2015 there were 2.52 million cars on Irish roads, 1.95 million of which are privately owned (i.e. not used for business).

Urban Sprawl in Ireland

As already mentioned, the **European Environmental Agency** is **extremely concerned** with the **rate at which Dublin City is sprawling** into the surrounding countryside. However, urban sprawl is occurring all throughout Ireland as **low-density housing** continues to be **built along exit routes** of towns. **Many roadways and commercial developments** have also **contributed to urban sprawl** around the country. Compared to other European cities, Dublin has an incredibly low population density, despite having an **area of 115 km²**. Dublin City has a population density of **4,588 per km²**. While this may seem **high by national standards**, a city such as Paris has a population density of over **21,400 per km²**.

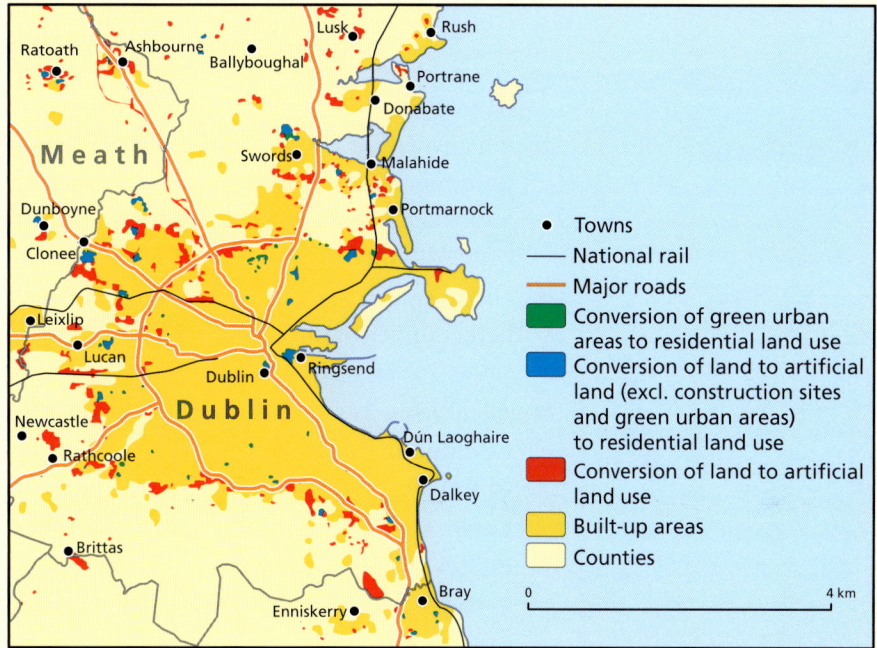

Fig. 6.5 Urban sprawl in Dublin

Map legend:
- • Towns
- — National rail
- — Major roads
- ■ Conversion of green urban areas to residential land use
- ■ Conversion of land to artificial land (excl. construction sites and green urban areas) to residential land use
- ■ Conversion of land to artificial land use
- ■ Built-up areas
- ▢ Counties

Causes

During the **Celtic Tiger era**, many **young couples** looked to **buy homes** for the first time. However, most people were **unable to afford homes** in Ireland's cities due to **inflated housing prices** and so they looked to buy **more affordable housing** in the **towns and villages surrounding** the **cities** instead. This led to the **rapid growth** of these **towns and villages** and the construction of large housing estates to accommodate first-time buyers. An example of this is **Ashbourne in Co. Meath**, which in **1970** had a **population of under 400**. By **2011** this number had risen to **11,355**.

In response to the **growing housing market**, more land surrounding **Ireland's cities was zoned** for **residential** and **commercial purposes** by county and city councils. This land was **bought by property developers** who built large uniform **housing estates**, regardless of whether there was a demand or not.

The construction of **several motorways linking Dublin** to the other major Irish cities encouraged further urban sprawl as the roads greatly **reduced travel times** in Ireland. This meant that people who **worked in the cities** could **commute longer distances** to work and

Fig. 6.6 Motorways converge in Dublin, which encourages urban sprawl.

this encouraged them to move further from the city to areas where **housing was more affordable**.

With **housing prices** at an **all-time high** during the **Celtic Tiger**, many property developers borrowed large sums of money to invest in housing projects all over Ireland. When the housing market crashed in 2008, many of these developers went bankrupt and left **several housing estates unfinished**. These 'ghost estates' have also caused **urban sprawl** in many towns and cities all over Ireland, where housing estates were being built in areas where there was little demand for them.

Consequences

- The **growth of small villages** and towns **without adequate infrastructure** to support them has put pressure on their surrounding rural environments. **Shortages of safe drinking water** and **insufficient wastewater plants** to cope with increased use have led to some environments becoming polluted.
- Urban sprawl has **extended outwards from Dublin** towards the **commuter belt** counties of the borders and midlands. This is seen in the census, which shows the largest population growths occurring along these counties.
- As more people are living further from city centres, there are increased commuting times to and from work. Currently **Ireland's average commuting time** is **double that of** the EU average.
- **Urban sprawl** leads to increased costs of **service provision** as new **housing estates** require **roads, sewage mains, water pipes, electricity** and **council maintenance** of green areas.
- Many **housing projects completed** during the **boom** were poorly planned, with many being **built on the floodplains** of rivers. These **homes** are **prone to flooding**, with many people now being **unable to acquire flood insurance**. Should their homes be flooded, these people will have to pay for repairs themselves.
- **Wildlife**, including **foxes and badgers**, are now a relatively **common sight in cities** such as **Dublin and Cork**, especially at night. As animals are being **forced out of their natural habitats**, they have no choice but to look for food in residential areas.

Solutions

The economic recession which began in **2008** put a halt to the **irresponsible and largely uncontrolled** building **developments**. In the aftermath of the **collapse of the housing market** a number of questions were asked, mainly: *How do we prevent this from happening again?*

There are a number of steps which can be taken in order to control urban sprawl in Ireland:

- Build **higher-density housing** such as that used in major cities around the world.
- **Reverse** the **doughnut effect** by **redeveloping inner city** areas in order to modernise residential areas.
- The development of **more substantial public transport** such as light rail, which should be **integrated with** any **new housing developments** in order to reduce the impact on the environment, e.g. Adamstown.

> **FACT**
>
> Records kept by the Environmental Protection Agency show that artificial surfaces in Ireland grew by 31 per cent between the years 1990 and 2000. In the eight years from 2000 to 2008, this increased by a further 25 per cent.

While these steps could greatly **reduce the impact of urban sprawl**, there are **fears of another housing craze** in the near future, with housing **shortages in Dublin** high on the agenda of the Irish government. Only time will tell whether we have learned from our mistakes or whether they will be repeated.

Heritage Issues

As a city expands outwards, developments may collide with **historic buildings** or **archaeologically valuable areas**. Therefore, it is important that these **sites are protected from future developments** so that the history and culture of these areas are protected.

⊙ **Fig. 6.7** Higher-density housing is a solution to urban sprawl.

The **Heritage Act** was introduced in **1995**, which ensures that heritage is taken into account before new developments are started. The Heritage Council of Ireland works to **protect, preserve and enhance our culture** by providing support, information and advice at local level.

The best-known case of a need for the Heritage Act protecting historic structures was during the discovery of **Viking Remains** at **Wood Quay** in Dublin city in the 1970s. The building of the Dublin Corporation Civic Offices destroyed much of the site before it was fully excavated. The artefacts that were saved can be seen in the **National Museum** in Dublin.

ACTIVE **LEARNING**

1. What is the surface area of Dublin?
2. How has increased car ownership contributed to urban sprawl?
3. What environmental problems have been caused by urban sprawl?
4. What factors caused urban sprawl to increase during the Celtic Tiger?
5. Explain two solutions to urban sprawl in Ireland.
6. What is the role of the Heritage Act 1995?

⊙ **Fig. 6.8** Traffic congestion in Dublin during evening rush hour

6.2 Problem 2: Traffic Congestion

In most cities of the world, traffic congestion has become an issue. In the developed world, **large numbers of people commute to and from the city** each day for work; while in the developing world, rising standards of living lead to **increased car ownership**. In both cases, **traffic systems** become **overwhelmed**, leading to congestion.

Causes

Traffic congestion occurs as a result of **increased car use**, leading to **slower travel speeds, longer commute times** and longer traffic queues. Roads around **urban centres** experience **high volumes of traffic**, which becomes extremely **heavy during** the busiest times of the day, namely **rush hour. Unless public transport systems** in cities are efficient enough to **accommodate large volumes of commuters, congestion** will occur. With over **2.5 million cars** on Irish roads, traffic congestion is an issue, especially in **Dublin**, which has an **average journey speed** of just **8 km/h**.

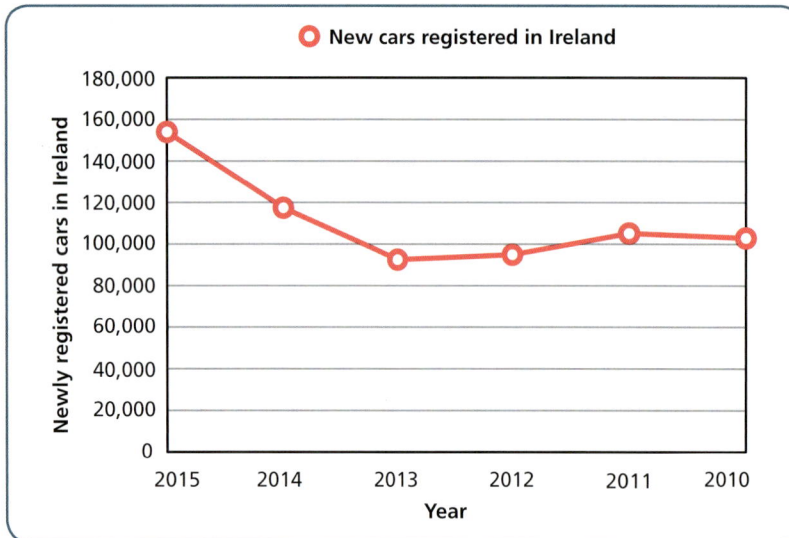

New cars registered in Ireland

⌃ **Fig. 6.9** Number of newly registered cars in Ireland

GEO **DICTIONARY**

Rush hour: time of the day in which traffic is heaviest; this normally occurs between 7:30 and 9:30 in the morning and 5:00 and 7:30 in the evening, when people are commuting to/from work

⌄ **Fig. 6.10** Fumes from exhausts harm people's health and the environment.

Effects of Traffic Congestion

Traffic congestion has a number of impacts:

Social Impact

Traffic congestion not only causes longer commuting times, it also causes **health issues** to regular commuters, such as **increased stress levels** and **high blood pressure**. When a person spends several hours of the day in his or her car, there is less time for physical exercise. This, combined with stress, has **adverse effects on a person's health**. Due to long commuting times, workers spend longer times away from home, which **impacts on family life**. Outside of the home, social lives are **negatively impacted**: there are **fewer opportunities** to become **involved** in the **local community**.

Economic Impact

Traffic congestion means cars spend long periods of time not moving, meaning **fuel is wasted** while the engine is idle. Furthermore, driving in an efficient manner is almost impossible, since drivers are **continually accelerating and braking**. This increase in fuel consumption adds to the **cost of commuting**. As fuel costs increase, haulage and delivery companies **charge more to deliver products** to shops. This additional **cost** is **passed on to the consumer**, making goods and services more expensive.

Environmental Impact

Increased pollution from **exhaust fumes** leads to **air pollution**, which in turn **impacts on people's health**. In the **UK**, over **5,000 deaths per year** are attributed to health issues caused by traffic in cities. Emissions from exhausts are a major contributor to **smog** in cities, while the exhausts themselves cause **noise pollution**.

Reducing Traffic Congestion

There are several measures that can be taken by urban planners to address the issue of traffic congestion.

- Rather than having traffic enter the town or city, **ring roads** can be used to **bypass** them, e.g. the **M50** in Dublin.
- Traffic systems such as traffic lights, **one-way streets** and **slip lanes** can greatly **reduce traffic congestion** by allowing traffic to move more efficiently.
- **On-street parking** can be banned in areas that experience **high traffic volume**, through the use of double yellow lines.
- The building of **flyovers or underpasses** means traffic can pass through busy junctions without having to stop.
- **Congestion charges** for driving through the city during busy times would encourage commuters to use public transport instead.
- Removal of toll booths on motorways can help with traffic flow, e.g. on the M50, which was also widened to six lanes.

While the measures mentioned above can be **effective in reducing the volume of traffic** entering an urban area, these measures are only **practical and fair** if there are sufficient **alternative** modes of transport available. In other words, it is unfair to charge hefty congestion fees for commuters driving to the city centre for work if there is not another viable option to get there. Therefore, it is essential to have an **efficient and relatively cheap mode of public transport** operating between the commuter belt and city centre. Such modes of public transport include:

- **Bus lanes:** Bus lanes make it much faster to travel through the city at busy times.
- **Park-and-ride facilities:** These facilities allow for commuters to park their cars outside the city centre and travel the rest of the way by bus. This reduces the overall number of cars entering the city.
- **Light rail:** Light rail services such as the Luas allow the quick and efficient movement of people from residential areas to the CBD for work.
- **Bike rental schemes:** These schemes allow commuters to use bicycles to travel around the city. This can be very effective when enough cycle lanes are provided.

CASE STUDY 📁

Traffic Congestion in Dublin

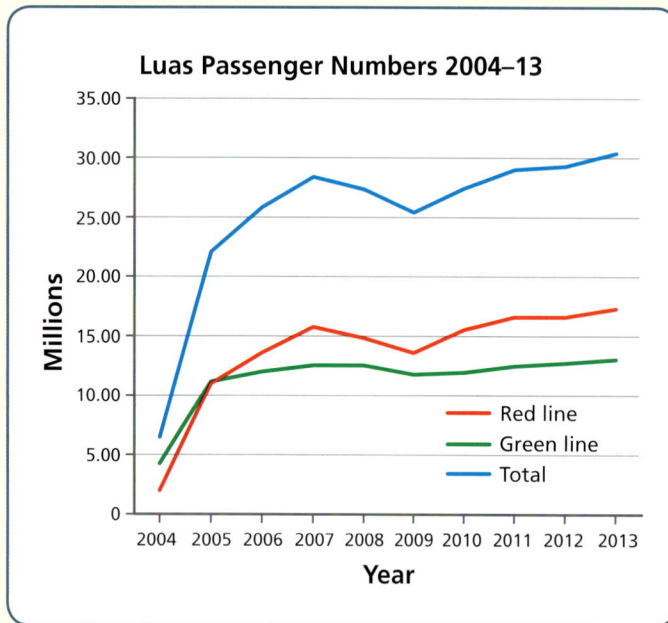

Luas Passenger Numbers 2004–13

⌃ **Fig. 6.11** Number of Luas passengers

Dublin is a **primate city** with a population in excess of **1 million living within its city boundaries**. As Dublin is the **core economic region** of the country, it is the **focal point of all major road and rail links**. All motorways (**M1–M11**) **connect to Dublin**, meaning traffic from all other major urban centres **converges in Dublin**, which leads to **congestion**. The Celtic Tiger era saw a **significant increase in** the level of **car usage** in or around the city. Today, almost **one-third of all new cars registered** in Ireland each year are registered in the **Greater Dublin Area**. As Dublin's **transport infrastructure was poorly developed**, it was unable to cope with such high volumes of traffic. This led to increasing levels of traffic congestion and a **government** decision to **invest** in the **development** of a more **modern transport system**:

- The **DART commuter rail line** was extended with increased services and **upgraded trains** and **carriages**.

- **Intercity train** services were improved to make them **more time-efficient** than travelling on motorway.

⌃ **Fig. 6.12** The M50 now has barrier-free tolling, which allows for free-flowing traffic.

- In **2004** two **Luas tram lines** were built to connect Dublin's suburbs to the city centre. In **September 2013**, work began on the **extension of the Luas lines** to include 13 new stops, eight of which are in city centre locations. The government is investing **€368 million** in the project and the aim is to have it fully completed and in **operation by 2017**. On average, **80,000 people** use the **Luas** to travel around the city **each day**.

- The **M50 was upgraded** to a six-lane motorway with an **automated toll bridge,** which helps traffic to move faster.

- **Heavy goods vehicles** no longer have to enter the city, as they can use the **Port Tunnel**. It is connected to the M50 and, therefore, to all other major routes in Ireland.

- **Quality bus corridors** (QBCs) were introduced, which have reduced travel times on Dublin Bus. **Dublin Bus** now carries **120 million passengers** per year, although numbers are falling due to the increasing popularity of the Luas.

FACT

Despite government investment, Dublin is the tenth most congested city in the world.

- The **bike rental scheme** was introduced in **2009**, which allows people to use a bicycle to travel around the city. Registered users have to pay a fee of just **€20 to avail of the scheme**, while the rental of the bicycle costs **50c per hour**.

- In its first year alone, **47,000 people** availed of the scheme, making it an undeniable success.

Despite the efforts made to tackle the issue of traffic congestion in Dublin, travel speeds continue to fall. As **90 per cent of commercial transport** in Ireland is done **via road**, the number of vehicles entering the city is still high.

ACTIVE LEARNING

1. What causes traffic congestion?
2. Describe the social and economic impacts of traffic congestion.
3. What measures have the Irish government taken to improve the issue of traffic congestion in Dublin?
4. For more information, read the following article from *The Irish Times* in 2014 in which traffic congestion in Dublin is discussed: **www.irishtimes.com/news/environment/dublin-is-world-s-10th-most-congested-city-1.1818738**.

6.3 Problem 3: Urban Decay

Urban decay occurs when **parts of a city become run-down**. This occurs when **formerly highly populated** and **economically active** areas of the inner city decline. Urban decay most commonly occurs in **formerly industrially-strong areas** in the **inner city** where **traditional factories** used to be located. These were **once areas of high employment**, such as Dublin's port. When these **industries decline or relocate to modern industrial estates**, the surrounding area's **populations move out** to more attractive locations such as the suburbs.

The inner city area suffers from **high levels of unemployment**, with many of the **old buildings** falling into **disrepair**, i.e. they decay. As these buildings are **among the oldest in cities**, they have **inadequate sanitation, poor heating** and suffer from **dampness**. The people left to live in the inner city are mainly **elderly, poorly educated** or those who are **unable to afford to relocate**. The **empty buildings** are **boarded up** and **attract anti-social behaviour**, e.g. **squatting** areas for people with **drug addictions. Crime rates increase** in these regions as a result of unemployment and poverty.

🔽 **Fig. 6.13** Urban decay in Dublin City

Absence of Community

Absence of community can occur for **both those who moved** to the suburbs and **those left living in the area**. In the inner city, many people **feel isolated** since their **neighbours have left**. This **removes the community aspect of life** for inner city residents. The **elderly** left living in the inner city, can often feel lonely or afraid, since **high crime rates** and anti-social behaviour increase.

Isolation can also occur for **the people who move** to the newly built suburbs on the outskirts of the city, as they **know few people in their new neighbourhoods**. Although living conditions are better, many people **leave the support of their family** members who remain in the city centre. Younger people who purchased property further from the CBD have to **commute longer distances to work**. The long and time-consuming journeys mean that they have **little time to become involved** in their new communities.

Urban Planning and Solutions to Urban Decay

Urban decay poses a **major challenge** for urban planners who **must develop strategies** to deal with the problems that arise. **Urban renewal** and **urban redevelopment** are used to **combat urban decay**, while the formation of **new towns combats** the **high levels of urban sprawl** caused by young people moving to the suburbs.

Urban Redevelopment

Urban redevelopment involves **demolishing older inner city buildings** and **rehousing their occupants** in newer suburban houses. The **former residential sites** can then be **redeveloped with new buildings** which can be used for **commercial, retail and office purposes**. An example of this is the **Dublin Docklands**, which you studied in Chapter 5.

Urban Renewal

Unlike redevelopment, **urban renewal does not involve changing the functions** of an area. Instead, **buildings, such as houses and apartments, are refurbished. Services and facilities** are also **provided** to ensure a better quality of life for residents in the area. Such services include **shops, schools**, crèches and other **children's services**. The Liberties in Dublin City has undergone urban renewal.

Ballymun Regeneration Project

In **1966** the government attempted to address the issue of urban decay in Dublin's **inner city** areas by **moving residents** to newly built **tower block apartments in Ballymun**. At the time, the high-rise accommodation was **considered to be one of the best examples of social housing in Europe**, with a total of **36 blocks of flats** built, and over **3,000 dwellings**. Some of the tower blocks were 15 storeys high. The construction of the blocks was **completed in 1969**, but it was not long until major problems began to surface.

Fig. 6.14 The Ballymun tower blocks caused many social problems.

- The buildings were **made of poor-quality materials**, meaning the apartments were **damp and cold**. The elevators rarely worked and the general maintenance of the buildings was poor.

- The government **failed to provide basic amenities** for the community, such as shops or recreational areas (e.g. playgrounds or green spaces).

- There was a **high level of unemployment** among the residents of the Ballymun towers. A **low percentage of children finished school**, with many dropping out at a very young age.

- The **people** who left the inner city **felt isolated from their families** and friends, leading to an **absence of community** in Ballymun.

- High levels of unemployment and low levels of education led to **increased alcohol and drug abuse** in the area, which in turn led to **increased crime rates**.

Urban Renewal

In **1997 Ballymun Regeneration Limited** was set up and given the task of **planning the renewal of the area**. The project was given a **budget** of **€2.5 billion** to be used to **create 5,000 new homes**, half of which housed the residents of the tower blocks and the other half of which was to be sold as private housing. It was hoped that this **mix of public and private housing** would lead to the creation of a better sense of community and **reduce social stratification** in the area.

Fig. 6.15 Aerial view of regenerated Ballymun

Besides housing, the project created a town centre with a **range of facilities** for the **30,000 people** living in the area. **Retail and commercial services** were built in the town centre to create employment for residents. Local sports and civic centres were also developed to provide recreational services for young people.

The project was **completed in 2014** with a tree-planting ceremony taking place in 2013 with the then Minister for Housing and Planning.

Tallaght: A New Town

In **1967** the **Wright Report** recommended the **development of three new towns** in western Dublin to accommodate the city's growing population. These towns were Blanchardstown, Lucan and **Tallaght**. It was hoped that these towns would help to **prevent urban sprawl** from occurring.

Until the 1960s Tallaght was a **small rural village** with a **population of about 2,500 people**. While **no official plan** was devised, Tallaght was **laid out as a new town** that was to be surrounded by rural lands. Initially, many of the **social and cultural proposals** were **ignored**, meaning that Tallaght was **not supplied with adequate amenities** for its growing population.

In response to issues caused by a lack of amenities, the **government developed a town centre with services** such as an **Institute of Technology**, a **hospital** and **shopping centres**. A **modern industrial estate** was also built to **provide employment** to the area's residents.

➤ **Fig. 6.16** Tallaght has been developed into a modern and well-serviced town.

Modern transport links have developed around the town, such as the M50 and the Luas tram line which connects Tallaght to the city centre. Today the population of Tallaght has grown to over **80,000 people**.

ACTIVE LEARNING

1. Describe why urban decay occurs.
2. How did the government try to address the issue of urban decay in the 1960s and why was it not successful?
3. Describe how Ballymun was regenerated/renewed.
4. For more information on the Ballymun Regeneration Project go to **www.omparchitects.com/en/projects/ballymun-regeneration-masterplan**

6.4 Problem 4: Environmental Damage

In this section, we will look at the environmental quality of urban areas, specifically air quality and water supply.

Air Pollution

It is estimated that more than **1 billion people around the world are exposed to dangerous levels of air pollution** each year. This has a devastating effect on health, with more than **1 million premature deaths each year**. Rapid levels of urbanisation have led to **increasing levels** of air pollution in cities throughout the world. The **two main sources** of pollutants of air in urban areas are:

- Burning of fossils fuels
- Car emissions.

Burning of Fossil Fuels

The burning of **fossil fuels**, such as **coal**, leads to the **formation of acid rain** and **smog**. Acid rain increases the rate of **chemical weathering of buildings**, statues and monuments, while also **polluting water supplies**.

Smog occurs when large amounts of **smoke** are released into the atmosphere and **mix with fog**. In the past, smog was a **major concern of many cities** with high levels of industry. Smog can **severely harm** the **health** of those who breathe it regularly, leading to **respiratory diseases** such as **asthma, emphysema** and **lung cancer**. Many cities have reduced smog by **banning bituminous coal** and allowing only **smokeless fuel** to be **used**. These measures have successfully **reduced smog levels** in cities such as **London** and **Dublin**.

As temperatures increase, ice caps become thinner due to melting

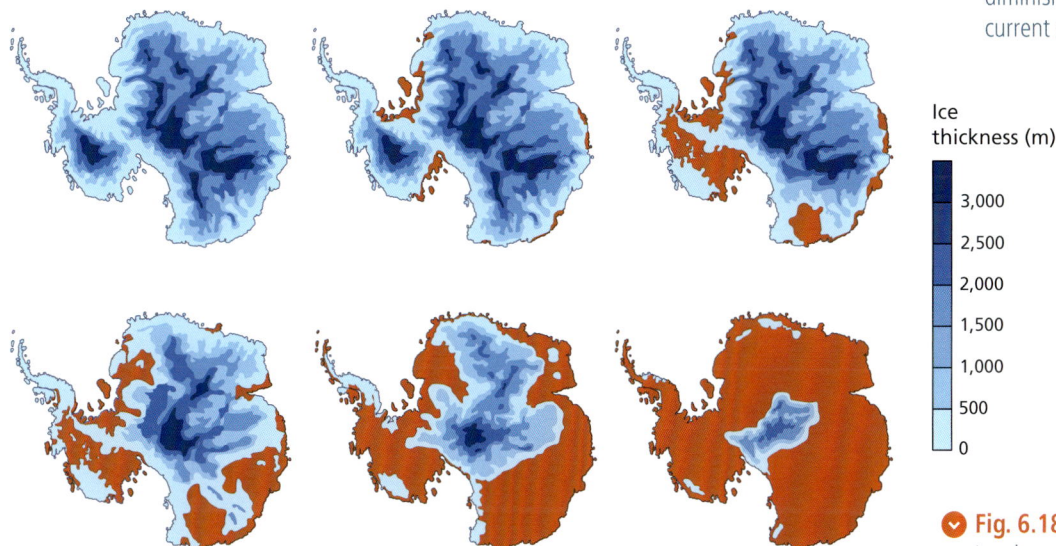

Ice thickness (m)

- 3,000
- 2,500
- 2,000
- 1,500
- 1,000
- 500
- 0

Global warming, which is largely caused by the **burning of fossil fuels, threatens** many cities in **low-lying regions** throughout the world. It is suggested that sea levels could be as much as **59 cm higher by the year 2100**.

Car Emissions

With smokeless coal introduced to many cities around the world, the **biggest threat to air quality** remains emissions for cars and other vehicles. Car exhausts emit harmful pollutants into the air, such as **nitrogen oxide and benzene**. Not only are these pollutants responsible for harming the environment but they also increase the likelihood of serious respiratory disease for people living in rural areas.

[A-Z] GEO **DICTIONARY**

Bituminous coal: also known as 'black coal'; it contains bitumen, a substance which produces soot when burned

◄ **Fig. 6.17** How glacial ice will diminish if we continue our current rate of fossil fuel use

▼ **Fig. 6.18** In 1952, smog in London was responsible for an estimated 4,000 deaths.

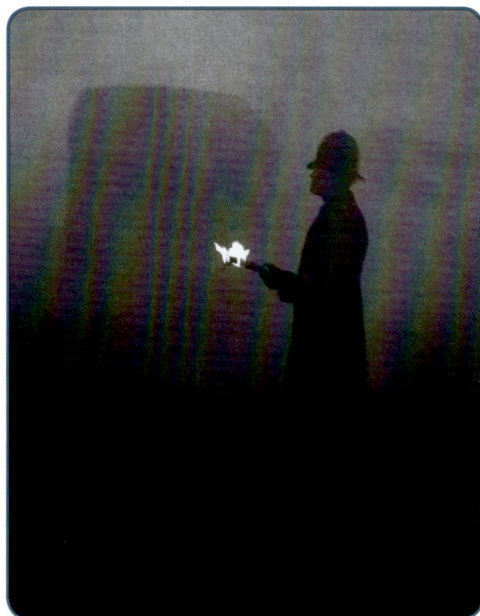

[A-Z] GEO **DICTIONARY**

Global warming: a rise in the average temperature of the Earth's atmosphere and oceans

Benzene: a harmful chemical found in coal and oil

Elective 5: Human CHAPTER 6

As cars are the **most popular mode of transport** in Ireland, air pollution for cars is a **major concern for the Irish government**. Despite technological investments made by car companies in reducing emissions, there has been an **increase in the number of cars owned** in Ireland, meaning any improvements have been cancelled out.

GEO DICTIONARY

Kyoto Protocol: an international protocol that aims to reduce global warming

Under the **Kyoto Protocol** countries must now **monitor the levels of harmful pollutants** being released into the atmosphere. Since 2010, the Irish government has given local authorities the responsibility of reducing the level of toxins being released into the atmosphere should they exceed the acceptable levels. The Kyoto Protocol will end in 2020, at which time it will be replaced by the **Durban Agreement**. Not all countries signed up to the Kyoto Protocol, but all countries **committed to cutting their carbon emissions** under the Durban Agreement.

Water Quality

Water is one of the most **important natural resources** that we have: all living things depend on it. The water we consume comes from a variety of **sources**, such as **rivers and lakes**. Water is taken from these sources and treated before being piped to urban areas. A number of factors impact on our water quality:

- **Contamination from agricultural activities**, such as slurry-spreading and run-off caused by heavy rainfall
- **Untreated sewage** entering our water supply, which causes algae blooms
- **Unsatisfactory treatment**, which leaves the water contaminated as it enters our supply.

CASE STUDY

Air Pollution in China

China's urban areas face major challenges if they are to overcome their air-quality issues. According to the World Bank, **16 of the 20 cities** with the worst **air quality** are located in China. It is estimated that some 20 per cent of the country's population breathes in heavily polluted air each day.

Causes

China's cities are **surrounded by heavy industries** and **coal-fuelled power plants** which emit tonnes of carbon, gases and soot into the atmosphere. The air pollution and smog in cities such as **Shanghai and Beijing** are often so bad that their airports are forced to close.

Coal is the **number one cause of air pollution** in China's cities. Roughly

Fig. 6.19 Air pollution in China

80 per cent of electricity and **70 per cent of the country's total energy** are produced from the burning of coal. Approximately 6 million tonnes of coal are burned each day in China. It is estimated that by **2030 there will be 400 million cars on Chinese roads**.

An improving standard of living in **China's eastern cities** has led to an **increase in car ownership**. With millions more cars being bought each year, there has been a rapid increase in the amount of **sulphur dioxide and other harmful gases** being released into the atmosphere.

Effects

Public health is being badly affected by air pollution, with **cancer** caused by absorbing harmful chemicals now the **number one cause of death** in China. Many children have died or become seriously ill as a result of lead poisoning.

China is now the **number one producer of carbon emissions** in the world, having overtaken the United States. As well as air pollution **impacting on urban areas**, an increase in **acid rain** as a result of increased sulphur has **damaged forestry** and agricultural land in rural areas.

Solutions

The most obvious solution to the increasing levels of air pollution in China is the **banning of coal-powered industrial and electricity plants**. Beijing has banned new coal-powered plants from being built in parts of the city where sulphur levels are already high.

The government has mapped out a **new five-year plan** in which it has listed a number of ambitious objectives to be achieved by 2020. The government has **ordered over 15,000 factories** to publicly **report figures** on air emissions each year.

The government has committed to have **20 per cent of its power** produced from **renewable** sources by **2030** and has invested over **$90 billion in cutting carbon emissions**.

In **2016** China overtook the US as the **number one producer of wind energy** in the world. China has invested over **$100 billion** in developing **renewable energy technologies**.

While China deserves credit for its move towards environmentally friendly energy production, it has a long way to go.

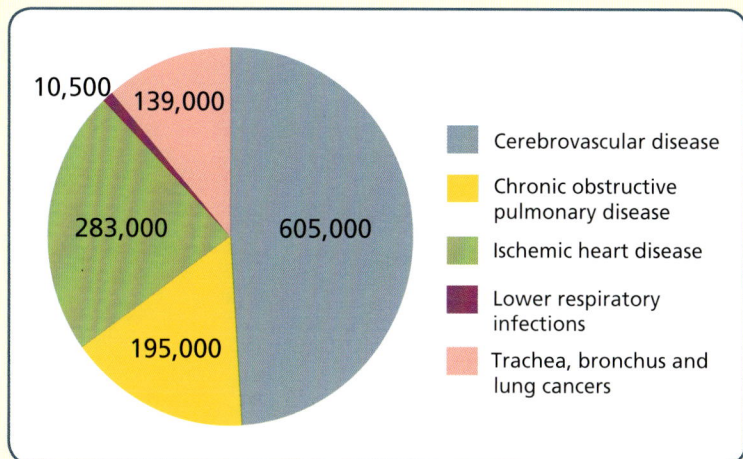

Pie chart legend:
- Cerebrovascular disease
- Chronic obstructive pulmonary disease
- Ischemic heart disease
- Lower respiratory infections
- Trachea, bronchus and lung cancers

Values shown: 10,500 · 139,000 · 283,000 · 605,000 · 195,000

Fig. 6.20 Deaths caused by air pollution in China

ACTIVE LEARNING

1. What are the main causes of environmental pollution in urban areas?

2. What factors have caused air pollution in China?

3. What measures has China taken to improve air quality?

6.5 Developing World Cities

As of 2016 there are **28 megacities** (population >10 million) in the world, most of which are in the developing world. However, given rapid growth in population and the poor economic situation of some countries, a number of problems can occur.

● **Fig. 6.21** The world's megacities

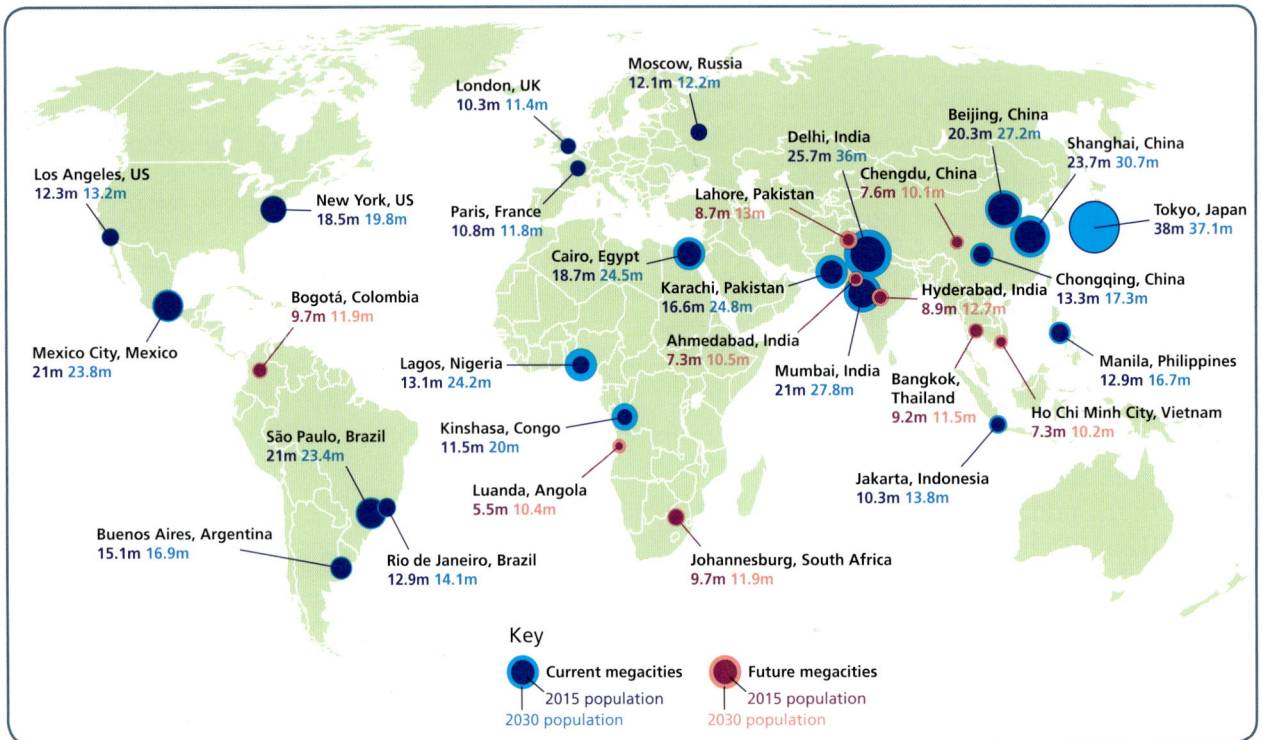

Fig. 6.21 The world's megacities

Moscow, Russia
12.1m 12.2m

London, UK
10.3m 11.4m

Delhi, India
25.7m 36m

Beijing, China
20.3m 27.2m

Shanghai, China
23.7m 30.7m

Los Angeles, US
12.3m 13.2m

New York, US
18.5m 19.8m

Paris, France
10.8m 11.8m

Chengdu, China
7.6m 10.1m

Lahore, Pakistan
8.7m 13m

Tokyo, Japan
38m 37.1m

Cairo, Egypt
18.7m 24.5m

Karachi, Pakistan
16.6m 24.8m

Hyderabad, India
8.9m 12.7m

Chongqing, China
13.3m 17.3m

Bogotá, Colombia
9.7m 11.9m

Mexico City, Mexico
21m 23.8m

Lagos, Nigeria
13.1m 24.2m

Ahmedabad, India
7.3m 10.5m

Mumbai, India
21m 27.8m

Manila, Philippines
12.9m 16.7m

Bangkok, Thailand
9.2m 11.5m

Ho Chi Minh City, Vietnam
7.3m 10.2m

Kinshasa, Congo
11.5m 20m

São Paulo, Brazil
21m 23.4m

Luanda, Angola
5.5m 10.4m

Jakarta, Indonesia
10.3m 13.8m

Buenos Aires, Argentina
15.1m 16.9m

Rio de Janeiro, Brazil
12.9m 14.1m

Johannesburg, South Africa
9.7m 11.9m

Key

Current megacities
2015 population
2030 population

Future megacities
2015 population
2030 population

Rural to Urban Migration

In many developing regions, e.g. poorer African countries, rural areas are extremely poor. Many people migrate from these rural areas **in search of food and shelter**. This leads to a rapid population increase in urban areas, with rural families providing a **better chance of survival** for their children in towns and cities.

Growth of Shanty Towns

Because of the rapid growth of urban areas as a result of rural to urban migration, **governments and authorities are unable to provide adequate housing** and services for their populations. As a result, people are forced to live in whatever forms of shelter they can find, leading to groups of poor-quality shacks or shanty towns. Globally, there are close to **1 billion people living in shanty towns**.

Traffic Congestion

In developing cities, traffic management is **extremely poor**, causing a great deal of traffic congestion and air pollution. **Newly industrialised countries** (e.g. **Brazil**) have experienced rapid economic growth. The wealthier a country becomes, the more cars are bought. This leads to traffic congestion.

Air Pollution

Air pollution is a **major problem in developing cities** because of high volumes of traffic and lower air-pollution safety standards.

The increase in air pollution has also led to an increase in **lung diseases**, which puts increased pressure on health services. The reduction of air pollution is closely linked to reducing the use of the car as the main source of transport, as well as introducing cleaner fuels for industrial power.

Waste Disposal

Waste disposal is **not correctly implemented in developing world cities** because of the high numbers of people. Waste is disposed of in huge **landfill sites,** which have a negative environmental impact. **Run-off** from these landfill sites causes **toxic waste** to seep into **water supplies** or **poison nearby farmland**. Many of the poorest city dwellers work as landfill pickers on these sites, collecting and sorting tins, cans, plastics, etc., which they then sell to recycling plants.

CASE STUDY 📁

São Paulo (Brazil)

São Paulo is the **largest city in South America**, with a population of **21 million** people. The city has experienced rapid population growth over the past number of years because of **high levels of inward migration** from the poorer parts of the country, e.g. **Sertão**. This population growth has put a large strain on the limited services available.

Air Pollution

São Paulo has roughly **6 million cars, 1 million motorbikes** and over **2,000 industrial plants**, making it **one of the worst cities in the world for air pollution**. Air quality has become **extremely poor,** leading to São Paulo receiving the nickname 'cough city' from its residents. Air pollution can be in the form of **particle matter (PM)** in the air (**e.g. dust and smoke**) or **poisonous gases (e.g. ozone, sulphur dioxide and nitrogen dioxide)**. These gases are the main contributor of air pollutants in the city, most of which are emitted by cars.

🔽 **Fig. 6.22** São Paulo has grown rapidly.

As **levels of air pollution increase**, so too do levels of **respiratory diseases**. The effect has led to the government implementing policies to try to reduce the severity of the situation. A number of transportation policies that restrict driving and reduce the emissions from vehicles and fuel content have been introduced. One such policy is '**Promoto**', which regulates the emissions from motorcycles. **Motorcycles emit 7 times** as much **particle matter** (PM) as cars do.

GEO DICTIONARY

Particle matter: pollutants in the air

Fig. 6.23 Air pollution in São Paulo

Promoto requires that motorcycle manufacturers reach the same standards as car manufacturers. **Reducing the sulphur content in diesel fuel** reduces air pollution and **ultra-low sulphur diesel** is **now available** in São Paulo. These policies have helped to reduce the level of air pollution by 21 per cent over a four-year period.

Traffic Congestion

Traffic congestion is another major problem in São Paulo. A **traffic jam of 293 km occurred one day in the city in 2009**. Congestion such as this is caused by a rapid increase in car ownership, with over 1,000 cars being bought every day in the city. The city is a **focal point for many roads**, which leads to large volumes of traffic passing through each day, reducing the **average speed of travel in the city to just 17 km/h**.

Operation Rota (Operação Rodízio) was introduced to **tackle traffic congestion**, meaning that cars were prohibited from being driven one day a week based on the last digit of their licence plate number. A **20 per cent reduction in traffic volume** is anticipated under this system. To date, 90 per cent of the population has abided by the rules which, in turn, has reduced air pollution by 15 per cent.

Shanty Towns (Favelas)

Roughly **20 per cent of São Paulo's population live in shanty towns/favelas** which **lack sanitation, water** and **health services**, and have a **high crime rate**.

Fig. 6.24 Favelas in São Paulo

These favelas initially formed in areas as a result of social stratification. At the beginning of the twentieth century, the wealthier population lived in the higher central districts of the city, while the poor were concentrated along floodplains and railway lines. However, since then the growing migrant population has led to favelas spreading throughout the city. It is estimated that 60 per cent of all population growth in São Paulo since the 1980s has been absorbed by favelas. The government removed favelas from the more valuable parts of the city. This has led to many large favelas being located on the periphery of the city.

There are a number of issues associated with favelas:

- Rubbish collections are not possible in favelas because of the narrow streets. This leads to a **high risk of fire** and the spread of **disease**.
- Favelas are constantly growing in São Paulo because accommodation there is **cheap and close to the workplaces of much of the population**.

In order to provide energy for homes in favelas, the authorities have developed a method of burning **methane from landfill sites** – which provides power to 7 per cent of the city's homes.

- The high rates of poverty make the population of the favelas vulnerable. Often, younger people are taken advantage of by criminal gangs who use them for selling drugs, prostitution and begging.

Solutions

In order to overcome problems, the Brazilian government has introduced a number of initiatives aimed at improving the lives of the city's poorest.

Site and Service Schemes

The government provides a site and a small concrete 'hut' with basic services such as water, electricity and sewerage systems. The migrant is given full ownership rights for the hut but is expected to finish the building at their own expense. Quite often these huts are completed between a group of migrants.

Self-help Schemes

Residents of favelas are given materials by the local council in order to improve existing shelters. Residents also set up community schemes to improve education and medical services, while local authorities provide electricity, water and sewerage disposal.

Housing Developments

Large sections of favelas are cleared, while their residents are removed to more modern housing elsewhere in the city. This also aims to reduce the level of social stratification occurring in the city.

Transport

São Paulo now has an underground Metro system which improves the movement of people while also reducing air pollution. New road, rail and bus services have been provided, while parts of the CBD are now pedestrianised.

Industrial Estates

New industrial estates with water supplies, sewage systems and electricity supplies are built close to favelas to provide business premises and jobs in areas of high unemployment.

The **burning of biogas** from landfills earns São Paulo **carbon credits under the Kyoto Protocol, earning €15 million to spend on environmental projects**.

Note!

The Case Study on São Paulo in Chapter 25 of *Earth Textbook* can also be used to answer this section.

ACTIVE LEARNING

1. Why have urban areas grown so rapidly in the developing world?
2. What are the main issues caused by rapid population growth in São Paulo?
3. What measures has the government taken to address these issues?

GEO DICTIONARY

Biogas: natural gas, such as methane, produced from the fermentation of organic material

6.6 Sustainable Cities and Cities of the Future

Rural to urban migration has been a common occurrence in all countries in the North since the beginning of the Industrial Revolution. However, with increasing levels of economic development in the South, new cities will develop and existing cities with continue to expand. Although urbanisation seems to have peaked in the North, all cities in the developing world have continued to grow rapidly as people leave rural areas in search of a better standard of living.

As you have already seen in this chapter, cities all over the world are **struggling to deal with pollution, traffic congestion** and **environmental issues** caused by such population increases. Therefore, since the trend of an increasingly urbanised world looks set to continue, it is up to urban planners to find solutions to existing problems such as urban sprawl, urban decay and inadequate services, while also reducing the impact on the environment is minimal.

Cities of the Future

Future cities will **need to be better planned** and **provide better services** than cities in existence today. The issue of **urban sprawl** is one of the most pressing and it can be **reversed only with more intensive use of existing lands** in city areas. In order for this to occur, **housing** will have to be **well planned and serviced** with modern and **reliable public transport** in order to **prevent traffic congestion** and **air pollution**.

Stricter use of **urban planning laws** and **well-developed policies** on the **zoning of land** will help to ensure that the **interaction** between **industrial and residential areas** is **reduced**. This avoids issues such as **contamination of water supplies** and **noise pollution**, and it **decreases the amount of traffic congestion** in residential areas caused by people commuting to work. For dormitory towns surrounding the city, **counter urbanisation** is a desirable measure to prevent further urban sprawl. This would mean that towns would develop **their own commercial and industrial centres**, making them independent from the main city in the area. Commuter towns close to Dublin have begun to show signs of counter urbanisation, e.g. **Navan and Drogheda**, which have their own commercial centres.

More emphasis on community will be needed in the planning of new towns. This can happen by allowing for more **community involvement**. This has occurred in Cloughjordan in Co. Tipperary, where residents have created goals and visions for their town. Policies such as these allow for better **social integration** and **avoid** issues such as **social stratification**.

Sustainable Cities

Cities will need to become both more **environmentally friendly** and more **people-friendly** in order to become sustainable. **Inner cities** need to become **pedestrianised** to **avoid** issues such as **traffic congestion and air pollution**. This would also **encourage people to live within the city** centre again and **prevent urban sprawl** and the **doughnut effect**.

Well-developed public transport **links** will mean less pollution and will help to make **city centres cleaner** environments in which to work and live. These **transport links** should also link to **residential areas** to **avoid high volumes** of city traffic.

ACTIVE LEARNING

1. Visit **www.thevillage.ie** for further information on Cloughjordan Village.

Fig. 6.25 A sustainable city

The **residential areas** themselves should be well planned, with **sufficient green areas** for **recreation and relaxation**.

Energy-efficient houses would greatly reduce the amount of energy used to heat homes, while **better waste disposal** practices and waste reduction programmes will greatly **reduce the carbon footprint** of cities.

ACTIVE LEARNING

1. How can strict planning laws address issues in future cities?

2. How would a pedestrianised city centre improve inner city areas?

ORDINARY LEVEL

1. (i) Name **one** city where traffic congestion is a problem.

    (ii) Explain the reasons why traffic congestion occurs in this city.

    (iii) Describe **one** solution to traffic congestion.

(i)	City named	4m
(ii)	Explanation: 9 SRPs @ 3m each	27m
(iii)	One solution described: 3 SRPs @ 3m	9m

2015 Q11B 40M

2. (i) Name one city in the developing world.

    (ii) Describe and explain reasons for the rapid growth of this city.

(i)	City named	3m
(ii)	Explanation: 9 SRPs @ 3m each	27m

2015 Q12B 30M

3.

Means of Travel to Work in a number of Irish Regions (%)							
Region	On Foot	Bicycle	Bus and Train	Motor cycle	Car	Lorry and Van	Work from home
West	7.9	1.4	2.1	0.2	68.3	9.7	10.4
Dublin	12.8	5.0	19.9	0.9	52.2	3.5	5.7
South East	9.1	0.9	1.3	0.3	69.3	8.9	10.2

Amended from CSO

The table shows the means by which people travel to work in a number of Irish regions.

The percentage of people working from home is also included.

ORDINARY LEVEL

Examine the table and answer each of the following questions.

(i) What was the most popular means of travelling to work?

(ii) Which region had the greatest total percentage of people travelling to work on foot and by bicycle?

(iii) Explain briefly why the Dublin region had the highest percentage of people travelling to work by bus and train.

(iv) List **two** problems that may be experienced in urban areas where a high percentage of people travel to work by car.

(v) List **two** ways authorities in urban areas attempt to reduce the number of people travelling to work by car.

All parts 6m each	30m

2014 Q11A 30M

4. (i) Name **one** city in the developing world.

(ii) Explain the problems experienced in this named city.

(iii) Describe **one** solution to these problems.

(i)	City named	4m
(ii)	Problems explained: 8 SRPs @ 3m	24m
(iii)	One solution described: 4 SRPs @ 3m	12m

2014 Q11C 40M

5. Describe and explain the measures being taken in towns and cities to solve the problem of traffic congestion.

Explanation of measure: 10 SRPs @ 3m	30m

2013 Q12B 30M

6. Examine the aerial photograph of Carrick-on-Shannon (see Fig. 4.33 on page 127).

(i) Using the usual notation (right background, etc.), give **two** locations on the aerial photograph where traffic congestion could be a problem in Carrick-on-Shannon.

(ii) Select **one** of the locations chosen in part (i) and, using evidence from the aerial photograph, explain why traffic congestion might occur at this location.

(iii) Examine in detail **one** possible solution to this traffic congestion.

(i)	Two locations @ 3m each	6m
(ii)	Explanation: 4 SRPs @ 3m each	12m
(iii)	Examination: 4 SRPs @ 3m each	12m

2012 Q11B 30M

ORDINARY LEVEL

7. **(i)** Name a developing or a developed city that you have studied.

  (ii) Explain **two** problems arising from the growth of the city named in part **(i)**.

 (iii) Describe **two** solutions to these problems.

(i)	City named	4m
(ii)	Two problems explained: Each problem 3 SRPs @ 3m each	18m
(iii)	Two solutions explained: Each solution 3 SRPs @ 3m each	18m

2012 Q11C 40M

HIGHER LEVEL

1. 'Problems can develop from the growth and expansion of urban centres.'

Discuss this statement with reference to **one** developing city that you have studied.

Named city	2m
Discussion: 14 SRPs @ 2m each	28m

2016 Q11C 30M

2. Discuss how the growth of urban centres can lead to any two of the following problems, with reference to examples that you have studied:

- Traffic congestion
- Urban decay
- Urban sprawl.

Example of urban centre	2m
Discussion of problem 1: 7 SRPs @ 2m each	14m
Discussion of problem 2: 7 SRPs @ 2m each	14m

2015 Q10B 30M

3.

Fastest-Growing Towns in Ireland				
Town	Region	Population 2006	Population 2011	% Population Change 2006–2011
Saggart	South Dublin	868	2,144	147
Courtown Harbour	Wexford	1,421	2,857	X
Newcastle	South Dublin	1,506	2,659	77
Carrigtwohill	Cork	2,782	4,551	64
Ballymahon	Longford	963	1,563	62

Amended from CSO

Examine the table above and answer the following questions.

(i) Calculate the increase in the total population of Newcastle, between 2006 and 2011.

(ii) Calculate **X**, the percentage change in Courtown Harbour's population, between 2006 and 2011.

(iii) State **two** reasons for the rapid growth of towns in South Dublin, between 2006 and 2011.

(iv) Explain briefly **one** problem caused by the rapid growth of Irish towns.

(v) Explain briefly **one** reason why the Census of Population is important for urban planning.

Five parts @ 4m each	20m

2013 Q10A 20M

4. Discuss **two** issues facing cities in the future in the developed world.

Two issues named @ 2m each	4m
Issue 1 explained: 7 SRPs @ 2m each	14m
Issue 2 explained: 6 SRPs @ 2m each	12m

2013 Q12C 30M

5. 'Authorities in developing world cities have attempted to overcome the problem of rapid urban growth.'

Examine the above statement with reference to example(s) you have studied.

Example named	2m
Examination: 14 SRPS @ 2m each	28m

2012 Q10B 30M

Questions on urban problems are very common, with all aspects of the chapter asked in past exam papers. In this section, we will look at Question 11C from the 2013 Ordinary Level paper. As with all questions, particular attention must be given to the wording of the question.

EXAM QUESTION

Describe and explain the problems caused by the rapid growth of a developing world city that you have studied.

2013 Q11C 30M

Marks Awarded
Developing world city named @ 3m
Problems explained: 9 SRPs @ 3m each

SAMPLE ANSWER

A developing world city that I have studied is São Paulo in Brazil [3m]. São Paulo has a population of over 21 million, which has grown rapidly due to inward migration [3m]. This large population growth has put a strain on the city's services: air pollution, traffic congestion and shanty towns have become serious issues [3m].

Problem 1: Air Pollution

There are roughly 6 million cars and 1 million motorbikes registered in São Paulo. There are also over 2,000 industrial plants, and this has led to high levels of air pollution [3m]. Air quality in São Paulo is poor due to the high levels of particle matter and poisonous gases, earning it the nickname 'cough city' [3m]. As the air becomes more polluted, there are more cases of respiratory diseases, so the Brazilian government is introducing a number of policies to help improve air quality [3m].

Problem 2: Traffic Congestion

Traffic congestion is another major problem in São Paulo. It is estimated that over 1,000 cars are bought in the city each day [3m]. As most major roads meet in the centre of the city, large volumes of traffic have led to traffic jams [3m]. Operation Rota aimed to improve traffic flow in the city by reducing the traffic volume by 20 per cent [3m]. It is thought that 90 per cent of

The answer is well focused and is structured in an examiner-friendly manner. The student immediately names the city being discussed, while all problems discussed relate specifically to that city, rather than general discussion. Headings prevent repetition and ensure maximum efficiency in terms of gaining marks and the time spent on this question.

the city's inhabitants comply with the operation. This has led to a 15 per cent reduction in air pollution in São Paulo [3m].

*Problem 3: Shanty Towns

Roughly 20 per cent of São Paulo's population live in favelas [*3m]. These makeshift shelters lack sanitation, water and health services and usually have a high crime rate [*3m]. Favelas developed as authorities were unable to house the high number of immigrants entering the city. This led to large shanty towns developing along the edges of the city [*3m]. Rubbish collections are not possible in favelas due to their narrow streets. This means that rubbish simply piles up. This increases the risk of fire and the spread of disease [*3m]. The high rates of poverty make the populations of favelas vulnerable, and many young people join criminal gangs in order to earn money [*3m].

Marks Awarded
Developing city named @ 3m
Problems explained: Best 9 SRPs @ 3m each
Total: 30/30

TOPIC MAP

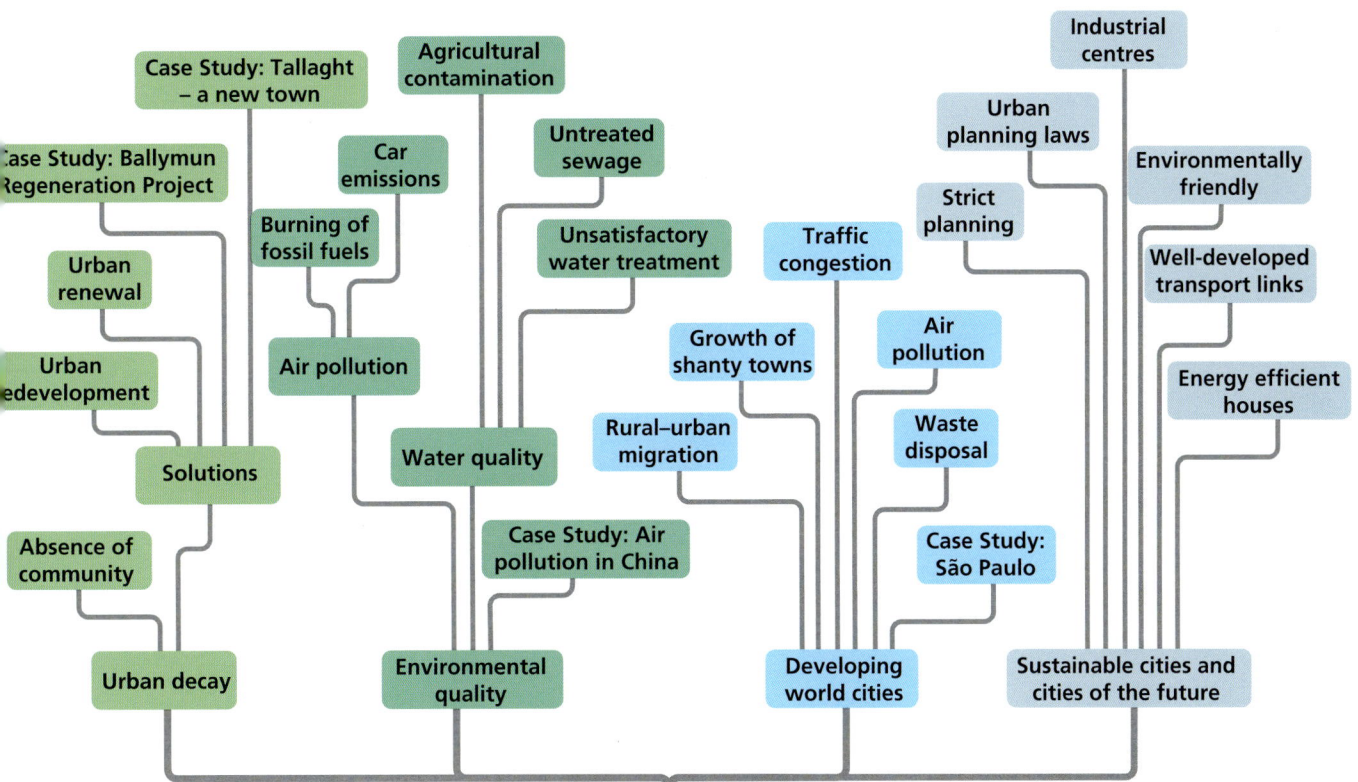

Urban Problems

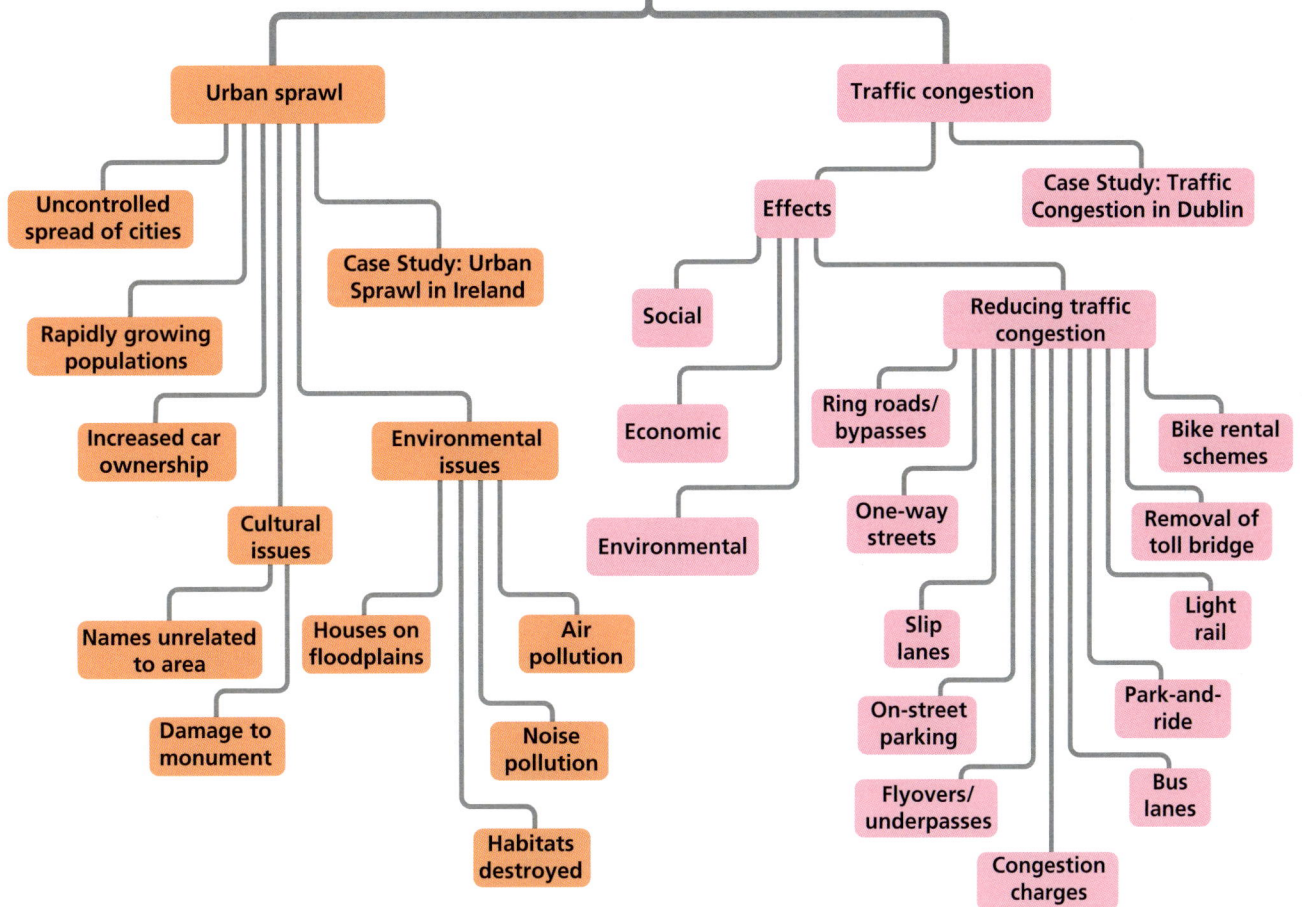

Environmental quality (green branch):
- Case Study: Ballymun Regeneration Project
  - Urban renewal
  - Urban redevelopment
- Case Study: Tallaght – a new town
- Solutions
  - Absence of community
  - Urban decay
- Car emissions
- Burning of fossil fuels
  - Air pollution
- Agricultural contamination
- Untreated sewage
- Unsatisfactory water treatment
  - Water quality
- Case Study: Air pollution in China

Developing world cities (blue branch):
- Traffic congestion
- Growth of shanty towns
- Rural–urban migration
- Air pollution
- Waste disposal
- Case Study: São Paulo

Sustainable cities and cities of the future (blue branch):
- Industrial centres
- Urban planning laws
- Strict planning
- Environmentally friendly
- Well-developed transport links
- Energy efficient houses

Urban sprawl (orange branch):
- Uncontrolled spread of cities
- Rapidly growing populations
- Increased car ownership
- Cultural issues
  - Names unrelated to area
  - Damage to monument
- Case Study: Urban Sprawl in Ireland
- Environmental issues
  - Houses on floodplains
  - Air pollution
  - Noise pollution
  - Habitats destroyed

Traffic congestion (pink branch):
- Effects
  - Social
  - Economic
  - Environmental
- Case Study: Traffic Congestion in Dublin
- Reducing traffic congestion
  - Ring roads/bypasses
  - One-way streets
  - Slip lanes
  - On-street parking
  - Flyovers/underpasses
  - Congestion charges
  - Bike rental schemes
  - Removal of toll bridge
  - Light rail
  - Park-and-ride
  - Bus lanes

Index

A

absence of community 166
absence of settlement 115
acacia 42
afforestation 48
Afghanistan 11, 18
agricultural revolution 55–6
Ahern, Bertie 69
AIDS 53–54, 58–59
air pollution 168–9, 170–1, 173–4
antiretroviral drugs (ARVs) 58, 59
apartheid, definition 69
asylum seekers 68, 77, 78
asylum shopping 78
austerity 76
Australia 7, 41

B

Ballymun Regeneration Project 167
bid rents 148
biomes 43
birth rates 10, 11, 16, 18
    influences on 11–15, 44, 49–50
    and religion 15, 25, 49–50
brain drain 62, 71
Brazil 22, 87–9
Bronze Age 2000–600 BCE 97–8
brownfield sites 135, 146

C

car emissions 169–70
carbon footprint 40, 60
carbon output 40
Carrick-on-Shannon 106, 151
Carrick-on-Suir 112
carrying capacity 41, 52, 55
Catholicism, and birth rates 15, 25, 49–50
Ceausescu, Nicolae 15
Celtic Settlement (600–500 BCE) 98, 102
Celtic Tiger era 41, 75, 159
Census of Ireland (2016), investigation of 27–8
central place theory 109–11
child mortality 17–18, 51–52, 54, 57
children 11, 51
    estimated cost of raising 12
    and forced marriages 20
China 12, 13–15, 40, 170–1
Christaller, Walter 109
cities
    developing worldwide 172–3
    and land values 148–9
    social stratification 144–5
    sustainable 175–7
civilisation 97
climate 6, 7
climate change 43–4
colonisation 7
commuter zone 24, 27, 86, 136
counter urbanisation 116

County Development Plans 116–17
crannóg 98
Croatia, Stage 5 demographic model 19
crop rotation 55
crossbreeding 55
culture, influence on overpopulation 49–50

D

Darfur, civil war 48
DART 164
death rates 10, 11–15, 17, 18
deforestation 46
demographic transitional model 16–19
    Stage 1: High Fluctuating Stage 16–17
    Stage 2: Early Expanding Stage 17–18
    Stage 3: Late Expanding Stage 18
    Stage 4: Low Fluctuating Stage 19
    Stage 5: The Senile Stage 19
dependency ratio 23
derelict 146, 147
desertification 40, 42, 46, 48
Dingle 102–3
diseases 17, 45, 57
dispersed settlement 114–15
donor region 68
    advantages of emigration 70–1
    disadvantages of emigration 71–2
dormitory towns 87, 138
dry points 99, 103
Dublin 24
    CBD 137, 143
    industrial area 138
    land use zones 137–8
    location of services 144
    Multi Nuclei Theory in 143–4
    open space 138
    population 27, 28
    residential land use 138
    social stratification 144, 145
    sprawling suburbs 28
    traffic congestion 164–5
Dublin Docklands 146–7
Dublin Docklands Development Authority (DDDA) 147
Dun Aengus promontory fort 98
Dungarvan, County Waterford 113
Durban Agreement 170

E

Early Christian Settlement (500–800 CE) 99, 103
Ebola Virus 17
ecological footprint 60–1
economic factors, and population distribution/density 24
economic liability 18–19
Educate Together 84
education
    and birth rates 11, 16
    and death rates 11
    and life expectancy 11
    of women 48, 49

Egypt 6
emigration 8, 41, 68, 69, 76
    and donor regions 70–2
    socio-economic factors 8–9
employment permits 76–77
Empty Diagonal (France) 29
Enniscorthy, aerial photograph 150
Environmental Protection Agency 160
environmental quality 168–70
Equal Status Act (2000) 84
Eritrea 44
erosion 43
Ethiopia 53–5
ethnic cleansing 82
ethnicity, definition 69, 81–82
ethos 84
Europe 5, 52
European Economic Area (EEA) 76–7
European Environmental Agency 157, 159
European Union (EU)
    Dublin System 78–9
    EU Blue Card 79
    FRONTEX 78–9, 80
    immigration policy 78
    Migration Policy 78–81
    Schengen Agreement 79

F
family planning 11, 21, 25, 49–50, 51, 54
famine 24, 43, 54
favelas 88, 144, 174–5
flint 97
flyover 163
food production 55–6, 57
food security 43
foreign direct investment (FDI) 71
Fortress Europe 79
forts 102
fossil fuels 169
France
    conflict in 82–3
    outmigration 29, 30
    population 19, 29–30
    religious issues 83–4
FRONTEX 78–9, 80
fulacht fia 98

G
Galway 28, 107–9
general practitioner (GP) 73
genetically modified foods 56
genetics 56
Germany 19, 53–4
ghettoisation 73
Gleninsheen Gorget 97
global hectares 60
government, and population distribution 8
government policy, and birth rates 12–15
Great Famine 7, 24, 41
Greece 19
green revolution 56, 59
greenbelts 137, 149
greying 19, 21, 53
gross domestic product (GDP) 61, 62
gullying 43, 49

H
Heritage Act (1995) 161
Hinduism 15, 51–2
hinterland 110, 111
historic factors, and population density/distribution 7, 24
HIV/AIDS 53, 58–9
Horn of Africa 45

I
IFSC 147
illiteracy 18
immigration 19, 30, 53, 68, 72–6
impermeable 43
India 18, 50–2
infrastructure, definition 55
internally displaced person (IDP) 68
Ireland
    asylum seekers 77, 78
    birth rates 25–6
    carbon footprint 40
    Census investigation 27
    children, estimated cost of raising 12
    and commuters 27–8
    dependency ratio 23
    ecological footprint 60–1
    economic factors 24
    economic recession 25, 26, 41
    emigration 7, 8–9, 24, 41, 69, 74–6
    fertility rate 27
    historic factors 24
    immigration 25, 74–5
    inward migration 41
    migration 85–6
    migration policy 76–8
    migratory pattern changes 74–6
    outward migration 24, 25
    physical factors 24
    physiological density 9
    population 4, 19, 21, 26–7
    population change over time 23–9
    population decline (1841–51) 24
    rural–urban migration 24, 85–6
    traffic congestion 87
    urban sprawl 86–7
Irish-Americans 7
Italy 50

J
Japan 19, 21–2

K
Kenmare, County Kerry 104–5, 120
Kilmallock, County Limerick 100
Kolkata 40
Koofi, Fawzia 18
Kyoto Protocol 170

L
labour deficit, definition 41
labour intensive 62
lag time 149
land use
    changes in 145–6
    Dublin Docklands 146–7
    planning issues 145–6

land values, in cities 148–9
laterite soils 43
Leinster, population increase 27
Lemass, Sean 24
lesser developed country, definition 15
life expectancy 11
linear/ribboned settlement 114, 115
Luas 164

M
Mali 40, 41
manufacturing industry 43
marginal land 56
medical technology 57
Mediterranean Coast 29
megacity/megacities 88, 172
melting pot 81
Mesolithic (7000–3500 BCE) 96–7
Mexico 18
migrant 68
migration
    barriers to migration 68, 70
    changes in migratory patterns 74–6
    definition 68
    ethnic issues 81–2
    forced migration 68
    net migration 68
    pull factors 68, 70
    push factors 68, 69
    racial issues 82
    voluntary migration 68
Migration Policy (EU) 78–81
monopoly 57
Morocco 18
multi-denominational 84
Muslim countries, fertility rates 50

N
National Development Plans 117
natural resources 40
    overuse in Sahel region 45–6
Neolithic (3500–2000 BCE) 87, 102
Netherlands 41
New Towns 1960 CE onwards 101–2
Newly Industrialised Economies (NIEs) 62
Niger, birth rates 44
niqab 84
Nord, The 29–30
Norman Settlement 1169 CE 100
North America 7
nucleated/clustered settlement 114, 115

O
Ogham stone 98
optimum population 42
outmigration 24, 25, 29, 30, 47–8
overcropping 46
overgrazing 45–6
overpopulation 40, 41
    and conflict 47–8
    definition 41
    effects of 46–8
    impact of technology 55–7
    influence of society and culture 49–50
    and migration 47–8

    possible solutions 48–9
    wealth and income levels 52

P
Pakistan 50
Paris 30
peak land value intersection 148
percolation 43
pesticides 56
physical factors
    climate 6
    drainage 6
    and population distribution/density 24
    relief 5
    resources 7
    soils 6
physiological density 9
planning issues 145–6
Plantation Town Settlements 1500–1700 CE 100–1
polygamy 83
population
    birth rates 10
    death rates 10
    developed countries 61
    developing countries 62
    and development rates 61–2
    measurement of change 10
    natural decrease 10
    natural increase 10
    optimum population 42
    world growth 3
population density 4, 5, 7, 41
    in France 29–30
    in Ireland 4, 24
    in Sahel region 6, 7
population displacement 8
population distribution 3–4
    factors influencing 4–9
    in France 29–30
    human factors 7–9
    in Ireland 24
    physical factors 5–7
population growth 55–7
population pyramids 20–2
poverty and population 52
prehistoric settlement 96–8
preventative medicine 45
primate city 24
Prohibition of Child Marriage Act 51
promontory fort 98
Purdah, women and 51–2

R
racism, definition 73
range 111
receiver/host region 68, 72–3
refugees 45, 68, 69, 78, 81
religion, and birth rates 15, 49–50
remittance money 71, 73
replacement rate 22
resource-based industry 116
resources, and population density 7
rezoning 134
right-wing political parties 79
Romania 12, 13–15

rundale system 115
rural depopulation 72, 73, 116
rural land use 149
rural planning 116–17
rural settlement patterns 114–15
rural–urban migration 172
        in Brazil 87–9
        in Ireland 24, 86–7
Rwanda 17

S
Sahel region
        birth rates 44
        climate change 43–4
        conflict 47–8
        deforestation 46
        desertification 40
        drought 43, 44
        drought-resistant grasses 49
        economic poverty 44
        environmental degradation 46–7
        famine 43
        fertility rate 45
        low carrying capacity 42
        migration 47–8
        natural resources, overuse and depletion 45–6
        overcropping 46
        overgrazing 45–6
        overpopulation 42–9
        population 6, 7, 42, 44–5
        poverty and population 52
        refugees 45
        rising cereal prices 44
        seasonal rains 43, 44
salad bowl, definition 84
São Paulo 40, 87, 88, 173–5
Saudi Arabia 50
Savannah, definition 42
sedentary farming 46
Seine Valley 30
settlement 96
        distribution and density 113
        functions of 106
        historic era 99–101
        new towns: 1960 onwards 101–2
        prehistoric settlement 96–7
        site 103
        situation 104
shanty towns 172, 174–5
Skellig Michael 99
smog 163
social stratification 138, 140–2, 144–5
society, influence on overpopulation 49–50
socio-economic conditions 8–9
soils, and population density 6
souterrain 98
South Africa 18, 58–9
specialist machinery 56
standard of living 11, 12, 20

stereotype, definition 82
sub-Saharan countries 11, 17, 20, 52
suburbanisation 116
Sudan 44, 47–8
surplus 57
sustainable cities 175–7
Sweden 7
Syria 8, 69–70, 79, 80–1

T
Tallaght: A New Town 168
threshold 110, 111
togher 98
tourism, and the Mediterranean Coast 29
traffic congestion 87, 94, 147–8, 155, 161–3, 172, 174–6, 185
        in Dublin 164–5
trusteeship 84
túath 98

U
underpass 163
underpopulation 41, 42
United Arab Emirates 18
United States 7, 9
urban decay 147, 165–6
urban hierarchy 110, 111
urban land use
        commercial 134–5
        industrial 135
        recreational land use 137
        residential 135–6
        transport 136
urban land use theories
        Theory 1: Concentric Zone Model 139–40
        Theory 2: Sector Model Theory 140–1
        Theory 3: Multiple Nuclei Theory 141–2
urban planning 134, 166
urban redevelopment 166
urban renewal 137, 166, 167
urban sprawl 29, 86–7, 157–8
        in Ireland 159–61

V
Viking Settlement 800–1169 CE 99

W
waste disposal 173
water 59, 170
Westport 119
women
        access to education 48, 49
        in India 51–2
Wright Report (1967) 168

Z
Zambia 11
zone of transition 139
zoning 134

Legend
Eochair

Ordnance Survey Ireland
Suirbhéireacht Ordanáis Éireann

DISCOVERY SERIES
SRAITH EOLAIS

M 1 — Mótarbhealach / Motorway (Junction number)

N 11 — Bóthar príomha náisiúnta / National Primary Road

N 71 — Bóthar tánaisteach náisiúnta / National Secondary Road

Carrbhealach dúbailte / Dual Carriageway

Bóthar príomha /tánaisteach náisiúnta beartaithe / Proposed Nat. Primary / Secondary Road

R 574 — Bóthar Réigiúnach / Regional Road

Bóthar den tríú grád / Third Class Road

Bóithre de chineál eile / Other Roads

Bealach / Track

Líne tarchurtha leictreachais / Electricity Transmission Line

Stáisiún cumhachta (uisce) / Power Station (Hydro)

Stáisiún cumhachta (breosla iontaiseach) / Power Station (Fossil)

Crann / Mast

Bealach / Track

Brú de chuid An Óige / Youth Hostel (An Óige)

Brú saoire Neamhspleách / Independent Holiday Hostel

Láithreán carbhán (idirthurais) / Caravan site (transit)

Láithreán campála / Camping site

Láithreán picnici / Picnic site

Ionad dearctha / Viewpoint

P Ionad páirceála / Parking

A T An Taisce / National Trust

Tearmann Dúlra / Nature Reserve

Feirm Ghaoithe / Wind Farm

Foirgnimh le hais a chéile / Built up Area

Ionad eolais turasóireachta (ar oscailt ar feadh na bliana) / Tourist Information centre (regular opening)

Ionad eolais turasóireachta (ar oscailt le linn an tséasúir) / Tourist Information centre (restricted opening)

i Ionad eolais turasóireachta / Tourist Information centre

Garda Síochána / Police

PO Oifig phoist / Post office

Eaglais nó séipéal / Church or Chapel

Ardeaglais / Cathedral

✈ Aerfort / Airport

Aerpháirc / Airfield

9 18 27 Galfchúrsa, machaire gailf / Golf Course or Links

Bealach rothar / Cycle route

Bealach comhréidh le comharthaí; Ceann Slí; / Waymarked Walks; Trailheads.

Loch / Lake

Abhainn nó sruthán / River or Stream

Canáil, canáil (thirim) / Canal, Canal (dry)

Líne bhur láin / High Water Mark

Líne lag trá / Low Water Mark

Trá / Beach

Bád fartha (feithiclí) / Ferry (Vehicle)

Bád fartha (paisinéiri) / Ferry (Passenger)

Teach Solais in úsáid / as úsáid / Lighthouse in use / disuse

Bádóireacht / Boating activities

Stáisiún traenach / Railway Station

Crosaire comhréidh / Level Crossing

Tollán / Tunnel

Iarnród tionscalaíoch / Industrial Line

Iarnród / Railways

Teorainn idirnáisiúnta / International Boundary

Teorainn chontae / County Boundary

Páirc Náisiúnta / National Park

An Ghaeltacht / Irish speaking area

Páirc Foraoise / Forest Park

Seilbh de chuid an Aire Chosanta / Dept. of Defence Property

Foraois bhuaircíneach / Coniferous Plantation

Coillearnach Dhuillsilteach / Deciduous Woodland

Foraois mheasctha / Mixed Woodland

Séadchomhartha Ainmnithe / Named Antiquities

Clós, m.sh. Ráth nó Lios / Enclosure, e.g. Ringfort

Láthair Chatha (le dáta) / Battlefield (with date)

SUMMIT INFORMATION

NOTE Over 600m summits must have a prominence of 15m. Between 400m and 599m a prominence of 30m and from 150 to 399m a prominence of 150m.

- Above 600m
- 599m - 400m
- Below 400m

The summit classification is courtesy the Mountain Views hillwalking community. The lists used, updated to 2009, include: The "Arderins" 500m list, The "Vandeleur-Lynam" 600m list, and other lists for smaller tops and county high points.

Mountain Rescue Base

Céim imlíne comhairde 10m / 10m Contour Interval

Céim imlíne comhairde 50m / 50m Contour Interval

Cuaille triantánachta / Triangulation Pillar

123 • Spota airde / Spot Height

Trasnú cliathráin / Graticule Intersection

IRISH NATIONAL GRID

Compiled and published by Ordnance Survey Ireland,
Phoenix Park, Dublin 8, Ireland.
Arna thiomsú agus arna fhoilsiú ag Shuirbhéireacht Ordanáis Éireann, Páirc an Fhionnuisce, Baile Átha Cliath 8, Éire.

This is a sample reference only

(Discovery Sheet 23)
Sample reference: G 103 079

Irish Transverse Mercator (ITM) **Not used on this extract.** is a newly derived GPS compatible mapping projection that is associated with the European Terrestrial Reference System 1989 (ETRS89). For further information on ITM and for coordinate conversion visit our website.

CENTRE OF SHEET ITM CO-ORDINATES:
EXAMPLE: ⊕ 499973E 827008N

SCALE 1:50 000
SCÁLA 1:50 000